Performance is alive and well in spite of the constraints imposed by pollution controls and unleaded fuel. To get back lost performance and meet emissions standards manufacturers have turned to twin cam multi-valve cylinder heads and fuel injection for many of today's engines.

employment. However, the fact that the engine has been built to function under these, and a wide variety of other conditions in no way indicates that the manufacturer doesn't know much about performance engineering. In fact, it surprises many enthusiasts to find just how much performance potential is built into present day engines. Engines may begin life as fairly hot performance units and then during their development be deliberately de-tuned for a number of reasons. It is reported by those within the factory that the intercooled Buick 3.8 turbo has its output limited by changing the computer "chip" because the standard rear axle isn't quite up to the task of drivers regularly doing drag starts. In some lands the Datsun 300ZX turbo is governed by a speedo-tripped fuel shut-off to a top speed of 127mph in the interests of affordable insurance premiums. Others can be de-tuned in the interests of economy, and so on.

Recently some testing was carried out on the Opel Corsa with an Ecotec 1.6 4-valve engine. The owner wanted a cheap but competitive dual purpose road/ clubsport car preferably with no internal engine modifications and about 150hp. This seemed a fairly tall order as the factory quoted the power output as being only 107hp at 6000rpm. First, the factory fuel injection system and electronic engine management system were scrapped. A new throttle body injection arrangement was fabricated from an old pair of Weber 42 DCOE sidedraughts as it was felt that commercially available 45mm bore throttle bodies as used on 220hp race engines would upset mid-range power. The new engine management system was a laptop programmable unit. Table 1.1 shows the excellent result and clearly demonstrates the tuning potential of today's engines.

Table 1.1   Opel Ecotec 1.6 dyno test

rpm	Test 1		Test 2	
	hp	Torque	hp	Torque
2000	34	90	34	89
2500	50	106	48	101
3000	64	112	61	107
3500	74	111	73	110
4000	88	116	84	111
4500	98	114	96	112
5000	105	110	110	116
5500	107	102	127	121
6000	108	95	142	124
6500	106	86	149	120
7000	101	76	152	114
7500	92	64	147	103

Test 1 – standard engine, standard inlet and exhaust, standard computer

Test 2 – standard engine, 42mm throttle body injection, standard exhaust, programmable computer, standard cams retimed to give best power range

I see many cars which have had their performance and economy spoiled simply because the owners had the "all smog gear is bad" mentality. True, some pollution devices do detract from performance and economy, but some improve both performance and economy. The early fuel evaporation system (EFE) is an example. Many carburated engines use this system to rapidly heat the inlet manifold, providing quick fuel evaporation and more uniform fuel distribution when the engine is cold. The rapid heating of the induction system allows slightly leaner carburettor jetting and reduces the length of time the choke is required. Exhaust emissions go down, cold driveability and performance improves, and fuel consumption decreases. Basically a good system, but many enthusiasts disconnect it, making their cars a real pig to drive when cold.

The air injection reactor system (AIR) is both good and bad, depending on the engine. On turbo engines the AIR system contributes to performance by significantly increasing exhaust gas volume and velocity at lower engine speeds. This aids the turbo to spool up to speed more quickly, increasing boost and reducing lag and low speed sluggishness. These and other pollution control systems will be dealt with in detail in a later chapter; however, these two examples illustrate the point that we need the correct outlook before making tuning decisions.

In fact at all times we need to make logical, not emotional, tuning decisions if we are to be truly happy with the end result. Avoid over-enthusiasm and accurately assess your engine. Write down what are its good and weak points. Write down what you want to achieve and then carefully think the matter through. I personally feel that too many modifications are made simply as something to brag to friends about, when in truth the enthusiast is quite disappointed with the result. So many modified cars are horrible to drive because the cam or the carburettor is too big. The only way to avoid this type of problem is to think the matter through carefully. Don't make changes for the sake of change. If the valves are large enough then why waste money fitting larger ones? If the standard carburettor is large enough and gives good economy then why fit a Weber or a Holley?

Think too about how long you want the engine to last. If the standard engine is plagued with rapid cam lobe wear, then a modified cam will aggravate the situation, so consider if you really want to replace the cam and rockers, say, every 15,000 miles. Perhaps you don't, so consider other ways of achieving your goal. Does the engine manufacturer fit a hotter cam in another model which would do the job, could the standard cam be advanced, would it be wise to leave the standard cam alone and get the desired result by cleaning up the head? All these options deserve to be considered. Maybe the engine is prone to fast valve guide wear. Obviously a high lift cam will exaggerate this weakness so think about the choices available to you. Roller tip rocker arms, chrome valve stems, bronze valve guides, a cam with less lift and so on.

Another consideration is the electronic engine controls. Many function interdependently so you can't disconnect or change any single part of the system; the total package has to be considered. For instance, the engine may be equipped with an electronically-controlled carburettor. Changing to a conventional carby will just foul up the electronics, so your modifications have to be planned around the retention of the standard electronic carburettor. Possibly the ignition is tied into the computer. This means that unless alternative "chips" are available, the advance curve cannot be altered. Hence camshaft options will be limited to what will work with the standard ignition advance curve. Also, the electronics probably incorporate a rev limiter, so if the engine is governed to, say, a maximum of 6000rpm, then component choices must be made with that fact in mind.

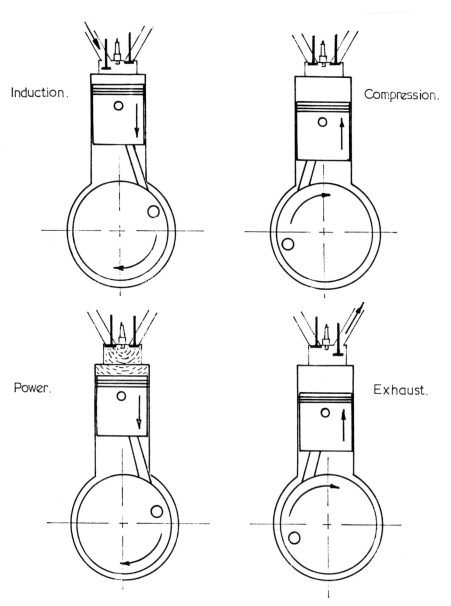

The four strokes; induction, compression, power and exhaust which take place in every cylinder each two revolutions (720°) of the crankshaft.

The same principle applies with fuel-injected engines. Most road fuel injection systems are a little fussy about cam changes. All will tolerate non-stock cams, but some systems have trouble getting the idle speed and mixture right unless a cam with a certain duration and lobe phase angle is selected. Some injection arrangements are air flow limiting; the runners may be small to give a broad torque curve or the throttle body could be on the modest side. Either situation restricts air flow so it would be useless planning a 200hp conversion if the induction system will flow enough air for only 180hp. Similarly with the injectors; if because of cost considerations the standard injectors have to be retained and they have a fuel flow potential of 150hp, then engine modifications need to be planned around that reality.

So that there is no misunderstanding of the basics of engine operation I will explain what goes on in each cylinder every two revolutions (720°) of the crankshaft. This type of engine is called a four stroke or four cycle engine because of the four distinctive cycles which occur during 720° of crankshaft rotation. These cycles are the induction stroke, the compression stroke, the power stroke and the exhaust stroke. First, as the piston goes down, the inlet valve opens fully and admits air and vapourised fuel to fill the cylinder (the induction stroke). On the compression stroke the piston rises, but compression does not commence until part way up the stroke when the inlet valve closes. As the piston approaches top dead centre (TDC), the spark plug ignites the fuel/air mixture. Compression of the burning mixture continues as the piston rises to TDC. The resulting pressure drives the piston down on the power stroke. Part way down on this stroke the exhaust valve begins to open and as the piston rises again to TDC, the burned gases are expelled out past the open exhaust valve (the exhaust stroke). Just before the piston actually reaches TDC, the inlet valve starts to lift off its seat to allow in the fuel/air mixture when the piston descends on its next induction stroke.

I have endeavoured to keep this book as non-technical as possible and eliminate information which would apply primarily to race and rally engine development. If you require more detailed information then I would suggest that you also read another of my books *Four-Stroke Performance Tuning* published by Haynes Publishing. In that book I delve far more deeply into combustion; cylinder head, exhaust and camshaft design; how Holley, Weber and SU carburettors work and how to tune them.

Chapter 2

The
Cylinder Head

Cylinder head design has come a long way in recent years and many moden engines now incorporate features which a decade ago would have been found only in purpose-built race engines. Most of the advances in port and combustion chamber design have been adopted as a direct result of pollution control. Early emission engines were inefficient, low hp fuel guzzlers. To get back lost power and efficiency, car makers had only a limited number of options open. Camshaft design couldn't be changed without upsetting emissions and economy. Exhaust design was already quite efficient so no easy gains could be made here. This left only cylinder heads and carburation. Some adopted fuel injection as an interim solution and most began intensive research into porting and combustion chamber design. The result today is a good number of family saloons sporting cylinder heads not too far removed from that found on the Cosworth DFV V8 Formula 1 race engine of 25 years ago.

This is not intended to imply that the cylinder heads fitted to current engines cannot be improved upon. They can be, but the modifications now required are much more subtle than in the past. Today's heads usually do not require the removal of very much metal from the ports or combustion chambers in performance/economy applications. Frequently the valve size is adequate too. For a long time I have maintained that big ports and big valves are not the way to go, particularly for street engines, and that principle is still true.

A large number of amateur head modifiers and even cylinder head shops still spend a lot of time doing what I call "sparkle and glitter" head jobs. They don't really change the shape of the ports or combustion chamber, and it is probably just as well they don't, given their obviously limited knowledge. What is more usual is to grind out the first couple of inches of port close to the manifold face, because that is the part easiest to get at with a grinder, and then finish off with a high polish. The combustion chamber is next to receive a sparkle job and probably big valves as well. The end result is a head that looks pretty and has cost a lot of money, but which in truth

actually reduces power and economy at most points in the rev range.

Many ordinary family saloons now feature high flow cylinder heads with large valves right from the factory. Only subtle port and valve modifications are necessary to unleash extra hp.

On a performance/economy engine we particularly need to keep gas speed up, otherwise the fuel will drop out of suspension and dribble into the combustion chamber in non-combustible droplets. This wastes fuel, reduces performance, washes lubricant from the cylinder walls and ups emissions. Hence we do not need to hog out the ports; some stock ports are a little too big anyway. Big casting protrusions can be ground down, but don't waste time smoothing and polishing. With few exceptions the majority of stock ports give good flow up to about 0.400in valve lift, some up to 0.450in lift. The principal impediment to high lift flow is the valve itself and the valve pocket (also called valve bowl) which is the area between the valve guide and the valve seat. Obviously then, the valve pocket is the part of the port on which to concentrate our modification efforts.

To understand better what happens when the ports are hogged out and big valves are fitted, take a look at Table 2.1 which shows the gas flow through two Chev heads. The first head with casting number "993" was originally fitted to low performance 350cu in cars and trucks in the early 70s. By American standards it is not a bad head, but it certainly isn't close to what is coming out of Japan and Europe. Note that inlet air flow fell on its face at about 0.400in valve lift, which is about where we would expect a stock head to stop increasing in flow. The second head was a full race head with big ports and valves modified to give good power up to 8000rpm with a high lift roller cam. For the price of just one of these you could buy a full set of alloy wheels and high-performance low profile tyres! The flow figures seem to indicate that the race head was far superior right through the valve lift range. (Incidently the race head kept on flowing well right up to 0.650in lift). However, for little more money than a reconditioning job the low performance emission heads were modified to produce the 15 third set of test figures. As can be seen these mildly modified heads outflowed the full race heads right up to 0.400in valve lift and at 0.450in lift, which is about the maximum we can reliably use on the street anyway, they were not too far behind. Actually, the flow figures at maximum lift are not terribly important as the valve only dwells there for an instant; however, it spends much more time at lower lifts opening and then closing as well.

Table 2.1   Chev Cylinder Head Flow Test

Valve Lift			Cubic Feet Per Minute Air Flow			
	Test 1		**Test 2**		**Test 3**	
	Inlet	**Exhaust**	**Inlet**	**Exhaust**	**Inlet**	**Exhaust**
0.100in	33	23	38	32	42	30
0.150in	49	34	57	50	63	48
0.200in	66	42	75	65	85	63
0.250in	84	55	93	74	105	70
0.300in	98	62	108	88	116	85
0.350in	110	67	120	96	124	94
0.400in	116	71	131	108	131	102
0.450in	117	74	141	115	133	105
0.500in	117	76	150	118	135	110

Test 1 – standard Chev 350 head with 1.94in inlet and 1.5in exhaust valve

Test 2 – fully modified Chev 350 race head with 2.055in inlet and 1.625in exhaust valve

Test 3 – slightly modified Chev 350 head with 1.94in inlet and 1.6in exhaust valve

Except for the valve pocket area, the ports on the emission heads were not touched. In the inlet valve pocket the first job was to cut away the lip formed by the original factory-machined 75° throat cut. This lip was not ground right down to leave a straight wall as many would think, rather it was radiused as shown to assist the air to turn into the cylinder past the valve head. The short radius on the port floor also required careful blending and smoothing. Next, the valve guide boss was slimmed down, but not shortened in the interests of long life, and the port roof at the sides of the boss radiused and smoothed. After this, the port was very gently blended into a conventional three angle valve seat.

On the exhaust side it was decided to replace the 1.5in valve with a standard Chev 1.6in exhaust valve. Some Chev heads can be only properly modified for good exhaust flow after a 1.6in valve is used, otherwise the valve throat shape ends up all wrong. Also these heads were to be fitted to a Corvette which was being stroked from 350cu in to 383cu in and I wanted good exhaust flow. The first job was to cut a new seat to accept a 1.6in valve. A large 60° cut was taken under a normal 45° seat to allow a generous radius to be ground on both the long and short side of the port. This again is where many would-be head modifiers go wrong. They tend to bore or grind the valve throat parallel below the 45° seat cut, which drastically reduces low and mid-lift exhaust flow. After blending the 60° throat cut into the port, the valve guide boss was then slimmed and the port roof at the sides of the boss blended and smoothed.

To further prove the point that ports do not have to be made larger to give good

16

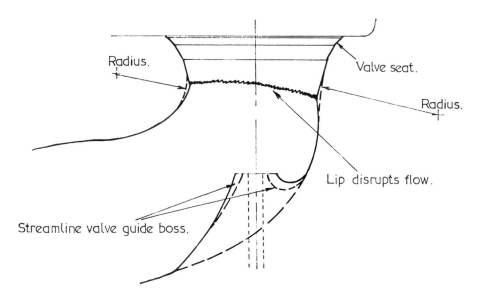

Radius.

Valve seat.

Radius.

Lip disrupts flow.

Streamline valve guide boss.

Radiusing the lip where the throat cut meets the cast inlet port promotes good air flow into the cylinder. If the port is ground right out to the edge of the valve seat, flow is spoiled.

flow in performance/economy engines, look at the example of a VW Golf 1.6 litre head. Standard, these heads flow fairly well, but they are restricted by tiny 1.34in inlet and 1.22in exhaust valves, and in the minds of many tuners by small ports as well. To dispel this idea just take a look at the flow figures in Table 2.2. On the inlet side flow dropped severely after 0.290in lift but in the exhaust port flow still wasn't too bad right up to 0.430in lift. In view of the small valves fitted it was decided not to waste time working on the valve pocket area or reshaping the valve underhead profile. Instead, suitably large valves would be fitted right from the start and then we would find out what sort of port modifications work.

The first step was to remove the standard valve seat inserts and fit high quality inserts (the standard inserts crack frequently), able to accept large 1.61in inlet and 1.34in exhaust valves. The standard ports were then roughly flared into the inside diameter of the inserts without any fancy work radiusing the throat or anything like that as I wanted to see just how well the standard head would work for a minimum outlay. As you can see from Test 2, the result was quite spectacular, proving that the small standard ports were well up to the task, even with a large increase in valve size. However, flow was still tapering off above 0.360in lift so some port modifications were tried to rectify this situation. The first move was to properly taper the valve pocket area right from the valve guide into the valve seat. This modification produced the figures shown in Test 3. Every modification tried after this gave better flow only at 0.470in lift which was of no value with a road cam, and as expected, some modifications reduced flow at all lifts up to 0.290in. On the exhaust side tapering the valve pocket into the wider valve throat didn't do anything one way or the other. The only modification which did any good, was to square the top of the exhaust port, where most flow occurs, over its entire length. This change produced the exhaust flow shown in Test 3. In view of the extra expense involved this work could not be justified for a road car as the larger exhaust valve by itself produced acceptable exhaust flow.

Table 2.2   VW Golf Cylinder Head Flow Test

Valve Lift		Cubic Feet Per Minute Air Flow				
	Test 1		**Test 2**		**Test 3**	
	Inlet	**Exhaust**	**Inlet**	**Exhaust**	**Inlet**	**Exhaust**
0.075in	21	17	22	22	24	23
0.150in	37	30	45	42	46	43
0.220in	51	38	64	53	65	57
0.290in	63	42	78	60	80	64
0.360in	65	47	86	66	86	72
0.430in	66	50	88	68	93	75
0.470in	67	51	89	70	95	78

Test 1 – standard 1.6 VW Golf head with 1.34in inlet and 1.22in exhaust valves

Test 2 – as above with 1.61in inlet and 1.34in exhaust valves

Test 3 – as above with ports modified

A nice straight inlet port like in the Golf and many modern ohc engines can be quite small and give good flow while pushrod engines with more tortuous bends require a larger port to allow acceptable flow. Looking at the illustration of the Chev inlet port you note that there is less flow on one side of the valve because the tight bend in the floor of the port restricts flow around that side of the valve. In fact in some heads flow along the floor of the port, and around the short radius into the combustion chamber, can be as little as 25% of the flow along the port roof and around the opposite side of the valve. Except at low valve lift the majority of mixture flows along the roof and around the more gentle radius into the engine. Hence with this type of head a larger port is necessary than if the port is good and straight, as the straight port has little variation in flow between the port floor and port roof.

Just how large the inlet port should be depends on a number of factors such as cylinder size, engine operating rpm, port shape, valve size etc. so a definite answer is not possible. However, it is true to say that the port must not be more than 0.82 times the valve diameter in the case of round ports, or more than 0.67 times the valve area in the case of rectangular or oval ports. Table 2.3 sets out inlet port sizes which I have found to work well in many applications. These are maximum recommended sizes; many engines will give fine performance with round ports up to 6% smaller in diameter and rectangular or oval ports up to 11% less in area.

Three and four valve heads usually do not require any change in inlet port diameter. If you wish to check, the port diameter should be 0.77 to 0.79 times the valve diameter.

As mentioned earlier, the part on which port modifications should be concentrated is in the area directly above and below the valve seat. To help the air turn into the combustion chamber the inlet pocket must not have straight walls as this destroys flow. Rather a venturi must be formed, as illustrated. At its narrowest point it should be 0.85 to 0.88 times the valve diameter. Sometimes manufacturers just do not

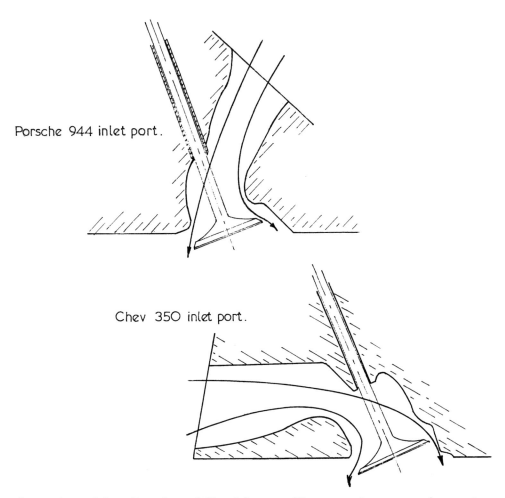

Porsche 944 inlet port.

Chev 350 inlet port.

Comparison of these Porsche and Chev inlet ports illustrates why many modern engines flow so well with relatively small but straight inlet ports.

Table 2.3   Inlet Port Size For Two Valve Engines

Cylinder Size (cc)	Port Diameter (in)	Port Area (sq in)
250	1.13	1.0
325	1.2	1.13
400	1.25	1.23
450	1.32	1.37
500	1.35	1.43
550	1.4	1.54
600	1.48	1.72
700	1.6	2.0

Note: with round ports the port must not be more than 0.82 times the valve diameter and with rectangular or oval ports the port area must not be more than 0.67 times the valve area leave enough metal in the valve pocket to form such a venturi, which leaves just two options. Either we have to be satisfied with less flow or if there is sufficient room in the combustion chamber and the budget is large enough, we can fit larger valves to give the required neckdown in the valve pocket.

Exhaust ports basically require similar modifications to the inlets. The valve pocket area must be radiused and have a throat diameter of 0.85 to 0.86 times the valve diameter. Then the port can open out to about 0.95 times the exhaust valve diameter as it approaches the manifold face. In road applications this is not terribly important as many engines work quite well with a port diameter only 0.89 times the exhaust valve size (for rectangular ports port area is 0.81 times exhaust valve area). If the exhaust ports are too small then grind the top half of the port larger, where most flow occurs. Round and oval ports can be squared at the top while rectangular ports can be made wider in the upper half. Do not lower or widen the floor of exhaust ports as this will create turbulent flow and encourage exhaust gas backflow into the engine.

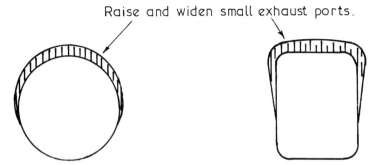

Exhaust ports which are too small should be raised and made wider in the top of the port, where most flow occurs.

A major constriction exists in the exhaust ports of emission engines with the AIR (Air Injection Reactor) system dumping directly into the exhaust port. To adequately support the air injector nozzle a substantial boss is cast in the port roof where most exhaust flow should take place. If it is possible to remove the AIR system, this should be done, then screw plugs in the holes left by the air injectors and grind the bosses away. This often will not be possible so it may be necessary to grind the injector nozzles and bosses down as far as practical, so as not to cause cracking of the port if the roof is fairly thin. If your engine does not have an air injector system but comes from a family of engines equipped with AIR, on some models the exhaust ports may have unused bosses cast in them which will have to be ground away for good exhaust flow. Turbo engines should not have the AIR system removed or rendered inoperative as it actually contributes to performance by increasing exhaust gas volume and velocity at lower rpm. This helps the turbo spool up to speed more quickly, reducing lag and low speed sluggishness.

Because the inlet and exhaust valves can pose a considerable restriction on flow both in and out of the engine, they must be of adequate size and of the correct shape to reduce flow impediments to a minimum. Many tuners by habit replace the stock valves with oversize items and in some instances, as with the 1.6 litre VW Golf, this is a wise move. However, many engines already have sufficiently large valves for road

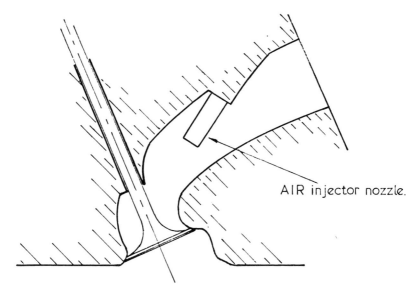

AIR injector nozzle and support boss badly impede exhaust flow because they partly block the top half of the exhaust port.

applications. What is required often is a subtle change to the stock valve shape to effect a good flow gain. There are advantages in retaining standard valves too; they are usually much cheaper than oversize racing valves, they are easy to obtain, the shape and length etc. doesn't change from one batch to the next, and they are usually available in a number of oversize stem sizes which allows the stock valve guides to be reamed out rather than replaced when the time comes to recondition the head. Some people worry about the quality of material used in standard valves but as a rule this is no longer a problem. All emission engines, and in particular unleaded fuel engines, are very hard on valves, hence only good heat and erosion-resistant materials can be used in stock engines. In fact many stock engines use materials in the valve heads very similar to that in competition engines. The secret to getting long valve life in today's engines is not better valve materials but more frequent reconditioning. A little valve guide wear and a rough or carboned up valve seat will soon lead to burned valves no matter what valve metal is specified. Some engines require a head reconditioning job as frequently as every 15,000 to 20,000 miles while others will still go 45,000 to 60,000 miles between valve jobs just like in the good old days.

Standard inlet valves flow much better when a simple 30° backcut is applied. The standard 1.94in Chev valve is typical of many mass produced valves but note in Table 2.4 how much flow improves when it is backcut as illustrated. As you can see, mid-lift flow was improved by up to 12%, which is as much flow gain as could be accomplished with many hours of grinding in the ports. Another relatively simple modification is to undercut the valve stem by 0.035in. In the Chev it produced a 7% flow gain at lower lifts. Care is needed with this latter modification to avoid valve stem fatigue and eventual cracking. The undercut area must be carefully polished and blended into the valve head and also the uncut portion of the valve stem.

Table 2.5 indicates the gains to be made from simple exhaust valve   21

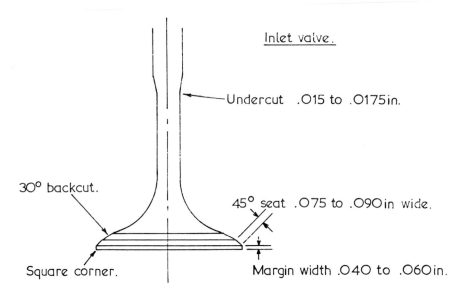

Simple valve modifications can produce as much flow increase as a lot of work in the ports. Inlet valves should be ground with a 30° backcut to blend the seat into the underhead radius. The stem is undercut over the distance between the valve guide and the underhead radius. A square corner between the valve margin and valve face reduces inlet backflow when a performance cam is fitted.

Table 2.4   Chev Inlet Valve Flow Test

Valve Lift	Test 1	Test 2	Test 3
0.050in	18	18	18
0.100in	33	35	38
0.200in	66	74	79
0.300in	98	109	112
0.400in	116	120	121
0.500in	117	117	118

Test 1 – standard Chev 1.94in inlet valve

Test 2 – standard valve with 30° backcut

Test 3 – standard valve with 30° backcut and 0.035in stem undercut

modifications. A 1.5in Chev exhaust valve was chosen for this comparison because of what looks like a very poor underhead shape. A 30° backcut improved the valve shape but flow went up only 3%, which just proves that backcutting does not work on some valves. Next a good radius was applied to the valve face/margin area. This modification picked up flow by over 12% at lower lifts. A 45° cut around the valve face would have worked just as well, but this tends to weaken the valve more than a radius job. The valve stem was not undercut as the exhaust valve stem shape in engines is very carefully established by factory testing for reliability. I know many exhaust valves have a terrible underhead stem shape which does restrict flow. However, that stem shape is required otherwise the heat of the exhaust gases

Table 2.5   Chev Exhaust Valve Flow Test

Valve Lift	Test 1	Test 2	Test 3	Test 4
0.050in	14	14	15	17
0.100in	23	23	27	29
0.200in	42	43	48	53
0.300in	62	64	66	75
0.400in	71	73	74	80
0.500in	76	77	77	81

Test 1 – standard Chev 1.5in exhaust valve

Test 2 – standard valve with 30° backcut

Test 3 – standard valve with 30° backcut and radiused face

Test 4 – 1.5in competition valve with 30° backcut, radiused face and 0.035in undercut stem

combined with their long term corrosive effects would erode the underhead area, precipitating minute cracks which eventually allow the valve head and valve stem to part company. The way around this is to fit expensive high grade competition exhaust valves with nice slim stems. These are of one-piece construction, not a head welded to the stem like many stock valves, and as such require a special aluminium bronze valve guide material to avoid stem scuffing and seizure. By way of comparison, Test 4 shows just how much flow improvement is possible when a competition valve with the correct underhead profile is used. This particular valve comes from the manufacturer with a 0.035in stem undercut. All that was added was a simple 30° backcut and a face radiusing job.

Standard exhaust valves can be modified as shown, with a 30° backcut and a radius to break the margin/valve face corner. If high quality one-piece austenitic stainless steel valves are fitted, the stems may be undercut to reduce their diameter by 0.035in.

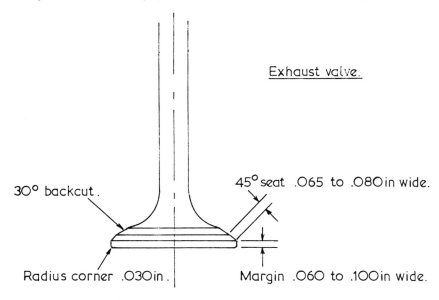

Exhaust valve.

30° backcut.

45° seat .065 to .080in wide.

Radius corner .030in.

Margin .060 to .100in wide.

Table 2.6 sets out the valve sizes which I like to see in a performance/economy engine with a two valve head. The performance difference between the minimum and preferred valve size is not very much in heads developed to give a good spread of power and economy. Theoretically, the bigger valves should flow more air at lower valve lifts and thus increase power output a little right through the range but it frequently does not work out that way. Car manufacturers have been doing a lot of cylinder head work both in-house and with the help of outside consultants for a few years now and they have fairly well worked out what size valves are most suited for road use.

Table 2.6   Valve Sizes For Two Valve Engines

Cylinder Size (cc)	Inlet Valve Diameter (in)		Exhaust Valve Diameter (in)	
	minimum	preferred	minimum	preferred
250	1.32	1.37	1.14	1.18
325	1.4	1.5	1.15	1.32
400	1.5	1.63	1.22	1.35
450	1.55	1.67	1.26	1.38
500	1.6	1.72	1.31	1.42
550	1.63	1.77	1.35	1.47
600	1.67	1.84	1.42	1.53
700	1.72	1.9	1.5	1.6

In the quest for more power and reduced pollution, a number of car makers are now offering engines with three and four valve cylinder heads. The arrangement of two inlet and either one or two exhaust valves in the combustion chamber allows for an increase in valve area over that possible with a two valve head, but contrary to what many believe and write, this increased valve area is not the real reason for the superior performance of a multi-valve engine. The power increase comes about primarily because the combustion chamber is a better shape with a spark plug igniting the fuel mix right in the centre of the combustion space. This brings about a more complete and progressive burn and results in more power. Additionally, with more valves there is more valve flow area at all lifts. Remember that air does not flow through a valve but around its periphery, thus flow area is equal to valve circumference multiplied by valve lift. An engine with a 1.725in valve has a valve area of 2.34sq in, while one with two 1.22in valves has a valve area also of 2.34sq in. However, the single large valve has about 40% less flow area at all valve lifts which restricts its maximum power potential.

Obviously regardless of the number of valves or their size, the combustion chamber wall must not block flow around any of the valve circumference if their full flow potential is to be realised. Years ago most heads had a restrictive bath tub combustion chamber which allowed reasonable flow around only approximately 40% of the valve's circumference. Fortunately today very few heads have such tight combustion chamber walls masking the valves. However, all heads with in-line valves do suffer from some valve masking no matter how well designed, and all the more so if oversize valves are fitted. The way to ease the problem is to grind away the combustion chamber wall which is in close to the edge of the valve. Ideally it would

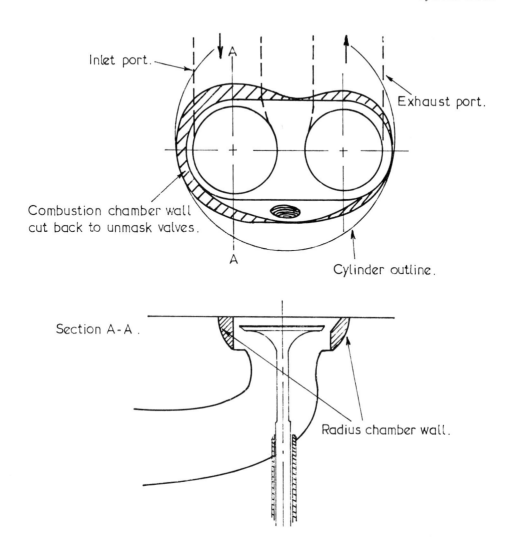

Inlet port.

Exhaust port.

Combustion chamber wall
cut back to unmask valves.

Cylinder outline.

A

A

Section A-A.

Radius chamber wall.

Combustion chambers with in-line valves will require some grinding to unmask the valves. A balance must be struck between high flow and good combustion. If the chamber wall is cut back as far as possible to improve flow, combustion may be slowed excessively and emissions could increase.

be good if we could have a passage between the edge of the valve and the chamber wall which is equal to the valve lift so that at 0.100in lift the wall is 0.100in from the valve, at 0.200in lift it is 0.200in from the valve and so forth. Such a chamber would probably flow reasonably well but the compression ratio would be very low and the mixture burn would be slow and inefficient. Hence a practical compromise has to be struck. The two ends of the chamber can only be ground back as far as the head gasket fire ring outline otherwise the head gasket will not seal. Around the inlet valve we want the chamber wall approximately 0.9 times the valve lift from the valve edge on the "live" or high flow side and about 0.65 times the valve lift from the edge of the valve on the "dead" short turn radius side. The chamber wall can be in much tighter 25 around the exhaust valve; about 0.7 times the valve lift on the high flow side of the valve and approximately 0.55 times the valve lift on the short turn radius side of the valve.

More and more modern engines are fitted with heads featuring semi-hemi or pentroof combustion chambers and inclined valves. With a few exceptions, the combustion chamber does not shroud the valves to any extent in these designs. So unless there is an obvious deficiency, leave these combustion chambers alone and spend your time getting the valve pocket and valve seats right.

All heads need accurately ground multi-angle valve seats to give good flow, and more importantly a perfect gas-tight seal for many thousands of miles. The actual seat angle should be 45°, 0.050in wide for the inlet and 0.070in wide for the exhaust. The outside diameter of the seat is 0.015–0.020in less than the inlet valve diameter and up to 0.010in less than the exhaust valve head diameter. The top cut to blend the seat into the combustion chamber is at a 30° angle and just wide enough to blend the 45° seat into the chamber roof. The throat cut is usually made at 60° but this is best determined on the flow bench as some inlets show superior flow with a fourth cut of 70–75° and exhausts can need a single cut of from 55–70°.

Some tuners like to use valve seats much narrower than I have suggested but this is not wise for road engines. Narrow seats flow better than wide seats only at very high lifts and at low and mid-lift they do not flow as well. Additionally, narrow seats pound out quickly which can lead to valve burning or lost performance. A valve gets rid of its heat primarily through the valve seat so if the seat becomes rough the valve head overheats, warps and finally burns.

The other heat flow path for the valve is via the valve guide to the engine

The inlet valve seat is cut 0.050 to 0.060in wide for long life. The outside diameter of the seat should be about 0.020in smaller than the valve head diameter. Because we want the valve as high as possible for good flow, the 30° topcut is kept less than 0.040in wide. The 60° undercut will be about 0.100in wide, blending into the factory throat cut.

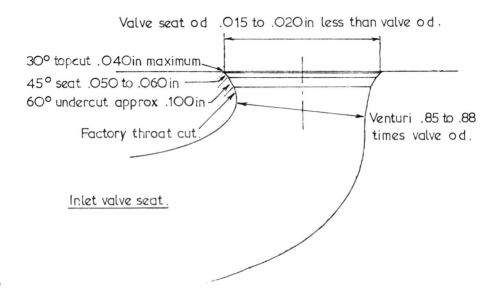

Valve seat o d   .015 to .020 in less than valve o d .

30° topcut .040in maximum

45° seat .050 to .060 in

60° undercut approx .100 in

Factory throat cut.

Venturi .85 to .88 times valve o d .

Inlet valve seat.

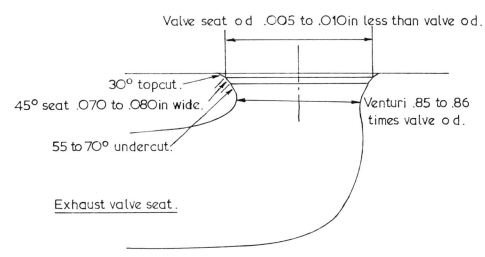

Valve seat o d .005 to .010 in less than valve o d.

30° topcut.
45° seat .070 to .080 in wide.

55 to 70° undercut.

Venturi .85 to .86 times valve o d.

Exhaust valve seat.

The exhaust valve seat is a little wider than the inlet to help get rid of the additional heat. The outside diameter of the 45° cut is almost the same as the valve head diameter because the valve will grow when hot. The width of the 30° topcut is not critical. In fact sinking the exhaust valves a little can help reduce mixture draw through and exhaust reversion. If a flow bench is not available stick to a 60° undercut and radius it into the venturi.

coolant, so do ensure that the guide and stem are not worn excessively. Primarily, the valve guide is responsible for accurately guiding the valve onto the valve seat, to effect a gas seal. When the guide and valve stem wear, this allows the valve to wobble as it seats, wearing the seat to an irregular shape. Again heat transfer is reduced so the valve head warps and eventually burns. In some engines though the problem can be much more serious than a burned valve; it can lead to a major blow-up! What can happen if the valve is very hot and the engine is running at higher rpm, is for the valve head to bend a couple of degrees relative to the valve stem. Each time the valve seats it bends back a different way, eventually fatiguing the stem. The valve head drops off and proceeds to hole a piston. Usually, welded two-piece valves are blamed for this type of blow-up but it is worn valve guides and worn valve seats which are the real problem.

Valve guides can only be accurately measured for wear after all the carbon baked into them has been removed. Generally, the clearance should be 0.001–0.003in for the inlets and 0.0015–0.004in for the exhausts. Don't rely upon your sense of feel, actually measure the clearance to ensure that it is within limits. If the clearance is excessive, the guides will have to be reamed and valves with oversize stems fitted. Alternatively, new valve guides may be fitted and the old valves can have their stems "paralleled".

Just as worn valve guides allow oil into the engine, upsetting combustion and perhaps causing detonation, so too can the absence of effective valve stem seals and oil splash shields. Personally I do not like the Teflon-type seals which press over the valve guide. In race engines that never see worn valve stems or guides they work fine but for road use where the stem to guide clearance is ideal for only a few thousand miles they just do not work. If there is sufficient room I prefer to use the common 27 "umbrella" type valve stem seal which fits firmly on the stem up under the valve spring retainer. Unfortunately, this seal will not fit inside some inner valve springs or dampers, and it may interfere with valve spring retainer to valve guide clearance with some high lift cams. The other common seal is the "O" ring type which is concealed between the valve stem, the collets and valve cap. This type is not as effective as an "umbrella" seal but will work well when used in conjunction with Teflon-type seals or under-retainer oil splash shields.

Faulty or the wrong type of valve stem seals, and the removal of oil splash shields, are probably the most common cause of excessive oil consumption, and a problem which is frequently underrated or overlooked. I have had freshly reconditioned engines brought to me which showed exhaust smoke at idle. Investigation showed that the oil splash shields had been left off. Replacing the shields stopped the smoke and cut oil consumption. Many race teams are now using umbrella seals in their production-based long distance race engines. Oil consumption has been halved in some cases. Overhead cam engines with inverted bucket type cam followers, which fit over the valve stem and valve spring, sometimes do not have valve stem seals fitted at the factory because this type of cam follower stops oil from getting onto the valve stem. However, oil vapour can be drawn down the inlet valve guide under high vacuum conditions. To prevent this, Teflon seals which press over the valve guide may be fitted on the inlets, cutting oil consumption and carbon deposits under the valve head and in the combustion chamber.

For the head to seal against the engine block it must be flat, with a stable and rigid deck and, of course, the correct type of head gasket must be used. Most alloy heads will experience sealing problems, due to a thin flexible deck, if more than 0.030–0.040in is machined off to reduce the combustion chamber volume. Some cast iron heads have such a thick deck that it is possible to mill off 0.100in if necessary, without any problems. 0.050–0.060in is a safer upper limit and this amount should suffice in most instances to restore chamber volume lost from unshrouding the valves. Chev cast iron heads made after about mid-1977 were cast thinner to reduce engine weight. These should not be machined more than 0.020in to avoid gasket problems. Whereas the earlier heavy heads have a straight deck edge under the spark plugs, the light heads have a projection between the head bolt holes under each spark plug.

Very few modern engines suffer head sealing problems in performance/economy tune if a little care is taken to select the correct type of head gasket. Usually the manufacturer's standard head gasket will be suitable; however I would not use a copper asbestos gasket or a stainless steel gasket. Naturally if the engine has been radically overbored, against my recommendation, then the standard gasket may lap

Lightweight Chev cast iron heads are very thin in the deck and should not be milled more than 0.020in to avoid gasket problems.

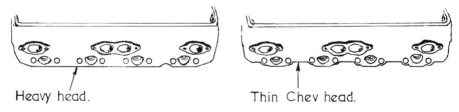

Heavy head.   Thin Chev head.

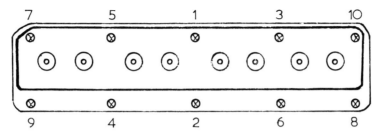

To avoid head warpage the manufacturer's tensioning sequence should be followed. Remember to increase the tension in about four stages. When removing the head, the tensioning sequence is reversed.

over the bore and be unsuitable. Also, where car makers have changed over to alloy heads for their latest engines do be sure to get the correct gasket set which suits an alloy head. A thin mild steel shim gasket will work well enough, if fitted the correct way up, with cast iron heads, but they will not effectively seal aluminium heads. The correct way to fit mild steel gaskets is with the channel rolled into them facing up as if to hold water. Mostly though head gaskets are a composition type with a mild steel fire ring. Some are coated around the water and oil holes with a sealer to prevent leaks. This sealer should not be removed with solvent as it does a good job of stopping water or oil seepage between the head and block. Regardless of the gasket material I always use a very thin coating of sealant; Rolls-Royce Hylomar for copper/steel/asbestos gaskets and non-hardening Permatex No. 3 for mild steel and composition gaskets. If the gaskets are factory pre-coated with a sealer I apply the sealer only around the gasket fire ring area.

When the head is fitted, the head bolts should have their threads buffed and oiled to ensure good tensioning. If the threads break into the water jacket delete the bolt thread oiling and apply a silicone sealant such as Silastic RTV. Then tighten the head bolts in the sequence recommended by the manufacturer. Note that this sequence is reversed for head removal. I always tension the head in progressive steps to prevent warpage. If the head tension was 80lbf ft I would first take all the bolts down to 30lbf ft, then 50, 70 and finally 80lbf ft. In about 15 minutes go over the bolts again. That's it for the moment if the head is alloy. With cast iron heads bring the engine to normal operating temperature and then re-tension the bolts. Final gasket set should take place after about 300 miles of driving, so then re-tension the head, either alloy or iron, again. This should not be done if the bolts break into the water jacket as leakage past the threads may result.

Chapter 3

Fuel and Compression Ratio

I don't think anyone has to be told that today's fuels are not what they used to be. Not too many years ago 100–103 octane five star fuel was freely available, allowing the use of compression ratios approaching 11:1. That situation has changed dramatically in just a few years because of pollution control and steep rises in crude oil prices in the early 80s. Today, the best leaded fuel is usually no better than 97–98 octane and the lead content is down from about 3 grams per gallon to 0.4–0.8 grams per gallon in many countries. In countries where pollution has become an issue, new cars have to make do with unleaded fuel. Some countries have only one grade of unleaded, of about 91–92 octane, while others have a high octane unleaded of 96–98 octane as well.

Since much confusion exists as to what octane ratings are all about it is best to have a look at the subject before we get into what options are open to us to improve the poor quality fuel situation which exists. Most people realise that we can get more power and better fuel economy with a high octane fuel because we can use a higher compression ratio, and perhaps more spark advance, without running into a detonation problem. However, many don't realise that simply changing from, say, 97 octane pump petrol to 100/130 Avgas, which has an octane rating of about 110, will not necessarily give any power increase. Actually, you could lose power if the engine was not modified, or could not be changed in any way to take advantage of the octane increase.

To understand this more easily, we have to delve back into history to see why a number system was introduced to grade fuels, and discover exactly to what the octane numbers refer. About the time of World War I, aircraft engines would suddenly self-destruct, through detonation. An engine might run just fine on one load of fuel, but punch holes in the pistons on the next batch. The fuels seemed to be the same, weigh the same, and may perhaps have come from the very same refinery.

The fuel companies tried chemical analysis in an endeavour to achieve parity from one lot of petrol to the next but, in spite of an intensive programme, they were not able to weed out the batches which were prone to produce engine knock. Therefore special fuel research engines, with a variable compression feature, were constructed to evaluate and grade fuels. Such a standard heavy-duty, single-cylinder test engine would be warmed up to a standard test temperature, run at standard rpm and load, and then have the compression ratio increased until the fuel being tested just produced engine knock. Its anti-knock quality would then be specified as its Highest Useable Compression Ratio (HUCR).

Even with every fuel test lab supplied with the same type of test engine, and using the same standard test procedure, it was discovered that the same fuel could test out with differing HUCR numbers in different laboratories. It was next decided that some unvarying standard was needed by which to calibrate the lab test engine. Two pure substances were chosen as reference fuels. The high reference fuel chosen was 2–2–4 trimethylpentane, what we commonly call iso-octane, while the low reference fuel was normal heptane (n-heptane).

Now it was decided that a fuel under test would be run in the variable compression test engine and its HUCR determined. Then a series of runs would be made with various mixtures of iso-octane and n-heptane until a blend was found which produced knock behaviour identical to the fuel being tested. At this point the quality of the test fuel would be rated in relation to the percentage of iso-octane in the reference fuel mixture which gave identical test results. For example, a fuel which behaved the same as a mixture of 90% iso-octane/10% n-heptane would be called 90 octane fuel. Using this standard test procedure, fuel of constant quality could be refined and supplied for a variety of applications.

Since that time a number of test procedures have come into use to simulate a variety of engine operating conditions. Motor spirit is usually rated according to the Research or Motor test methods. Both measuring techniques use the same single-cylinder, variable-compression test engine, but as indicated in Table 3.1 the Motor method employs a greater engine speed and a higher inlet mixture temperature than the Research test. Hence the Motor method is a more severe test, and generally yields octane numbers 6 to 12 less than the Research test as shown in Table 3.2. This distinction is important, as it informs us that the Motor Octane Number (MON) is more relevant to today's engines, and in particular turbo engines which operate at high inlet temperatures, than is the Research Octane Number (RON).

Table 3.1   Comparison of Motor and Research test procedures

	Motor Octane Test	Research Octane Test
Inlet air temperature	148.9°C	65.6°C
Engine jacket temperature	100°C	100°C
Engine rpm	900	600

The spread between the Motor and Research numbers is known as the fuel's sensitivity and it is very important to understand what this distinction is exactly. Because intake temperature affects different fuel compounds in various ways it is possible for a company to come up with a fuel which has a high Research number (or a high Pump Octane Number) of say, 97 but by the Motor test that same fuel would only rate as, say, 85 octane. Hence it would perform as an 85 octane fuel in a modern   31

Table 3.2   Octane test comparison

Research Octane Number	Motor Octane Number	Pump Octane Number
90	83	86.5
92	85	88.5
96	88	92
98	90	94
100	91.5	95.8
105	95	100
110	99	104.5

Note: the octane numbers in this table are approximate only and will vary by as much as 2 from one fuel to another

emissions or turbo engine with high inlet temperatures. However, on another day the same fuel company could use a different blend of fuel compounds, depending on what was available in storage or the type of crude oil being "cracked", and produce a fuel again with a Research octane of 97, but with a Motor number of 89. This is why there is this frequent complaint of "bad fuel". The Research number may legally be up where the company says it is, but because of the sensitivity of the blending compounds the fuel could be performing like low octane stuff because of the high inlet temperatures common in modern engines. Years ago, when high lead levels were usual, this sensitivity problem seldom surfaced as lead tends to "cushion" fuel sensitivity. However, with today's unleaded and low-lead fuels, fuel sensitivity will continue to cause us problems in modern engines for as long as Research octane figures are used as the industry standard to rate commercially available fuels.

In America the service station pumps carry a Pump Octane Number (PON) rather than the Research Octane Number usual on pumps in other parts of the world. This rating is the average of the RON and MON:

$$\frac{RON + MON}{2}$$

but it does not completely overcome the problem of fuel sensitivity. For example, a 92 PON fuel may have an 88 Motor rating and a 96 Research rating. However, fuel with a 92 PON from the same company may test out at 86 Motor and 98 Research because of the blend of compounds used in another batch. Hence even with this system the octane could vary by 2 points (88 to 86 Motor) as the engine of today with high inlet temperatures sees it.

The Supercharge test is applied to aircraft fuels which exceed 100 octane numbers, as the other tests obviously become meaningless at anything over 100 octane. The Supercharge Octane Numbers (SON) are really performance numbers obtained by linearly extending the scale beyond 100. In this test the reference fuel is iso-octane plus lead. Two tests are involved, the F3 and F4, which explains why aircraft fuels have a dual rating such as 100/130. The first number refers to the F3 test, which simulates a supercharged engine running on a chemically-correct fuel/air mixture, as when cruising. The F4 number gives an indication of the fuel's performance rating with an enriched mixture and increased supercharge boost, as would be supplied during aircraft take-off or during combat conditions.

There are really only two types of Avgas freely available today, both rated 100/130. The old green coloured 100/130 is a high lead variety with 4.5 to 6 grams of tetraethyl-lead (t.e.l.) per gallon while the newer blue coloured Avgas has 2 to 2.7 grams of lead per gallon.

The anti-knock properties of hydrocarbon fuels are related to their molecular structures. The paraffins, such as normal heptane and kerosene, are long chains of carbon and hydrogen held together by weak molecular bonds which are easily broken by heat. Iso-octane is a member of the iso-paraffin family. These have a branched chain structure that form stronger bonds to resist detonation better. The cycloparaffins (or napthenes) also have good anti-detonation properties with their hydrogen and carbon atoms well bonded in a ring-shaped molecule. The aromatic fuels, such as toluol, have a ring-shaped structure with very strong bonds. This explains why they have such good anti-knock characteristics.

The chemical composition determines just how rapidly the fuel will burn and whether it will be resistant to detonation at high compression pressures and temperatures. The fuels with weak molecular bonds break up and burn spontaneously (i.e., without being ignited by the combustion flame initiated by the firing of the spark plug) at lower temperatures and pressure than fuels with strongly bonded structures. Some fuel additives, such as the aromatics, make excellent anti-detonants because they burn slowly and don't oxidise or burn completely until combustion chamber temperature and pressure is very high. Such additives therefore inhibit, or slow down, combustion. Hence a high octane fuel will not increase power unless the engine actually needs a fuel which is chemically stable at high temperature and pressure. Obviously, if the engine does not have a compression ratio and spark advance great enough to produce high combustion pressure and temperature, then the high octane fuel will not burn completely during the early phase of the power stroke, resulting in loss of power.

Table 3.3 shows the results of fuel tests carried out on a 4.1 litre Buick. Because the engine was being developed to run on 92 octane unleaded the compression ratio was kept down to 8.8:1. The cam was a Phase III grind with 210° inlet and exhaust duration and 0.425in lift. In each test the total ignition advance was changed to achieve the maximum hp figures indicated, at 5000rpm. In all, six different fuels were

Table 3.3   Comparison fuel test of 4.1 litre Buick

Fuel	Test 1		Test 2	
	hp	Advance	hp	Advance
92 unleaded "summer A"	212	28°	220	31°
92 unleaded "summer B"	219	30°	223	32°
92 unleaded "winter B"	208	26°	215	29°
97 unleaded "summer A"	215	30°	222	33°
97 leaded "summer A"	218	30°	221	33°
100/130 Avgas "green"	222	40°	224	44°
100/130 Avgas "green"	210	30°	213	33°

Test 1 – heat to inlet manifold

Test 2 – heat blocked off to inlet manifold

tested; two different brands of 92 unleaded "summer" blend, a 92 unleaded "winter" blend from the same company as fuel B, a 97 unleaded, a 97 leaded with 1.8 grams per gallon, and "green" Avgas.

In the first series of tests the inlet manifold was heated to check the sensitivity of the fuels and in the second series the manifold heat passage was blocked to prevent flow through it. Note that this modification may not be suitable in cooler climates as the engine could lose some economy and cold driveability. As can be seen, the high octane unleaded was very temperature sensitive, as was the low octane unleaded from the same company. Both fuels only worked really well with reduced intake charge temperature. The 100/130 Avgas, as expected, made good power but required a lot of advance. When the advance was cut back, the power dropped.

The 92 winter blend was thrown in to show what effect fuel volatility can have on performance. In summer (or at higher altitudes) we don't want the fuel vaporising too easily and causing vapour lock. However, in the winter the fuel must vaporise easily, and stay in vapour to allow easy starting and acceptable driveability while the engine is below normal operating temperature. To achieve these fuel characteristics the fuel companies change the fuel blend according to the season and the altitude. At the risk of over-simplification what they do is blend in more of the volatile "front-end" molecules (also called "light ends") which vaporise and fire more easily. This brings another problem; that of reducing the shelf life and the octane rating as these molecules are released into the atmosphere. The more light ends, the shorter the shelf life, and the quicker the fuel loses octane level, which can be as much as 2–4 octane numbers. Apparently this is a problem with some high octane unleaded as well, so if you live away from the city in a location where there is a lower turn over of fuel you may often be getting old or out of season fuel which will require the use of a lower compression ratio to compensate.

The compression ratio has always been of interest to engine tuners, even more so today with the need to achieve the best possible fuel economy and power on low octane and unleaded fuel. In the past tuners liked to see the compression ratio pushed up as high as possible because high compression has always been equated with high horsepower. I agree that the compression ratio should be as high as practicable, but often the manufacturer has already found the limit and built his engines accordingly. If this is the case then all we can do is check that production tolerances have not lowered the ratio significantly below that which the makers intended.

The actual value of compression ratio which may be used in any engine is dependent on the design and size of the combustion chamber, the cam timing and overlap period, and the fuel octane rating. In the case of turbo engines we need to add the boost pressure and intake charge temperature as well. Generally speaking, small "fast burn" pentroof and semi-hemi combustion chambers and longer duration cams permit the use of a higher compression ratio than bathtub or wedge chambers and short duration cams. For example, the 1.6 litre four valve Toyota Corolla with a 81mm bore and pentroof chamber will run quite happily with standard cams on a 9.4:1 compression ratio burning only 92 octane unleaded fuel. With mild cams the compression can be upped to 10:1. Conversely, the 5 litre Holden with open wedge chambers and a 101.6mm bore will tolerate no more than a true 8.8:1 compression ratio with a mild cam on the same fuel. Increasing the fuel octane rating to 97 permits a compression ratio of 9.3:1 to be employed.

Research has indicated that increasing the compression ratio from 8.5:1 to 10.5:1 will result in a 10 to 12% fuel saving, with improved torque and acceleration as a bonus. Unfortunately, such a large jump just will not be tolerated with the fuel now available. Some tuners feel that the compression ratio can be pushed way up and then the ignition timing backed off to stop detonation. If this is done, the engine loses responsiveness and fuel efficiency. Table 3.4 indicates the result when this was tried on a 5 litre Holden. A Phase IV cam with 212° inlet and exhaust duration and 0.443in lift was used in all tests. In the first test, stock compression was used. It was supposed to be 8.5:1 according to the manufacturer, but in reality was a true 8.2:1. The engine made good power and torque on 30° total ignition advance. For Test 2 the compression ratio was increased to 10.8:1 but the engine wouldn't take full load without detonating severely so the timing was backed off until the detonating was eliminated at 19° total advance. With the distributor recurved to suit, the engine produced the figures indicated. The test was a disaster, with power down at all engine speeds. Added to this the engine sounded dead on the dyno and without the crispness that it had previously shown. Perhaps the "rattling" while the ignition timing was being sorted had damaged the pistons and rings which could have contributed to the poor power figures. Before stripping the engine to determine if this was a problem, a 50/50 fuel mix of 97 unleaded and Avgas 100/130 (106 Research octane approximately) was prepared to see if the engine would respond to good fuel. Test 3 shows the results with the distributor recurved and 35° total advance. The engine really responded to the change and showed just how much high compression and good fuel is worth in outright power. For Test 4 the compression was brought down to a more realistic 9.3:1. The distributor was recurved and total advance set at 27°. This increased maximum power by 8hp at 5000rpm over that in Test 1 and would have resulted in a fuel saving of around 5 or 6% on the highway. These tests clearly show that getting the compression ratio up within the limits of available fuel will give better performance. However, going too far and then backing the timing off will not solve the problem. The result will be lost power and generally sluggish performance.

Table 3.4   Compression ratio comparison test of 5 litre Holden

rpm	Test 1		Test 2		Test 3		Test 4	
	hp	Torque	hp	Torque	hp	Torque	hp	Torque
2000	109	286	102	269	117	306	112	294
2500	141	297	136	286	150	315	144	302
3000	174	304	167	292	183	320	179	313
3500	208	312	196	294	216	324	211	316
4000	237	311	219	288	248	326	241	317
4500	251	293	232	271	265	309	256	299
5000	257	270	241	253	270	284	265	278
5500	247	236	219	209	256	244	249	238

Test 1 – 8.2:1 compression ratio, 30° total advance, 97 octane fuel

Test 2 – 10.8:1 compression ratio, 19° total advance, 97 octane fuel

Test 3 – 10.8:1 compression ratio, 35° total advance, approximately 106 octane fuel

Test 4 – 9.3:1 compression ratio, 27° total advance, 97 octane fuel

Although a fuel blend was used during the testing of this engine I do not really recommend mixing fuel for road use for a number of reasons, namely; inconvenience, no guarantee of blending agents being freely available in all localities, possible damage to catalytic converter and oxygen sensor, danger to health from compounds being mixed, danger from fire.

In lands where only low octane leaded (91–93 Research) is available at the pump, enthusiasts have been tempted to blend in high octane unleaded (96–98 Research) in an attempt to get a higher octane leaded fuel. However, engines not designed for unleaded fuel require a minimum 0.05–0.1 grams of lead per litre for general use and 0.1–0.2 grams of lead per litre for high performance use to avoid valve and valve seat damage. Hence, if 92 octane leaded containing 0.2 grams of lead per litre was blended 1:2 with 98 octane unleaded, the resulting fuel would contain almost 0.07 grams lead per litre and have an octane rating of 96. Such fuel would be suitable for general use at moderate engine speeds and occasional high speed/high load bursts. Blended 3:2 these fuels would be suitable for high performance use with a lead content of 0.12 grams per litre and an octane level of 94.4 Research.

If your engine is designed to operate on leaded fuel do not use straight unleaded otherwise the valves and seats will soon be damaged. Running the occasional tank of unleaded through the engine will not hurt, providing leaded is used for the next fill. Using leaded fuel in a car designed to burn unleaded will not cause engine damage, in fact it will make life easier for the valves; however the lead will wreck the catalytic converter and in time also the oxygen sensor.

For those enthusiasts who engage in a little weekend competition driving, a little more advanced fuel blending may be in order providing the engine components are up to handling more turbo boost or more spark advance to take advantage of high octane fuel. At the present time there are a large number of concentrated octane booster additives on the market which are designed to convert pump petrol, either leaded or unleaded, into racing fuel. When blended in the correct proportions boosters which work will raise the octane rating of fuel about 5 points; double strength they raise the octane by up to 8 points. Some companies claim that their boosters will produce 108–110 octane fuel, equivalent to Avgas 100/130, but I have not found this to be true. In fact a number of boosters will give only a 2 octane increase. One booster which does work is *104+*. Mixed at normal strength this booster will give a true 5 points octane increase, allowing about 2–4° increase in spark advance or around an extra 2–3lb boost. Mixed double strength *104+* has little additional effect on some fuels, but with many fuels will yield an 8 point octane boost. To take advantage of this increase another 6–8° spark advance or up to 3–5lb more boost would be required.

When using these concentrated additives, there are two points you must keep in mind. The first is that American concentrates are usually marketed in US quarts, which equal 946cc as opposed to the Imperial quart of 1136.5cc. Therefore, if you live outside the USA you will have to carefully work out the blending ratio for the liquid measure used in your country. The second point is with regard to mixing technique. Don't just pour a can of octane booster into a drum of fuel and expect it to blend properly. What is preferable is to mix the concentrate with about 2–3 gallons of petrol, give the drum a good shake, and then add this mixture to the untreated fuel.

Avgas 100/130, either "green" or "blue", is also an excellent octane booster for weekend competition, but remember if the catalytic converter is left in place this leaded fuel will wreck it. A 50/50 blend should give as much octane as is required for weekend competition, around 106 octane with 98 unleaded and about 104 with 97 leaded.

For years enthusiasts have blended products such as toluol (Methyl Benzine), benzol and acetone with petrol to produce an octane increase. This worked well in the past when the octane level of petrol was boosted by the addition of large amounts of lead. However, current unleaded and low lead fuels may already have a percentage of either toluol or benzol, in particular, blended in to reach the required octane rating stated on the service station pump. Hence the addition of more of these products does not guarantee an increase in octane rating. At times a 1:4 toluol/petrol blend may permit the turbo boost to be wound up from 10 psi to 14 psi, but on another day you may punch holes in the pistons because the octane level has not risen significantly because the base fuel has already been loaded up with toluol and/or benzol. It all depends on what the refinery has available to it on any given day. If they have plenty of toluol or benzol in storage they will take this cheaper route to bring the petrol up to the required octane level. However, if the storage tanks of benzol and toluol are low then they will use more extensive refining to bring the petrol up to the required octane rating.

For a few years now water injection has been hailed by some as the perfect knock suppressor. I do not agree and apparently none of the car manufacturers do either. Water does not contribute to the combustion process, rather it takes heat and hence energy out of the combustion flame as it is converted to steam. This slows combustion, so unless the water is actually injected when the engine is under a heavy load, power and economy are lost. Many systems which I have seen inject too much water, not properly vapourised, and at the wrong level of engine loading. Some people use a 50/50 water/alcohol mix because the alcohol at least does contribute to the combustion process. However, this is not without its problems either; the alcohol in combination with water causes top cylinder and piston ring corrosion, shortening the life of the engine.

Now, I will not deny that some very sophisticated systems are appearing with special jets to "fog" the water, and complex electronic management to ensure that the correct quantity of water, usually at about 80 psi, is injected. These systems are very expensive and I question the need to go to this expense when for far less money, and superior results, toluol injection could be fitted. Turbo race cars may have no alternative but to use water injection as the regulations often require that ordinary pump petrol be used. However, this constraint does not apply to road cars, so in high boost/high compression engines toluol injection is an option worth considering.

In the most simple toluol injection systems a fifth injector sprays pure toluol into the inlet air stream under high boost or high engine load conditions. The fifth injector can be activated by a pressure switch connected to the inlet manifold, or it may be activated by a switch connected to the throttle plate. The complete system incorporates a small fuel tank of 5–10 litres for the toluol, a high-pressure fuel injection fuel pump, a fuel injector, a fuel feed line and a fuel return line. To maintain fuel pressure a fuel injection system pressure regulator may be used, or alternatively a "pill", a restrictor, may be fitted in the fuel return line.

When precise control of the fifth injector is desirable a more sophisticated system is called for, with the toluol injector being pulsed by a mapped electronic 37 management system. With this type of system the quantity of toluol injected would vary according to such things as turbo boost, engine rpm, engine load and inlet air temperature.

Because toluol drops out of vapour fairly easily, some consideration must be given as to the most suitable location for the extra injector. In turbo engines the fifth injector can be fitted at the intercooler outlet, while in non-turbo applications it is usually best located just before the throttle plate.

Because a number of modern engines have a knock sensor which relays back to the ignition chip that ignition retard is momentarily required, some tuners indiscriminately push up the turbo boost or the compression ratio. They figure that since this system is in place they will let it prevent engine knock. This is definitely not the way to go. You may impress a few people telling them how much boost or compression that your engine is able to run, but that is about the limit to what you will gain out of the exercise. As shown earlier in Table 3.4 too much compression just reduces maximum power no matter how good the ignition retard system. Some manufacturers also deliberately run too much compression and leave it to the knock sensor to keep them out of trouble. This usually is done to improve part throttle fuel economy, which is good for advertising, but also in America the manufacturers have to meet the government corporate fuel consumption levels averaged over the total number of vehicles produced. A higher compression than desired will allow some engine models to squeeze through without upsetting the delicate equation for the other engine models. For the same reason you will find that some engine models are available in very limited numbers and then only with a certain gearbox and rear axle combination so as not to put a dent in the corporate average fuel consumption figures.

Just how much compression or boost is desirable with today's pump fuel? As I indicated earlier there are far too many factors involved to give an accurate answer, but the figures shown in Table 3.5 will give a guide to the compression ratio suitable for naturally aspirated engines with a reasonably quick burn combustion chamber, a Phase II or Phase III cam, and a squish clearance of no more than 0.045in. For a turbo engine I like to see the compression ratio up at 8:1 to give reasonable part throttle economy and acceptable off-boost performance. For the engine to live with an 8:1 compression ratio boost will have to be limited to the level indicated in Table 3.6. Note that the boost levels with an intercooler refers to an effective unit which reduces the intake charge temperature by 50–60°C. Some intercoolers are far less effective, reducing charge air temperature by only 25–30°C.

Some tuners suggest that you don't concern yourself with intercooler size, but rather increase the boost and install an intercooler water spray. This is dangerous advice for several reasons. If the factory installation provided a maximum 7 psi boost the intercooler core or tanks could "blow", without suitable strapping and reinforcing,

Table 3.5   Compression ratio for naturally aspirated engines

Bore diameter mm	91–92 octane	96–97 octane
76	9.3:1	9.8:1
83	9.2:1	9.7:1
90	9.0:1	9.5:1
100	8.6:1	9.0:1

Table 3.6   Turbo boost/compression ratio

Compression ratio	91–92 octane	96–97 octane
7.7:1	7 psi	9.5 psi
7.7:1 intercooled	11 psi	14 psi
8:1	6 psi	8.5 psi
8:1 intercooled	10 psi	13 psi
8.5:1	5 psi	7 psi
8.5:1 intercooled	7.5 psi	10 psi
9:1		5.5 psi
9:1 intercooled		8 psi

at say 13 psi boost. To be really effective a water spray system has to dump a lot of water onto the intercooler, but if the spray system is not carefully metered and/or the intercooler is too cold, that water will not rise off as steam but will end up under the tyres causing serious traction problems. Competition cars regularly have a 30 litre water tank which is sufficient for about 30 miles on the race circuit or rally stage, but many road kits which I have seen have a tiny 3 or 4 litre plastic bottle. When the water bottle empties under boost it is meltdown time for the pistons.

The actual compression ratio is the relationship between the total volume of the cylinder, head gasket and combustion chamber, with the piston at BDC (bottom dead centre) and the volume contained in the space between the piston crown, head gasket and combustion chamber at TDC (top dead centre). This is expressed by the formula:

$$CR = \frac{CV + CCV}{CCV}$$

where CV = cylinder volume
CCV = combustion chamber volume

Naturally CV is the engine capacity in cc divided by the number of cylinders. CCV however is not so easy. This volume is made up of the combustion chamber volume, plus the volume that remains above the piston when the piston is at TDC, plus the volume caused by the thickness of the head gasket, plus the volume of the dish if dished pistons are used, or minus the amount displaced by high top pistons if these are fitted.

When we know what compression ratio we want then we can calculate what the volume CCV should be to give that ratio using the formula:

$$CCV = \frac{CV}{CR-1}$$

Assuming the engine has 500cc cylinders and we want a compression ratio of 9.2:1 then:

$$CCV = \frac{500}{9.2 - 1} = \frac{500}{8.2} = 61cc$$

39

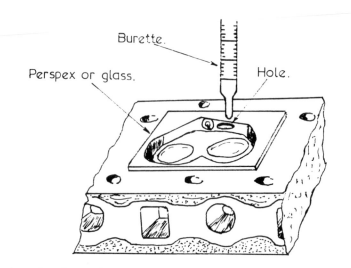

The combustion chamber volume is measured using a burette. For road engines the volumes do not have to be carefully equalised.

To find what the actual value of CCV is in our engine we first must physically measure the volume of the combustion chamber using a burette filled with liquid paraffin (kerosene). Incidentally, the combustion chambers should have been equalised in volume so that for road engines, there is not more than a 0.1 change in compression ratio from cylinder to cylinder. This means that if the pistons are the same level below the top of the block at TDC then an engine with 300cc cylinders will have a variation of no more than 0.5cc between the largest and smallest combustion chamber. For a 500cc cylinder the spread between the largest and smallest should not exceed 0.8cc and for 700cc cylinders the spread is 1cc.

If the engine has pistons which are either dished or high top, or have valve cut-outs, then the increase or decrease that they are causing has to be measured. For instance, if the cylinder bore is 90mm in diameter and the piston crown at the edge is

When dished or high top pistons are fitted, or if the piston crown has valve cut-outs, the volume has to be measured so as to ascertain the compression ratio.

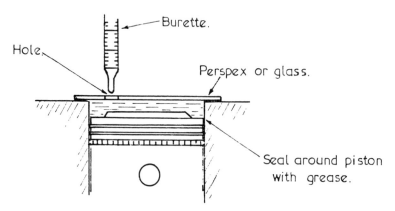

6mm from the block deck, using the formula:

$$V = \frac{\pi D^2 \times H}{4000}$$

where $\pi = 3.1416$

$D =$ bore in mm

$H =$ height between piston crown edge and block deck in mm

this volume should be:

$$V = \frac{\pi \times 90^2 \times 6}{4000} = 38.2cc$$

If on measuring the volume with a burette it is found to be 27.2cc, the lump on top of the piston decreases CCV by 11cc (38.2 – 27.2 = 11).

If the piston in this example had a dished top and the volume as measured by the burette was 52.7cc then the dish volume would be 14.5cc, increasing CCV by 14.5cc (52.7 – 38.2 = 14.5).

The above formula is also used to find the volume of the head gasket by measuring the thickness of a used, and thus compressed, gasket. If the pistons are flat tops and they are below the block deck at TDC, the same formula is used to find this volume as well.

To assist in equalising compression and combustion pressures, the crown of every piston should rise to approximately the same point in each cylinder. This is called the deck height or deck clearance. I like to keep the squish clearance between 0.035 and a maximum of 0.045in to assist combustion and cylinder scavenging. Hence if the compressed thickness of the head gasket is 0.030in then the deck clearance

A tight squish clearance of 0.035 to 0.045in speeds up combustion. The squish clearance is the sum of the compressed thickness of the head gasket and the piston deck clearance.

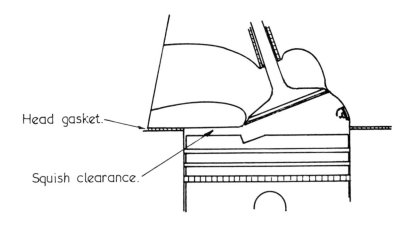

Head gasket.

Squish clearance.

required will be 0.005 to 0.015in. Usually, to achieve this figure the top of the block will have to be milled. Note in a road engine that it is not essential for all pistons to rise to the same height in each cylinder; a variation of 0.005in is acceptable.

Most people take the easy way out and simply mill the head to change the compression; however, I feel that this should only be done, if necessary, after the deck clearance has been reduced. As I said, I like to build a good deal of squish into an engine by having the piston rise to 0.035 to 0.045in from the face of the cylinder head. This causes the piston to squish the fuel/air charge from the edges of the cylinder toward the spark plug. The fast moving gases meet the spark plug and quickly carry the combustion flame to the extremity of the combustion chamber, thus reducing the risk of detonation.

With the passing of time more benefits of building squish into the engine have come to light. The mixture being purged across the combustion chamber from the squish areas homogenises the fuel/air mixture more thoroughly and also mixes any residual exhaust gas still present with the fuel charge. This serves to speed up combustion by preventing stale gas pockets from forming. Such pockets slow down, and in some instances can prevent, flame propagation.

Turbulence caused by the squish effect also serves to enhance heat transfer at the spark-initiated flame front. Without proper heat transfer, jets of flame would tend to shoot out toward the edges of the combustion chamber, prematurely heating the surrounding gases to start off the cycle leading to detonation.

If you can't get the compression ratio up where you want it from milling the block and the head then do not go and fit high top pistons. These have no place in a road engine, and I don't like using them in race engines either. A big compression

The piston squish band should be as wide as the cylinder head squish area to ensure good combustion. Additional spark advance usually restores power losses when the squish band is too narrow, but fuel consumption and exhaust emissions both increase.

lump on the piston crown masks the spark plug and retards flame travel after ignition, and then often upsets complete cylinder scavenging during the exhaust cycle. After ignition, we want the flame to travel uniformly across the piston dome and back toward the squish area. Any abrupt protrusion on the piston crown will disrupt the flame front as it moves across the piston, leaving pockets of mixture that are only partially ignited or completely unburned. A low, 2–3mm high, flat or circular dome is necessary with some semi-hemi combustion chambers to get the compression ratio up. These low domes do not cause much trouble if they do not mask the spark plug and are free of abrupt edges.

Whenever dished or reverse dome pistons are fitted to lower the compression, the outline of the dish should ideally be a mirror image of the outline of the combustion chamber. This means that the piston has a squish surface which exactly matches the cylinder head squish area. Unfortunately, pistons machined to mirror the combustion chamber tend to be much more expensive because of the intricate machine operations involved. Hence, car manufacturers tend to use lower cost pistons with a central dish and narrow squish band or an offset dish which places a large squish area over to one side of the piston crown. When the piston squish band is as wide as the cylinder head squish area the required squish effect is produced. However, the squish band on some pistons is much narrower than the cylinder head squish area, and some tuners when lowering the compression ratio of high boost turbo engines also machine the squish band too narrow.

Chapter 4

The Camshaft

A cam swap is an easy and inexpensive way to transform most present day engines. With the right cam a ten per cent power increase is usually attainable without much loss in fuel economy. But if the wrong choice is made, it could transform the car into a sluggish fuel guzzler which fails emissions inspections.

In spite of all that advertising would have you believe, a camshaft is a simple device designed to open and close the inlet and exhaust valves in harmony with movement of the piston within the cylinder. The inlet lobe pushes the inlet valve open just before top dead centre (TDC) on the induction stroke and keeps it open until well after bottom dead centre (BDC) to let the inertia or momentum of the high velocity fuel/air mixture literally ram in additional mixture as the piston moves upward on the compression stroke. The exhaust valve is opened by the camshaft exhaust lobe during the combustion stroke. Most of the effective expansion power of combustion is over by mid-stroke so the exhaust valve is opened well before BDC to allow the cylinder pressure to "blow down" before the piston commences up on the exhaust stroke otherwise power would be lost pushing the gas out of the cylinder. The valve is left open until a little past TDC to use exhaust gas momentum to scavenge the cylinder efficiently. The inlet valve is opening again during this period, called the overlap period, to allow the small vacuum created by the movement of exhaust gas out of the cylinder to assist in drawing fresh fuel/air mixture into the inlet tract and cylinder.

The theory sounds good but in practice it does not work out like this, except over a narrow 2000–3000rpm range. At low engine speeds the incoming fuel mixture has little velocity and correspondingly little momentum, so as the piston starts up on the compression stroke, mixture is pushed out past the open inlet valve into the inlet tract. Less mixture is available for combustion, hence a 3 litre engine can perform as though it is a 2.0 litre unit.

A similar situation occurs with late exhaust valve closing. Because the outgoing exhaust gases have low inertia at low rpm, the downward movement of the piston, now on the inlet stroke, will actually cause burned gas to turn around and be drawn

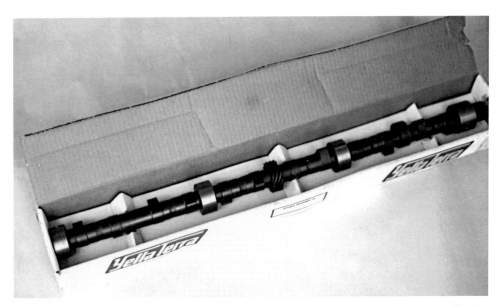

Swapping the standard camshaft for a performance item is one of the most cost-effective changes which can be made. However, selecting a cam that is too wild will wreck low speed driveability and fuel economy, and could cause failed emissions tests.

right back into the cylinder. These hot gases occupy considerable cylinder volume, volume that should have been filled by combustible fuel mixture. This exhaust gas goes on causing trouble by slowing combustion of much of the fuel mix and blocking combustion of the remainder. As will be discussed later, some manufacturers use both

At lower rpm late closing inlet valves allow mixture to be pushed out of the cylinder back into the inlet tract.

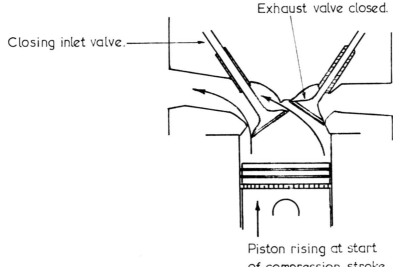

Exhaust valve closed.

Closing inlet valve.

Piston rising at start
of compression stroke.

45

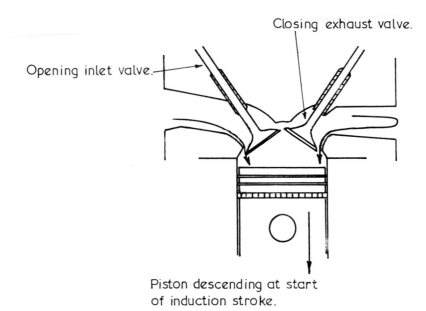

Opening inlet valve.

Closing exhaust valve.

Piston descending at start
of induction stroke.

*At lower rpm late closing exhaust valves allow exhaust gases to be drawn back into the
cylinders.*

late inlet and exhaust valve closing, by retarding the cam or wide lobe separation angles to reduce cylinder pressure and combustion flame speed. This lowers the emission of nitrogen oxides (NOx). Good for emissions but potentially destructive of performance and economy.

The other flaw in inertia gas flow theory is evident during the overlap period. At certain higher engine rpm, dependent on exhaust system and combustion chamber design, the fuel/air mix will be drawn down the inlet tract, across the combustion chamber and then out past the open exhaust valve due to the inertia created by the spent exhaust gas leaving the cylinder from the previous cycle. The larger the cam overlap period and the more efficient the exhaust system, the greater the potential for this to occur. The end result is more pollution, excessive fuel consumption and less power.

By now it should be evident that selecting the ideal performance/economy cam involves more than merely reading some persuasive advertising in a car magazine and picking a cam timing figure that seems appealing. To assist in your understanding we must go back to the basics. Then you will grasp more of what the camshaft numbers game is all about.

The illustration depicts the various features of every cam lobe. The base circle should be a constant radius from the cam centre. It allows the valves to seat and dissipate heat and permits the valve train time to settle from shock after each opening/closing cycle. The ramp (or clearance ramp) takes up slack in the valve train and commences gently lifting the valve. The flank rapidly accelerates the valve open, the nose slows valve train motion to a stop, and the following flank accelerates the valve back down toward its seat where the closing ramp takes over to gently lower the valve onto the valve seat.

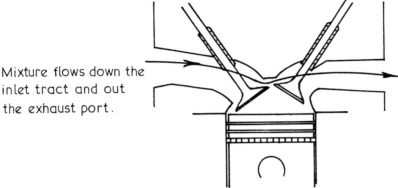

Inlet and exhaust valves both
open during overlap period.

Mixture flows down the
inlet tract and out
the exhaust port.

Piston near TDC at the end
of exhaust stroke.

At mid-range and higher rpm, mixture may be drawn out past the open exhaust valve due to exhaust gas inertia and a long valve overlap period.

A performance cam has lobes with shorter ramps than stock and longer, steeper flanks to open the valves more rapidly and keep them open longer.

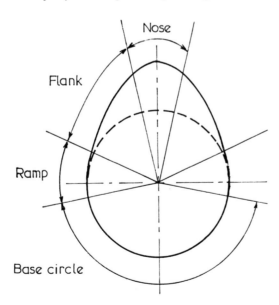

Nose

Flank

Ramp

Base circle

    That is all very simple; the problem arises when you wish to purchase a cam and you want to compare one manufacturer's cam timing figures with another. In the USA nearly everyone times their cams from a 0.050in cam lift point but most car makers time their cams from when the lifter (cam follower) commences to move. In all countries no standard system is used. Some are timed at 1mm cam lift, others at   47

0.004in, 0.006in, 0.010in, 0.015in and 0.020in. To further confuse the situation a number of cam grinders time their product at 0.010in valve lift for hydraulic lifter cams and at "lash point" (when valve clearance is taken up) for mechanical (solid) lifter cams. It has been suggested that comparing cam timing figures is much like comparing buildings by measuring the length of their shadows without taking into account the position of the sun in the sky. To illustrate the problem with which the enthusiast is confronted when trying to make some sense of advertised timing figures we will consider the mild Chevrolet "929" cam which I classify as a Phase I cam. According to the factory, the intake valve opens 26° before TDC and closes 90° after BDC while the exhaust opens 84° before BDC and closes 46° after TDC. Durations of 296° inlet and 310° exhaust, figures which are taken at lash point, could have one thinking that this is a wild race cam. Measured at 0.006in lift the duration is approximately 254° inlet and 262° for the exhaust, figures which could still indicate a sporty cam. However, measured at 0.050in lift the true nature of the cam is revealed; 195° duration for the intake and 202° for the exhaust, a truly mild cam! Hopefully, one day everyone will adopt the same system, such as has been done by American cam manufacturers.

In Table 4.1 I have set out a variety of cams to suit a number of performance/economy considerations. The numbers refer to cam duration measured at 0.050in cam lift.

Table 4.1   Camshaft Duration for Performance/Economy

Duration at 0.050in cam lift

Rocker arm ratio	1:1		1.15:1		1.25:1	
Cam type	Inlet	Exhaust	Inlet	Exhaust	Inlet	Exhaust
Phase I	208–212°	210–216°	204–208°	206–212°	202–206°	204–210°
Phase II	216–220°	214–224°	212–216°	210–220°	210–214°	208–218°
Phase III	224–228°	218–226°	220–224°	214–222°	218–222°	212–220°
Phase IV	230–232°	220–228°	226–228°	216–224°	224–226°	214–222°
Phase V	236–242°	224–230°	232–238°	220–226°	230–236°	218–224°

Rocker arm ratio	1.4:1		1.5:1		1.65:1	
Cam type	Inlet	Exhaust	Inlet	Exhaust	Inlet	Exhaust
Phase I	197–201°	199–205°	194–198°	196–202°	190–194°	192–198°
Phase II	205–209°	203–213°	202–206°	200–210°	200–202°	196–206°
Phase III	213–217°	207–215°	210–214°	204–212°	206–210°	200–208°
Phase IV	219–221°	209–217°	216–218°	206–214°	212–214°	202–210°
Phase V	225–231°	213–219°	222–228°	210–216°	218–224°	206–212°

What I refer to as Phase I cams are very mild, good low speed torque grinds. The exhaust duration should be no greater than 6° more than that of the inlet. Valve lift would be around 0.390in inlet and up to 0.410in exhaust. Cams of this type are fitted to pre-emissions 350 Chevs, current 350 Chev Corvettes and the Porsche 911 turbo.

Phase II cams also are mild, good low speed torque grinds, but there will be a minute loss of torque below about 1200rpm. The exhaust duration should be no greater than 4° more than the inlet. Valve lift would be up to 0.415in on all lobes.

Usually these cams will give better fuel economy than the standard cam providing driving habits do not change to take full advantage of the additional power available.

Phase III cams are my preferred performance/economy compromise grind. A little torque is lost below 1500–1700rpm but there is no problem with power brakes, power steering, air conditioner operation or a standard torque converter in auto transmission vehicles. The idle is smooth but a "cammy" note may be discernible if rowdy straight-through mufflers are used on some 6 and 8 cylinder vehicles with hydraulic lifters. The exhaust duration should be 4–6° less and certainly not more than that of the inlet, otherwise economy may be lost. Valve lift would be up to 0.420in however, if roller tip rocker arms are used, or if it is an overhead cam engine which doesn't have rocker arms, such as the VW Golf, the lift could be up to 0.440in on the inlet. I do not like lifting the valves too far in road engines as valve guide wear increases rapidly. Depending on driving style there should not be any loss of fuel economy. This is the warmest cam that I would recommend for turbo engines as the low compression ratio which is necessary with turbocharging combined with a longer duration cam would seriously reduce low speed power and flexibility.

Phase IV cams are really not an economy grind in engines larger than approximately 3.5 litres and should not be used in any vehicle which is overgeared. Engines smaller than 2 litre do not show much loss in economy and engines up to 3.3 litres would normally suffer a serious loss of economy only under stop-start driving conditions. There is a loss of flexibility under 2000rpm but power accessory function is not affected. The idle will be a little "cammy" in 6 cylinder engines with hydraulic lifters. Inlet valve lift would be up to 0.460in if roller tip rocker arms are fitted. The exhaust lobe should have up to 10° less duration and up to 0.050in less lift to maintain fuel efficiency and a wide power band.

What I refer to as Phase V cams have very limited application, and would only be used in engines up to around 1.8 litres. Note that the above valve lift figures are for two valve engines. Four valve engines would usually run 0.040–0.060in less lift.

Some people will no doubt question using a cam with less exhaust lobe duration and lift than the inlet. True the majority of performance cams have virtually identical inlet and exhaust lobes or the exhaust lobes may have more lift and duration. However, I have found that road cars with restrictive exhaust systems gain very little performance from exhaust lobes with extended duration and higher lift. On the contrary, often low speed performance and economy is reduced because of exhaust gas "draw-back" diluting the fuel/air charge and then at higher rpm fuel consumption may also increase due to fuel draw through into the exhaust during the overlap period. Cams with the inlet and exhaust lobes suggested for Phase III, IV and V may not be available off the shelf but most cam manufacturers will oblige with special grinds on request.

Table 4.2 shows the effect of cam timing on horsepower and torque. The test engine was a 229cu in (3.75 litre) Chev V6 equipped with stock 4 barrel carb and manifold, stock cast exhaust manifolds feeding into a single 2.5in exhaust, stock cylinder heads machined to raise compression to a true 8.8:1 and fitted with standard valves backcut to improve flow, and budget 1.52:1 roller tip rocker arms.

The stock cam was very, very mild; milder in fact than most standard cams. Hence a simple cam swap unleashed more power in this example than would usually be realised. The cam used in Test 2 caused very little loss of low speed torque and in   49

Table 4.2   Effect of Cam Timing on Horsepower and Torque

rpm	Test 1		Test 2		Test 3		Test 4	
	hp	Torque	hp	Torque	hp	Torque	hp	Torque
1750	63	189	63	190			60	180
2000	73	193	73	191	68	180	72	189
2500	93	196	96	202	88	186	95	199
3000	108	190	118	206	107	188	115	201
3500	123	185	135	203	123	184	137	206
4000	129	170	148	194	152	200	155	203
4500	134	156	153	179	173	202	165	193
4750	123	136	152	168	173	191	171	189
5000			137	144	176	185	162	170
5250					168	168	143	143

Test 1 – stock cam 0.365in inlet and 0.392in exhaust lift, 176° inlet and 194° exhaust duration

Test 2 – Chev marine cam 0.415in inlet and exhaust lift, 202° inlet and 210° exhaust duration

Test 3 – Phase IV cam 0.460in inlet and exhaust lift, 218° inlet and exhaust duration, 110° lobe centres

Test 4 – Phase III cam 0.446in inlet and 0.420in exhaust lift, 212° inlet and 206° exhaust duration, 108° lobe centres

the 2500–3500rpm range where we spend most of our time driving there is a good hp and torque increase. For Test 3 another off the shelf cam was chosen to check just how well the stock carb/manifold/head combination breathed. As can be seen in the table this cam did not give good power until 4000rpm, which is way above the usual cruise speed of most 6 cylinder cars. With a better design inlet manifold, extractor-type tubular exhaust headers and twin 2¹/₄in exhausts, this cam would have made about 195hp. A special cam with a low lift, short duration exhaust lobe was ground and fitted for Test 4. Compared with the marine cam used in Test 2, it lost a little low speed torque but had better power above 3000rpm.

The next aspect of the camshaft to be decided upon is the lobe phase angle, which can also be referred to as the lobe separation angle or just simply as the lobe centres. This angle fixes the actual position or phasing of the lobes on the camshaft and in turn determines the opening and closing points of the inlet and exhaust valves expressed in degrees of crankshaft rotation. For example, if the lobe has been ground to push the inlet valve to its maximum lift at 110° after TDC, and to open the exhaust valve to its peak at 110° before TDC, the camshaft is said to have a lobe separation angle of 110° (110° + 110° ÷ 2 = 110°).

Predominantly performance road camshafts are ground with a lobe separation angle of from 108 to 112 degrees. In most instances a narrow angle favours mid-range power while a wider angle increases peak power at the expense of low rpm power. Just why this transpires can be better appreciated when we compare two camshafts having identical lobe contours of 270° advertised duration but lobe separation angles of 108° and 112° respectively. The cam ground in 108° centres will have timing figures of

Lobe separation angle.

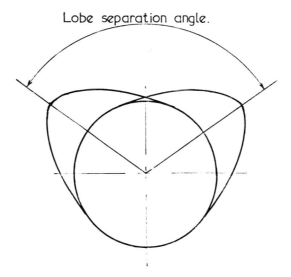

The lobe separation angle fixes the relative phasing between the inlet and exhaust lobes.

27/63, 63/27, meaning that the inlet valve will theoretically commence lifting off its seat 27° before TDC and close back onto its seat 63° after BDC while the exhaust valve begins to open 63° before BDC and closes 27° after TDC. The 270° cam ground on 112° centres has timing figures of 23/67, 67/23.

The difference between numbers like 27/63, 63/27 and 23/67, 67/23 may not appear too significant so what makes the two cams change engine power and fuel consumption characteristics? The most obvious distinction is the valve overlap period of 54° for the cam ground on 108° lobe centres (27 + 27 = 54°) and 46° for the cam with 112° lobe centres. With mild cams the additional overlap will have little effect, except to perhaps enhance cylinder filling and power at mid-range engine rpm. Hotter cams from Phase IV and upward will have a rougher idle because of the longer overlap, and of greater concern at certain higher rpm, fuel consumption could become excessive because of mixture draw-through.

The timing of the exhaust opening event is of little consequence and frequently can be varied by up to 8° before a change in horsepower or torque is detected. If a particular engine has an extremely inefficient exhaust it is sometimes helpful to open the exhaust earlier and increase "blow-down" time, thus reducing losses due to literally pumping exhaust gas out of the cylinder by the upward movement of the piston.

The timing of the inlet opening event is of more importance only when hotter, long duration profiles are utilised. If the inlet is opened very early, the piston's upward movement on the exhaust stroke may force exhaust gas into the inlet tract causing dilution of the fuel/air charge. This problem is compounded particularly if the entire exhaust system, including the exhaust valve and port, are very inefficient, as exhaust gas pressure could be quite high even very late in the exhaust cycle.

From a performance/economy viewpoint the intake closing event is the most important. We want to hold the intake open as long as practicable to extend the length

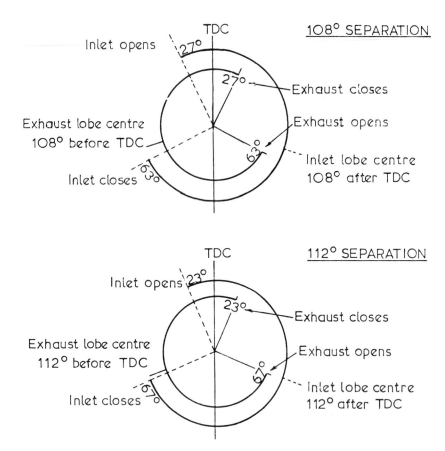

This timing diagram illustrates how changing the lobe separation angle alters the valve timing of a 270° duration camshaft.

of the induction period but we do not want the intake valve closing so late that the piston moving up on the compression stroke actually pushes a portion of our power-producing fuel mixture out of the cylinder and back into the inlet tract. This reverse flowing intake mixture (called reversion pulse or reversion flow) can cause more problems by actually blocking and then slowing intake flow into the cylinder on the next induction stroke. In extreme examples the reversion pulse reaches back to the carburettor venturis and disrupts the fuel metering signal. Reducing the lobe phase angle has the effect of closing the inlet valve earlier thus reducing low rpm reversion and increasing lower rpm horsepower and torque. Increasing the phase angle generally increases the peak torque and horsepower rpm because the induction cycle is extended by a few degrees (in this example 4°).

In road engines which are forced to run lower compression ratios when compared with race engines I tend to favour narrower lobe displacement angles to pick up mid-range power and improve fuel efficiency. However, this benefit can be offset to some extent because of the less efficient exhaust evident with road vehicles, which necessitates a somewhat wider lobe phase angle. There aren't any rules, because engines have no regard for rules, but I would suggest the following which I have found to apply in the majority of performance/economy applications. The majority of 4 cylinder engines require 108° lobe centres; some larger engines around 2 litre may work better with a cam ground to 110° lobe phasing. Pushrod type 6 and 8 cylinder engines with an rpm limit of up to 5500,108° lobe displacement with Phase I, II and III grinds; 110° with Phase IV grinds. Overhead cam 6 cylinder engines with a 6500rpm limit, 110° with Phase I, II and III grinds and 112° lobe phase angle with Phase IV grinds.

Table 4.3 shows the typical effect of changing the lobe displacement angle. Initially, a cam with long duration was chosen as the owner wanted BMW-type performance with a simple cam change and head clean up. Also the exhaust had to be quieter than stock which required the use of a restrictive 2.25in system. Because of the long duration and tight exhaust, the first cam was ground on 115° centres. It produced good top end power but like a BMW it didn't accelerate too well below 4000rpm in the higher gears which frustrated the owner when driving in city traffic. Another cam was then ground on 112° centres. It knocked the power off above 5000rpm but restored some lost lower rpm power.

Table 4.3   Effect of Cam Lobe Centre Change on 3.3 litre Holden

	Test 1		Test 2		Test 3	
rpm	hp	Torque	hp	Torque	hp	Torque
2000	67	176	61	161	64	169
2500	87	183	79	165	84	177
3000	108	189	104	182	105	184
3250	122	197	118	191	120	194
3500	130	195	130	195	132	198
4000	144	189	148	194	149	195
4500	147	171	163	190	162	189
5000	140	147	171	180	168	176
5250			163	163	154	154

Test 1 – stock engine and exhaust

Test 2 – Phase V cam 0.430in inlet and 0.410in exhaust lift, 222° inlet and 218° exhaust duration, 115° lobe centres

Test 3 – Phase V cam as above with 112° lobe centres

It does not always work out according to written theory. The 350 Chev in Table 4.4 was being built for maximum economy and anything over 250hp would be a bonus. An off-the-shelf cam was fitted for the first test but as it was felt that a cam with 108° lobe centres may give even better mid-range power and economy, the second cam was then installed. The result was the opposite to that expected; the bottom end dropped off a little and peak power improved slightly. There was no detectable change in fuel consumption at half and full throttle testing on the dyno.

Another device which we can use to change the characteristics of a camshaft is timing variation by advancing or retarding the camshaft. A number of manufacturers supply their cams ground advanced or retarded. This can be discerned by checking the timing figures. For example, the timing may be 30/60, 66/20. The first step is to find   53

Table 4.4   Effect of Cam Lobe Centre Change on 350 Chev

	Test 1		Test 2	
rpm	**hp**	**Torque**	**hp**	**Torque**
2000	121	319	120	315
2500	155	326	153	322
3000	204	357	201	352
3250	217	350	219	354
3500	232	348	233	350
4000	251	330	249	327
4500	258	301	259	302
5000	244	256	249	262

Test 1 – Phase II cam 0.453in inlet and 0.431in exhaust lift, 206° inlet and exhaust duration, 110° lobe centres

Test 2 – Phase II cam as above with 108° lobe centres

the inlet and exhaust lobe duration. The inlet is 30° + 180° + 60° = 270°; while the exhaust open period is 66° + 180° + 20° = 266°. Next we calculate when the inlet and exhaust valves are at their maximum lift in relation with the crankshaft. Unless the cam has asymmetrical lobes (we will discuss these later) the full lift point must be midway between the opening and closing point. Hence in this example the inlet valve will be at peak lift 135° (270° ÷ 2 = 135°) after it begins to open and the exhaust valve will be lifted to its maximum 133° after it commences opening. For the inlet we subtract the valve opening point (30° before TDC) from the half duration figure (135°), so the valve is fully open at 105° after TDC (135° – 30° = 105°). The exhaust calculation is similar except that we subtract the exhaust closing angle (20° after TDC) from the half duration figure (133°). Hence the exhaust lobe is at its peak lift point 113° before TDC (133° – 20° = 113°). To find the lobe separation angle the full lift angles are added together and divided by 2, with the answer being 109° (105° + 113° ÷ 2 = 109°). If the cam had been ground or installed with split timing (called "straight up") maximum inlet lift would have occurred at 109° after TDC instead of 105° after TDC, and the exhaust valve peak lift would have been at 109° before TDC and not 113° before TDC. This tells us that the cam has been ground 4° advanced ie the inlet and exhaust valves are opening and closing 4° earlier than in the straight up position.

The timing diagram illustrates the effect of advancing a cam having identical inlet and exhaust lobes with an advertised duration of 270°. The first cam has the lobes ground on 112° centres with a timing of 23/67, 67/23. The second cam has the same lobe profile but ground with a displacement angle of 108°, which gives a timing of 27/63, 63/27. By advancing the first cam 4°, using an offset timing gear key, the timing becomes 27/63, 71/19. Closing the inlet valve 4° earlier reduces reversion and improves power and economy in the rpm range where we drive most of the time. Also, opening the exhaust valve 4° earlier may help exhaust efficiency a little.

Now by comparing the cam on 112° centres advanced 4° with the cam ground on 108° centres, you may wonder why bother going to the trouble to have a cam specially ground with the timing advanced, or why bother making an offset timing gear key to do the same thing when the inlet opening and closing events finish up the same 27/63? Why not simply install a cam with 108° lobe centres? Well, it could be that we want

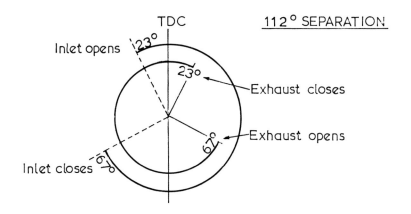

TDC — 112° SEPARATION

Inlet opens 23°

23° — Exhaust closes

— Exhaust opens 67°

Inlet closes 67°

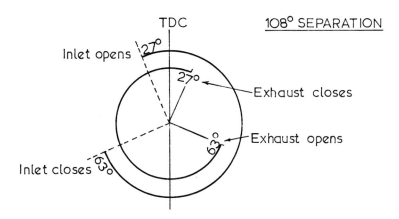

TDC — 108° SEPARATION

Inlet opens 27°

27° — Exhaust closes

— Exhaust opens 63°

Inlet closes 63°

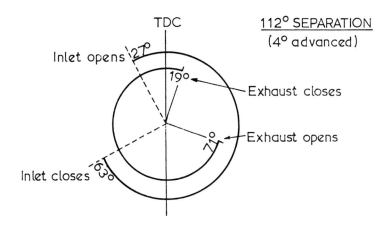

TDC — 112° SEPARATION
(4° advanced)

Inlet opens 27°

19° — Exhaust closes

— Exhaust opens 71°

Inlet closes 63°

Advancing a cam causes the valves to open and close earlier, which improves mid-range power and economy.

less overlap to improve idle quality and fuel economy in some Phase IV and wilder cams. Also, we may wish to open the exhaust valve very early (71° before BDC compared with 63° before BDC) because of an inefficient exhaust.

Again there are no rules, but there are few instances where I would run a cam straight up or retarded. Usually, I install cams with 108 to 110° lobe centres 4 or 5° advanced to keep low rpm cylinder pressure as high as possible. This is very important if the compression ratio has to be purposely low because of turbocharging or the compulsory use of unleaded or other low octane fuel. Some tuners and a number of car manufacturers install their cams retarded by anything from 2 to 8°. Usually, tuners do this because they are convinced that high compression ratios must be better, if only on paper in their advertising, and to get away with high compressions they have to ensure that some mixture is pushed back out of the cylinder past a late closing inlet valve, to avoid pinging at low rpm under load. Also, the exhaust lobes frequently have up to 14° longer duration than the inlet to ensure that exhaust gas is drawn back into the cylinder before the exhaust closes. The exhaust gas then dilutes the fuel/air mixture with non-combustible molecules, which disrupts and slows combustion and avoids detonation. Manufacturers retard their cams, usually not to run higher compression ratios, but to reduce the emission of nitrogen oxides (NOx). Fuel mixture diluted by exhaust gas burns more slowly and cooler, reducing the formation of NOx. The end result is reduced driveability at lower rpm and increased fuel consumption at cruising speeds.

Many enthusiasts inquire as to whether they should 'degree-in' their performance cam, or just line up the stock timing marks and hope for the best. The latter is not a viable option, particularly for ohc engines, as any milling of the head and/or block moves the cam timing, usually into a retarded position. However, this does not demand that the cam must be degreed. For example, when the stock cam is being retained and the engine design allows for easy cam movement into an advanced or retarded position I simply run the engine and move the cam around to give the desired power characteristics on the dyno. If the cam is a fairly mild non-stock grind with which I am familiar I often follow the same "fit and dial-in on the dyno" procedure. Wilder cams and cams which I don't know are always degreed first, valve to piston clearance is checked and then they are moved about with the engine running on the dyno.

As you now understand something of the science of cam timing you are in a position to decide exactly how you wish to degree-in your cam. For example, the cam may be ground retarded by 2°, so do not be afraid to set the cam 5° advanced if you feel that is what the engine needs. On the other hand the cam may be ground 3° advanced and you want it advanced 5°, but after timing the cam you find that the cam is actually 4° advanced. This would not be worth correcting as few engines are affected by anything less than a 2° timing correction.

After the cam is fitted with the stock timing marks lined up, the next step is to find where the cam is in relation to the crankshaft. In other words, is it advanced or retarded, and by how many degrees? To check this you will need a degree wheel or a 360° protractor at least 8in in diameter which can be bolted to the nose of the crankshaft. Also needed is a dial gauge to measure cam lift and a good solid pointer that can be fixed under a convenient bolt and lapped over the front of the degree wheel.

Firstly, TDC must be precisely determined and for this a positive stop is and pistons too at times. When fitting a belt take care not to kink it, and if reusing the belt ensure that it will rotate in the same direction as when previously fitted. I always fit belts in such a way that when facing cylinder No. 1 the belt's lettering is correctly orientated.

The majority of car enthusiasts look at economy purely from the viewpoint of fuel consumption. However, I take a much broader view. To my mind economy involves buying functional and not gimmicky parts at the right price and then maintaining everything properly to achieve the best service life. For example, it is false economy to fit old cam followers to run on a new cam as the old followers will soon wreck some of the lobes. It is also false economy to buy a bargain untreated cam. The lobes (not the bearing journals) should be given a treatment called by a variety of names such as Lubriting, Parkerising or Parko-Lubriting. The cam is treated after the bearing journals have been taped by being plunged into a high temperature bath of phosphoric acid. This acid etches open the pores of the freshly machined lobes so that they retain oil more effectively. Next, the cam receives a phosphate coating to aid break-in. To assist break-in lubrication even further I recommend that the lobes and followers be coated with a mixture of high pressure Hypoid 140 gear oil and moly disulphide. The first 10 to 15 minutes is the critical period for a new cam so it is essential that engine speed be maintained at 2000–2500rpm during this period to ensure adequate oil flow to the cam and lifters.

I am often asked if hydraulic lifters should be changed to a more "exotic" type and an appropriate cam fitted. Well, for many years I was no fan of hydraulic lifters and cams, but now hydraulic lifter cams give performance equal to, and in some instances better than, solid lifter cams in milder applications up to what I classify as a Phase IV grind. Solid lifter cams and roller lifter cams do have the advantage of a smoother idle with grinds hotter than Phase V and in race engines they will improve power output, but for performance/economy road engines hydraulic lifter cams work very well and there is less noise and less maintenance.

Some cam manufacturers are now producing street roller cams to suit both hydraulic roller and solid roller tappets. Unless the stock engine has a hydraulic roller, I do not use these in economy road engines. I can get all the power that most drivers want along with good economy using simple and reliable flat tappet grinds. If, however, someone wanted his 350 Chev to make 450hp I would use a roller cam.

A little time back a few of the cam people were making a lot of noise about their special asymmetric cams which they had just developed. These are nothing new, some of the car makers have been using asymmetric grinds in their family sedans for many years, but no doubt the advertising induced a number of people to pay considerably more money in the belief that this type of profile is better or more powerful than the common symmetric profile. Actually, few cams have a true symmetric profile as many have short opening ramps and closing ramps perhaps 10° longer, but as we are really only interested in performance cams in the area past where the clearance ramps finish and commence, we normally view the lobes as being symmetric i.e. the opening side of the lobe has the same profile and duration as the closing side of the lobe. Asymmetric lobes on the other hand have an opening flank a few degrees shorter than the closing flank.

Out of curiosity I purchased one of these super asymmetric grinds to see what the fuss was all about as previously I was convinced that whilst this type of profile   61

The lobes of this cam were wrecked because worn cam followers with dished faces were used. To avoid this type of damage, fit new or refaced lifters when replacing the camshaft.

basically reduced valve train noise, it didn't seem to give any extra power. What I found was interesting; yes, the cam did give a good wide power band just as the manufacturer claimed but this wasn't attributable to the asymmetric cam lobes which only varied by about 4° on the opening and closing flanks. What really helped the power band was the exhaust lobe which had around 15° less duration than the inlet.

Some of the cam advertising about high valve lift can also be misleading. As mentioned earlier, high lift increases valve guide wear, but with reground cams there is another problem. Unless a new virgin blank cam (billet cam) is used, the only way more lift can be attained is by grinding the base circle diameter smaller. This reduces the actual diameter of the camshaft, weakening the part. Thus as a cam lobe commences to push open a valve, the shaft bends a little, which changes the valve timing and also reduces the amount the valve is lifted. Therefore a cam with an advertised lift of, say, 0.430in may, in fact, lift the valve a true 0.395in if it is a solid lifter grind. Cam flex could account for 0.013in of lost lift; valve clearance 0.018in and valve train flex about 0.004in. I have seen reground cams with advertised lift figures differing by as much as 0.022in give identical valve lifts when installed, purely because the big lift cam flexed so much, due to the shaft diameter being reduced excessively, and cam bearings being too few and too far apart.

Chapter 5

The Valve Train

The first vital link in the valve train of pushrod type engines and some overhead cam engines is the cam follower (also called tappet, lifter or bucket). It has the work of changing the rotating motion of the camshaft to up and down motion. The contact point between the lifter and cam lobe is the most heavily loaded spot in the engine. The loading can be as high as 300,000lb in^2, which is one reason why cam followers require more than just casual attention when a performance cam is used.

Contrary to popular opinion, lifters are not flat; they are ground with a spherical radius of 37–75in which, depending on their diameter, means that they are about 0.003in high in the centre. This spherical radius, along with a cam lobe taper angle of 3–16 minutes, and a tappet offset of approximately 0.050in from the middle of the cam lobe, causes the tappet to rotate. The rotation reduces cam and lifter wear; in fact if the lifter doesn't rotate, the lobe will be worn right down in 15 minutes. For this reason only new cam followers or re-radiused cam followers should be fitted with a new cam.

For the pushrod engine there are three basic types of lifter; the solid flat lifter, the standard hydraulic flat lifter, and the high rate bleed-down Rhoads-type hydraulic flat lifter. Some people would also include mushroom solid flat lifters, hydraulic roller lifters and solid roller lifters, but these are really only suited for use in super-performance engines.

The standard solid and hydraulic type lifters function effectively with the mild cams required in performance/economy applications. However, if you are modifying an engine which has a reputation for rapid lifter wear then it would be wise to fit lifters made of better material. These are often available from the larger cam manufacturers and component suppliers like TRW and Sealed Power.

The Rhoads hydraulic lifter was designed to allow the use of long duration hydraulic cams without losing too much low speed performance. This is accomplished by a vertical slot ground all the way down the lifter's inner piston. As the lifter begins to rise on the cam lobe, oil is allowed to leak past the piston, thereby allowing the   63

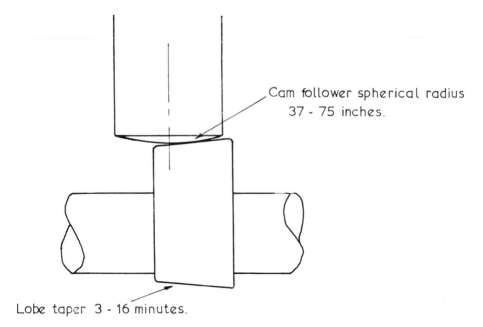

Cam follower spherical radius
37 - 75 inches.

Lobe taper 3 - 16 minutes.

To ensure long cam lobe life only new or re-radiused cam followers should be fitted when the cam is changed.

lifter to bleed down slightly at low rpm. Valve opening is delayed, reducing the cam duration by 10–15 degrees and reducing lift by about 0.020in at idle. The engine thus sees an improved idle and increased vacuum. As engine speed increases, there is less time to bleed off oil pressure, so by about 3000–3500rpm the cam's full potential duration and lift are restored.

From my testing I have concluded that the Rhoads lifter is a waste of time with mild, short duration cams, such as would be used for economy and performance. Used with long duration hydraulic cams of about 240–250 degrees measured at 0.050in lift they do work as claimed. I know of no good reason except perhaps less maintenance, to use such a long duration hydraulic cam. In excess of about 225 degrees duration (with 1.5:1 rockers) a mechanical cam has it all over an hydraulic. It idles more smoothly, has better low speed power and will rev about 500rpm higher. Additionally, the mechanical cam is much quieter at idle. An hydraulic with Rhoads lifters can produce a good deal of clatter at idle, particularly if the oil temperature is high or if the oil pressure is a little low.

The next link, in pushrod engines at any rate, is the pushrod. Little needs to be said about the pushrod except that it should be straight and rigid. Whenever rockers are replaced, the pushrods should also be replaced as the two wear a pattern together. For the same reason when engine rebuilding is carried out, the rockers and pushrods must be reinstalled together in the same location. In economy/performance engines there is no necessity to replace the pushrods with special chrome-moly or carbon fibre items. The standard article is more than adequate; I have seen hi-tech pushrods buckle in engines where the stock component showed no sign of failure.

Rocker arms provide the subsequent valve train link. Except for the riveted or

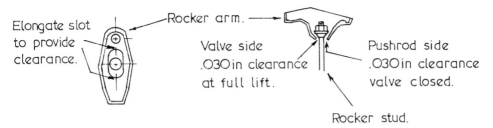

When a high lift cam is installed it may be necessary to elongate the slot in pressed-type stud-mounted rocker arms to avoid rocker to stud fouling.

welded pressed steel rockers found in a few engines, nearly all stock arms are suitable for use in mildly tuned engines using up to Phase V cams. The stud-type rocker arms fitted to many V8 engines and some 6 cylinder engines may require modification to avoid rocker to stud fouling when high lift cams are utilised. The clearance between either end of the rocker arm slot and the stud with the valve closed and also fully open should be measured using a wire 0.030in thick (a straightened paper clip will do).

Many enthusiasts are now fitting expensive high lift roller tip rockers in their street engines. I consider this to be a waste of money which could be used in more beneficial ways to bring real performance and economy. Generally, high lift rockers are used in the belief that more valve lift guarantees more power. Yet a slightly warmer cam would have done exactly the same thing at less than one third the price. If the cam has 0.280in lift, swapping from 1.5:1 to 1.6:1, rockers will theoretically increase valve lift by 0.028in to 0.448in. The same performance increase could be had by using a cam with the same lift and about 4 degrees more duration measured at 0.050in lift. From my testing I would recommend high lift rockers in maximum performance road and race engines or in engines which have standard rockers with a ratio well below 1.4:1. For engines like the BL "A" series fitted to the Mini and Metro it is difficult to get reasonable valve lift with the standard 1.25:1 rockers. In these engines I recommend a 1.4:1 or 1.5:1 rocker and a cam duration about 10 degrees shorter than would typically be used with the standard rocker arm. To reduce valve guide wear resulting from the changed rocker geometry and increased lift, rockers with a roller tip should be used when changing from 1.25:1 to 1.5:1 rockers.

Engines fitted with high lift cams which actually lift the valves in excess of about 0.420in do have reduced valve guide wear and improved valve seat life when roller tip rocker arms are used. However, high quality extruded aluminium arms with needle roller bearings and needle roller tips are not necessary for mildly tuned engines. Competition Cams have a fine range of budget roller tip rockers available to fit popular American engines. Being only a little more expensive than the stock rocker arm they represent a good investment in maximum valve guide, and valve seat, life.

Many engines have less than ideal rocker support arrangements which can lead to reliability problems in some instances and poor valve train control in others, when modified camshafts and heavier valve springs are used. An absolute must is to have pressed-in rocker studs pinned as these have been known to pull out, even with the stock cam and valve springs. A more expensive solution which would only be justified if a cam hotter than Phase IV is installed is to fit screw-in rocker studs. The studs must   65 be sealed to prevent seepage if the thread breaks in to the water jacket. Shaft-mounted rocker arrangements may require a number of improvements. Light alloy posts are not very rigid and should be replaced by steel posts to improve the valve train. Usually the shaft itself is up to the task, but the separation springs fitted between the rocker arms are best replaced by tubular steel sleeves. While doing this, pay attention to obtaining sleeves of the correct length to centralise each rocker over its respective valve.

The majority of modern engines are of overhead cam design with a combination rocker arm-cam follower. Shaft-mounted units give little trouble and can be used with a new camshaft after being refaced and Parko-Lubrited, providing that play between the rocker and rocker shaft is minimal. If there is excessive play, the rockers will have to be re-bushed or replaced and new shafts will be necessary. Ball mounted rocker-cam followers such as are used in the Ford Pinto wear rapidly and must be replaced along with the ball studs when a new camshaft is fitted.

Adequate cam and follower lubrication is of major concern in either type of overhead cam engine. Hence when a new cam is fitted, and at regular intervals, thoroughly inspect all oil passages and ensure that there is a good uninterrupted flow of lubricant to each cam lobe.

Many twin overhead cam engines and a few single overhead cam engines use an inverted bucket-type cam follower to transmit cam lobe motion directly to the valve. This type of follower is exceedingly durable and does not present any reliability problems, except in some super performance road applications. Unless the followers have worn flat or concave, they can be reused when new cams are installed.

One problem that is potentially damaging occurs in engines like the Fiat twin cam and VW Golf single cam which use inverted bucket tappets with a valve clearance adjusting shim inserted in the top. Because of a limited range of shims being available, it can be necessary to use "lash caps" on top of the valve stems to lift the bucket within adjusting range when reground cams with a smaller than stock base circle diameter are used. Providing a dab of grease is applied to each lash cap they will not jump out of place, creating problems during assembly; however, due to manufacturing tolerances the lash caps could be bearing against the collets rather than the valve stem. To avoid this possibility measure the recess in each lash cap and compare the figures with the amount each valve stem projects above the collets. Any

Machine lash caps to clear collets by 0.020in.

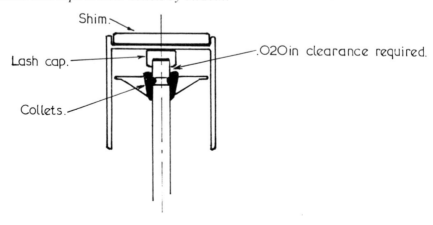

lash cap which does not clear the collets by 0.020in should be machined to increase the clearance.

Regardless of the type of valve train, very few engines present any difficulties when it comes to the design of valve spring retainers and collets (valve stem locks). If the engine has a known reliability problem in this area then steel valve spring retainers of a better material should be used; do not fit aluminium retainers. Some tuners feel that it is necessary to replace rotator-type retainers with fixed retainers, but this is usually unnecessary unless a Phase IV or V cam is being used. The rotator-type valve retainers are fitted usually to the exhaust valves of emissions engines to cause the valve to rotate. This cleans the valve and seat of carbon and evens out valve head temperatures, reducing valve erosion and burning. Rotators are not necessary on the inlets, but they do a good job of extending exhaust valve life and reduce the frequency of valve regrinds. If in your brand of engine they do not have a reputation for cracking and allowing a dropped valve, leave exhaust valve rotator-type spring retainers in place.

Not all valve rotation systems are desirable. The type mentioned above where the centre of the spring retainer clamps solidly to the valve stem usually are reliable but some manufacturers have resorted to a rotator system which creates huge problems with dropped valves. With this arrangement the collets lock solidly within the spring retainer but the valve stem is a "floating" fit within the collets. This allows the valve freedom to rotate inside the collets and clean the valve seat. In time the constant friction between valve stem and collet causes considerable wear, allowing a dropped valve. If your engine has this type of valve rotation, the two collets will actually butt together when installed rather than having a gap between their ends. What must be done is grind off the faces of the collets so the two halves tightly clamp onto the valve stem and have a good gap between their ends.

In economy/performance engines the valve springs have an easier life than in race applications, hence very stiff, high rate springs, are neither desirable nor necessary. The primary requirements for a valve spring are that it must be durable and with a spring rate sufficiently high to seat the valve and keep the valve train in constant contact with the camshaft lobe up to the maximum recommended engine

Collets which butt together allow the valves to float and turn. In time the collet groove wears, causing a dropped valve and probably a holed piston as well.

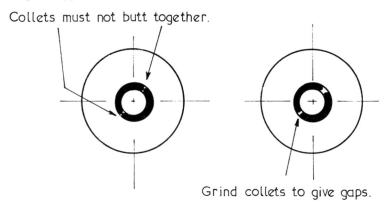

Collets must not butt together.

Grind collets to give gaps.

rpm. In road engines valve springs seldom suffer durability problems; cracking or sagging prematurely. However, it is wise to remember that they do not last forever when teamed with modern cams which feature high lift, rapid acceleration lobes. Therefore when the head is removed to freshen up the valves and seats, do measure the length of each spring uncompressed and then have the spring rate checked on a spring tester. If the compressed pressure is more than 10lb less than specified, the springs should be replaced and if any spring shows signs of sagging then all of the springs require replacement.

A number of tuners instinctively replace standard springs with high rate springs when a cam swap is made. Frequently this is unnecessary; most stock springs are adequate for Phase III cams and in some engines the stock springs require replacement only when race cams are fitted. Unless they are really essential, high rate springs actually accelerate engine wear. In addition to increased cam lobe and follower wear there is also more wear on the rockers at the pushrod cup, the pivot, and at the valve contact point. If the on-seat pressure is also high then valve and seat erosion speeds up. Engines with stud-mounted pressed metal rocker arms may experience cracking of the rockers which would necessitate the use of expensive needle roller competition rocker arms. Always consult with your cam manufacturer and ascertain just what spring rate is required with his cam. He should be able to tell you the required on-seat pressure and the full lift pressure necessary to keep the valve train in harmony at maximum engine speed. With that information it can be seen if the standard springs are up to the task.

The cam people may, for example, specify an on-seat pressure of 70lb and a full lift pressure of 180lb. On checking your workshop manual specifications you find that the car makers state that the standard springs have a pressure of 65lb at a compressed length of 1.5in and a pressure of 135lb at a compressed length of 1.25in. This may not appear to be of much value as you know from measuring them that the fitted length of the valve springs (the partially compressed length of the spring with the valve seated) is 1.47in and as the theoretical valve lift is 0.435in then the compressed spring length at full lift will be 1.055in. (Note in this example valve clearance is 0.020in so true valve lift will be 0.415in, assuming no deflection of the camshaft or rockers and assuming true to ratio rocker arms; many are not, it is not unusual to find rockers supposedly 1.5:1 with a true ratio closer to 1.45:1.) We can calculate from the specifications that the stock springs have a spring rate of 280lb per in because compressing the spring from 1.5in to 1.25in increased the pressure from 65lb to 135lb. Hence 0.25in compression brings a 70lb increase in pressure, therefore the spring rate is 280lb per in (70lb ÷ 0.25 = 280lb per in). Knowing the spring rate, the on-seat pressure at 1.47in and the full lift pressure at 1.055in can be easily calculated. If at 1.5in the pressure is 65lb then at 1.47in it will be 73.4lb (65 + [280 x 0.03] = 73.4lb) and at 1.055in it will be 189.6lb (65 + [280 x 0.445] = 189.6lb) so the standard springs should have sufficient pressure. However, it would be wise to actually measure the pressure on a valve spring tester.

Having determined that the spring pressure is satisfactory does not establish that the stock springs are suitable because the valve springs may stack solid with no clearance between coils before full lift is reached. All valve springs require what is termed working clearance between coils. Depending on the spring manufacturer this can vary from as little as 0.005in between coils to as much as 0.020in, the majority of springs requiring about 0.010in. Perhaps the simplest way to check the minimum length the spring can be safely compressed is to slip feeler strips of the appropriate thickness (or brass shim stock) between each coil and then fully compress the spring in a vice and measure its length. For the springs to be suitable this figure must be no more than the full lift valve spring length which we calculate by measuring the length of every spring with the valve seated and then deducting the valve lift from the smallest seated length. Let us assume that the seated lengths vary from 1.45in to 1.47in and the valve lift is 0.415in (theoretical lift 0.435in minus valve clearance of 0.020in). The minimum spring compressed length will be 1.035in (1.45 - 0.415 = 1.035), hence to be suitable our valve springs would have to be shorter than 1.035in when measured in the vice fully compressed with feeler strips between all coils, to avoid coil binding and valve train and cam lobe damage.

With modern high lift cams it is also possible for the valve train to become solid due to the bottom of the valve spring retainers hitting the tops of the valve guides at full lift. It is easiest to check for this condition with the head removed and without valve springs. Firstly, set a telescopic gauge or a snap gauge at the full lift valve spring length. Then fit the valve spring retainers and collets to each valve, pulling them up tightly. Next in turn push each valve to the simulated full lift position and determine that there is at least 0.060in clearance between the valve spring retainer and valve guide. If the clearance is less, metal can be ground from the retainer up to the maximum of about 0.040in. When more metal removal is necessary it will have to be cut from the valve guides.

The next thing we must take care to do correctly is adjust the valve clearance (valve lash). The cam grinder will supply a clearance figure for the inlet and exhaust valve. If he gives a "cold" clearance he means just that; the engine should not have been run in the previous five hours. The "hot" clearance is for an engine at normal operating temperature. It is important to maintain correct valve clearance to allow the valve to seat properly and transfer its heat to the valve seat. If the valves are run tight to quieten them, valve burning could result.

Setting the valve clearances accurately is not difficult; it just requires a little time and thought. Firstly, let me point out that it will be impossible to do a good job if the contact face of the rocker or the tip of the valve stem has a dip worn into it. The feeler

High lift cams may cause the valve spring retainer to contact the valve guide at full lift. Therefore before assembling the head ensure that there is at least 0.060in clearance in the simulated full lift position.

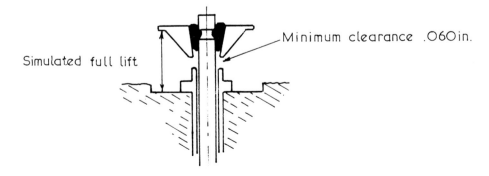

blade will be too wide or too rigid to fit into the dip, hence the clearances will be wrong. When we measure the clearance the lifter should be fairly close to the centre of the base circle of the cam lobe. This is no problem with overhead cam engines as it is easy to see when the cam follower is on the base circle. There is a difficulty, however, with ohc engines using rocker-type cam followers which employ a swivel foot to contact the valve stem as the foot easily rolls over, resulting in inaccurate clearance adjustments. To overcome this situation I prefer to adjust the clearance by inserting the feeler strip between the cam lobe and rocker. When doing it this way it becomes necessary to reduce the clearance because of the effect of the rocker arm ratio. Therefore if the clearance at the valve is 0.013in and the rocker ratio is 1.45:1, then the clearance measured at the cam lobe will be only 0.009in (0.013 ÷ 1.45 = 0.009).

Pushrod-type engines require a little more thought because it is not possible to see when the lifters are on the base circle of each cam lobe. Knowing that both the inlet and exhaust valve are closed at TDC on the compression stroke simplifies matters as the lifters obviously must be on the base circle at that moment. Starting with the No. 1 piston on TDC on the compression stroke (the rotor button will point to the No. 1 plug lead) adjust the clearance. Then turn the motor over to bring each piston in turn, according to the firing order, to TDC and adjust the clearances as you go. To make this task easy mark the crank pulley with TDC marks for all the cylinders; 4 cylinder engines will have one mark 180° around from the No. 1 and No. 4 mark, 6 cylinder engines will require two new marks each 120° from the original, and 8 cylinder engines will require three new TDC marks spaced 90° apart.

Adjusting the valve train of engines with hydraulic lifters is quite different. The majority of manufacturers recommend that the adjustment be done with the engine hot and running. They suggest that each rocker be slackened off until it emits a distinctive "clacking" sound and then the adjuster should be taken down one half to one full turn. To increase the rpm at which the lifters "pump up" I suggest that the adjusters are taken down only one quarter turn. An alternative method is to slacken off each rocker with the engine stopped, then run the engine for a few seconds to completely fill the lifters with oil. Next, with the engine stopped and the lifter on the base circle, turn the pushrod within the fingers, tightening the rocker at the same time. When some resistance to turning the pushrod is felt, note the position of the adjusting spanner and tighten the rocker adjusting nut a further quarter of a turn.

Unfortunately, to reduce costs a number of car makers no longer make any provision to adjust hydraulic valve systems. Hence when the head or block deck is machined, or a cam is fitted with a smaller than standard base circle, you will have to take special steps to obtain the correct valve adjustment. The simplest, but more expensive way, is to use adjustable pushrods. These are also fiddly to adjust. An effective and less expensive method is to raise or lower the rocker arms by either shimming up the rocker pedestals or machining the pedestal base to lower them. Firstly, to determine if shimming or machining is required, turn the engine so that No. 1 piston is at TDC on the compression stroke. Next fit the two pushrods and rockers for this cylinder and tighten the pedestal studs down finger tight. If there is clearance between the two rockers and valves, fully tighten the pedestal studs and then measure and record the clearance. Repeat this procedure for all the other cylinders, measuring and noting the clearance. After this divide each clearance figure by the rocker ratio and then add 0.040in to 0.050in divided by the rocker ratio to each figure. This

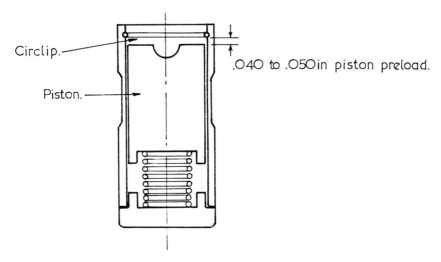

Circlip.

Piston.

.040 to .050in piston preload.

Hydraulic lifters must be preloaded otherwise the rockers and valves will clatter. Normal piston preload is 0.040in to 0.050in.

appears complicated so consider an example. The engine has 1.5:1 rocker arms. The clearance is 0.030in on the No. 1 inlet valve and 0.021in on the No. 1 exhaust. Dividing each clearance figure by the rocker ratio gives us 0.020in and 0.014in respectively. Adding 0.040in and 0.050in divided by the rocker ratio increases each figure by 0.027 to 0.033in. Hence the inlet figure becomes 0.047 to 0.053in and the exhaust figure becomes 0.041 to 0.047in. These figures represent the amount which will be machined from the base of the pedestals to preload the lifter the required 0.040in to 0.050in.

On the other hand it is possible that when the pedestal studs are taken down finger tight there is a gap between the base of the pedestal and the cylinder head. In this case measure and record the gap for each pedestal. Next, multiply each figure by the rocker arm ratio. If the resulting figures are somewhere between 0.040in and 0.050in then the pedestals can be fully tightened down as the lifter preload will be correct. However, if the figures are less than this, the pedestals will require shimming. Consider the example of an engine with 1.5:1 rockers. The gap under No. 1 inlet pedestal is 0.015in and under the exhaust 0.018in. The gap required for correct preload is 0.040in to 0.050in divided by the rocker ratio ie 0.027in to 0.033in. Therefore shim thickness will be 0.012in to 0.018in and 0.009in to 0.015in respectively.

Chapter 6

The Exhaust

Subtle changes to the exhaust system can unleash a lot of horsepower without any decrease in fuel economy. In fact usually the opposite is true; a free flowing exhaust ordinarily reduces fuel consumption. With race and rally engines a lot of testing is necessary to get the exhaust tuning just right. However, with road engines using mild economy cams and fitted with mufflers, exhaust tuning is far from a precise art. A lot of money can be wasted buying parts which are totally unnecessary for muffled road cars.

For example, while testing a 3.3 litre Holden it was decided that a special extractor-type header was required. The owner wanted a high power output but being limited to a Phase V cam, so as not to upset the electronic fuel injection sensors, this was proving to be a little elusive. It appeared that the next obvious place with which to gain more power was from the exhaust. The standard engine came fitted with an extractor header which did not appear to be very efficient. The extractors were a 6–3–1 type with small diameter 1.375in primary pipes approximately 12 to 17in long. The secondaries were 1.625in diameter and of a similar length leading to a 2in o/d collector. What was strange considering the firing order 1–5–3–6–2–4 was the unusual primary pipe combinations. Cylinders 1 and 4 were connected, as were 3 and 5, and 2 and 6. This did not appear to make any sense except to perhaps increase work area around the engine when installed.

The first change was to fit an off-the-shelf 6–2–1 header with "standard" straight six pipe connections; cylinder 1, 2 and 3 joined together and 4, 5, 6, together. The primaries were again small at 1.375in and the secondaries were 1.75in. This exhaust made virtually identical power as the stock header above 3500rpm, but below that it lost on the average about 1hp. Next, a special one-off header was fabricated to experiment with different pipe diameters and lengths. After several trials the best exhaust was found to be a 6–3–1 system with 1.5in primaries 16in long, and 1.75in secondaries 20in long, leading to a 2.5in outlet. The primaries were connected conventionally; cylinders 1 and 6, 2 and 5, 3 and 4. The end result was an exhaust costing a lot of money which gave a mere 2 to 4hp more than the stock pipes that had appeared to be so inefficient.

This is just one example of how money can be wasted, but invariably I find that with small cams and mufflers even very odd, inefficient-looking tubular headers work just as well as nice looking headers with big diameter equal length pipes. Cast iron manifolds sometimes are not all that bad either. Some of the Japanese and European car makers cast their exhaust manifolds very well; almost as well as tubular headers. Often it will be found that these cast manifolds virtually duplicate tubular headers. The correct cylinders are joined together and the cast "branches" are frequently up around 10 to 12in long to reduce exhaust contamination from one cylinder to another cylinder.

Really this, along with less exhaust restriction, is the reason why tubular headers are fitted. The basic idea is to connect the primary pipes so that the exhaust gas from one cylinder will not pressurise another cylinder. Taking a typical four cylinder engine with a 1–3–4–2 firing order, it can be seen that at the end of its exhaust stroke No. 1 cylinder will tend to draw in exhaust gas being expelled under high pressure from the No. 3 cylinder when a standard cast iron manifold which connects all four exhaust ports is used. Naturally No. 3 in turn will draw in exhaust gas from No. 4, No. 4 will draw in gas from No. 2 and so on. To overcome this problem a tubular header or a cast iron manifold with branches up around 10 to 12in long is necessary on 4 and 8 cylinder engines when cams hotter than Phase III are utilised.

The exact design of the header is not really so important with economy cams. The primary tubes may be connected 4 into 1 or 4 into 2 into 1 (also called tri-y) and

This Mustang V8 header doesn't look very efficient; the pipes are small in diameter and they are nowhere near equal length. However, with a mild performance/economy cam fitted the engine makes about the same power as with big diameter equal length tube headers.

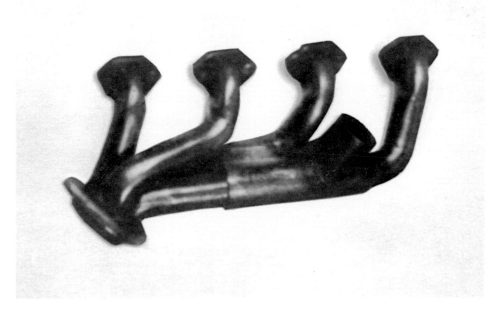

the tubes should be at least 12in long to be really effective. When cams up around 240° duration at 0.050in lift are used, 4–1 headers usually show more top end power and 4–2–1 headers give better mid-range power. Table 6.1 indicates the pipe size which should be aimed for when selecting a header. Actually in performance/economy applications I consider ease of maintenance with the various header types fitted to be more important than the pipe sizes. For this reason I tend to favour 4–2–1 or short tube (ie 12–16in) 4–1 headers to gain maximum working space around the engine. I regularly waste a lot of time working on customer's cars which have been equipped with ill-designed headers. The most common problem on V8 engines is not being able to get all of the spark plugs out without first unbolting the headers! Other common problems on all engines are not being able to adjust the steering box, or remove the oil filter and starter motor with headers fitted. Some header manufacturers do not seem to care very much about maintaining a safe working clearance between header pipes and such things as steering arms, firewall, starter motor, alternator, air conditioner

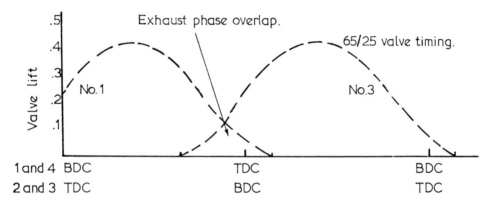

When an exhaust manifold connects all the exhaust ports of a 4 cylinder engine together, the gases exiting one cylinder can contaminate another cylinder, diluting the fuel/air mixture.

4 into 1 tubular headers cut out exhaust gas contamination between cylinders on 4 cylinder and V8 engines. However, long branch headers like these seriously limit working space around many engines.

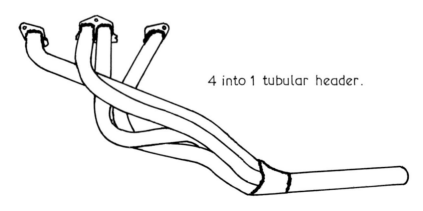

4 into 1 tubular header.

compressor etc. It is annoying belting pipes with a hammer to gain clearance and it is expensive replacing electrical components over-heated by the close proximity of header tubes.

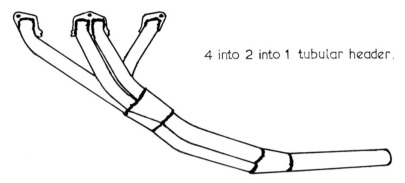

4 into 2 into 1 tubular header.

This 4 into 2 into 1 header is for 4 cylinder engines. It allows more working space around the engine than a 4 into 1 system and mid-range power is usually superior as well.

The pipe connections are quite different for 4 into 2 into 1 headers for V8 engines than those for 4 cylinder units. Note that the connections for the left and right cylinder banks are also different. A balance pipe should be fitted between the exhaust pipes of all 6 and 8 cylinder engines with twin exhaust systems.

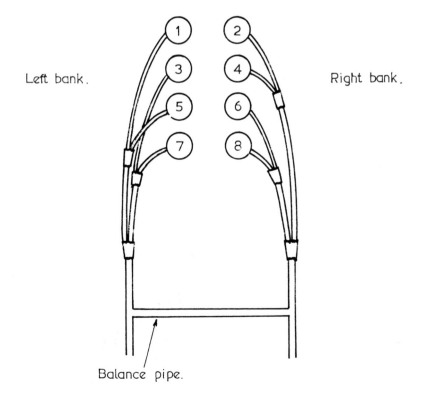

Left bank.

Right bank.

Balance pipe.

Table 6.1   Header pipe sizes for 4 and 8 cylinder engines

| Cylinder Size (cc) | 4 into 2 into 1 header | | 4 into 1 header |
	Primary pipe size (in)	Secondary pipe size (in)	Primary pipe size (in)
250	1.25 dia x 12 to 18 long	1.5 dia x 15 to 24 long	1.25 dia x 15 to 30 long
325	1.25 to 1.375 dia	1.5 to 1.625 dia	1.25 to 1.375 dia
400	1.375 to 1.5 dia	1.625 to 1.75 dia	1.375 to 1.5 dia
500	1.375 to 1.5 dia	1.625 to 1.75 dia	1.5 to 1.625 dia
600	1.5 to 1.625 dia	1.75 to 1.875 dia	1.625 to 1.75 dia
700	1.625 dia	1.875 to 2.0 dia	1.625 to 1.75 dia

Note: all pipe lengths are as shown for 250cc cylinder size
all pipe diameters are outside diameters

Table 6.2 shows what sort of power increase can be expected with various exhaust manifold types. The test engine was a 305cu in Chev V8 with emissions gear. The carb was a standard 4 barrel Quadrajet on a stock inlet manifold with a 1in spacer and the centre divider cut down. Early model 307 heads milled to increase the compression ratio to 9:1 were given a valve seat and throat job. Backcut 1.84in inlet and 1.5in exhaust valves were fitted. The cam was a Phase III grind with 108° lobe centres, 212° inlet and exhaust duration and 0.412in lift. In all tests a twin 2.25in exhaust and mufflers were attached. A 2in balance pipe (cross-over pipe) interconnected both engine pipes.

In the first test Chevrolet's most poorly designed (from a performance viewpoint) cast iron manifolds were used. These connect each of the four exhaust ports together and discharge into the exhaust pipe at the rear of the engine. For the second test "ram horns" Chev cast manifolds were used which dump their gases into the exhaust pipe in line with the centre cylinders. Because of improved flow and reduced cylinder contamination with exhaust gas, power increased considerably right through the power range. For the final tests several tubular headers were tested with similar results. Headers with 4 into 1 primaries 1.625 dia x 28in long lost power below 2500rpm while those with 1.5 dia x 28 long primaries gave more power below

Table 6.2   Exhaust comparison testing of 305 Chev

| rpm | Test 1 | | Test 2 | | Test 3 | |
	hp	Torque	hp	Torque	hp	Torque
2000	107	282	110	290	112	295
2500	137	287	139	293	141	296
3000	169	295	175	306	178	312
3500	201	302	208	312	212	318
4000	228	300	237	311	238	313
4500	241	281	248	289	254	296
5000	252	265	259	272	264	277

Test 1 – Chev cast iron "rear discharge" manifold

Test 2 – Chev cast iron "rams horns" manifold

Test 3 – 4 into 2 into 1 headers

Some stock cast iron exhaust manifolds work better than others. The centre dump Chevrolet "ram horns" manifolds are much more efficient than the rear dump design.

3000rpm without giving away anything at 5000rpm. The power figures shown for Test 3 were produced when 4–2–1 headers were fitted. These had 1.5 dia x 15in long primaries and 1.875in dia x 20in long secondaries. This system gave marginally superior power right through the power range than either 4–1 system. As can be seen, when a mild cam is installed and mufflers are fitted, tubular headers do not necessarily unleash a whole lot more power if the cast iron manifolds are of the centre outlet "ram horns" type.

A popular myth says that the first modification on small capacity high rev engines is to get rid of the stock exhaust manifold as they knock off a potential 7–10 hp. Yes, at times I have seen that sort of power increase when tube headers are fitted, but the results shown in Table 6.3 are more typical of what I regularly find, as the standard manifold on modern engines is generally very efficient. This Opel engine was stock except for a carefully modified head and mild Phase II cams with 0.370in lift. The exhaust manifold was ground to match the ports to the gasket cut-outs.

No doubt you have seen advertisements claiming huge power increases when headers are fitted and there was probably a nice graph showing the relative power outputs to prove the point. I won't say that such claims are untrue but usually these power comparisons are made with a standard manifold and standard small bore exhaust to prove how inefficient the manifold is, and then for the second test headers and a large bore system, or perhaps no exhaust system at all if the company is totally unscrupulous, are used to prove how headers benefit power output. This is not to say that headers are of no value as they will show some power improvement. However, 77

Table 6.3   Exhaust comparison testing Opel Ecotec 1.8 litre

	Test 1		Test 2		Test 3	
rpm	hp	Torque	hp	Torque	hp	Torque
2000	41	107	38	101	41	107
2500	54	113	51	107	51	108
3000	67	118	64	113	63	111
3500	80	120	79	118	78	117
4000	97	128	94	124	93	123
4500	112	131	107	125	110	129
5000	131	138	130	137	132	139
5500	138	132	141	135	139	133
6000	148	129	149	130	147	128
6500	153	124	156	126	155	125
7000	146	110	148	111	144	108
7500	130	91	128	90	133	93

Test 1 – standard Opel exhaust manifold

Test 2 – tubular 4 into 1 headers, 1.625in x 36in long

Test 3 – tubular 4 into 2 into 1 headers, 1.625in x 15in long primaries, 1.75in x 23in long secondaries

this improvement should be weighed carefully against their cost and the inconvenience which headers can cause. I would not consider their use on 4 and 8 cylinder engines with small Phase I or II cams as headers really only begin to show their worth with Phase IV cams and warmer.

Six cylinder exhaust manifolds fall into two categories; very good or plain horrible. Fortunately, very few straight sixes use a cast iron manifold which connects all exhaust ports together and dumps through a single outlet. This type of manifold creates a lot of exhaust back pressure and because of overlapping exhaust open periods each cylinder will draw in high pressure exhaust gas from two other cylinders during its exhaust cycle. Even Phase I cams are out if this type of manifold is retained.

Nearly all modern straight sixes utilise a "split" type cast manifold which joins cylinders 1–2–3 to one outlet and joins cylinders 4–5–6 to a second outlet. The split manifold works very well even with wild road cams as there is very little overlap of exhaust cycles. Tubular headers will give marginally more economy because exhaust gas flow is a fraction better, but they will not give an increase of more than a couple of horsepower when performance/economy cams are fitted.

Table 6.4 shows the effect of exhaust manifold and exhaust system changes on a 229cu in V6 Chev. The engine was outfitted with stock 4 barrel carb and manifold, stock cylinder heads milled to raise compression to a true 8.8:1 with a valve seat and throat job, stock backcut inlet and exhaust valves, Phase IV cam with 218° inlet and exhaust duration at 0.050in lift and 0.460in inlet and exhaust lift, and 1.52:1 budget roller tip rocker arms.

It can be seen that headers raised the power level only a little over what was produced with stock cast iron manifolds. However, swapping to a free flow dual exhaust gave very good results. At cruise speed the engine developed about 5hp more

"Split" type cast manifolds allow good exhaust flow on 6 cylinder engines. This 2.6 litre Mercedes produces 162hp with full emissions gear and CAT converter; enough to push the 190E to 130mph.

and in the upper power range power was up by 10 to 16hp. This is a big power increase for a small amount of work and a minimal outlay of money.

Table 6.4   Exhaust comparison testing of 229 Chev

	Test 1		Test 2		Test 3		Test 4	
rpm	hp	Torque	hp	Torque	hp	Torque	hp	Torque
2000	68	180	71	186	69	182	70	184
2500	88	186	90	190	89	187	91	191
3000	107	188	113	198	107	188	111	195
3500	123	184	129	193	125	187	129	194
4000	152	200	162	213	154	202	162	212
4500	173	202	183	214	176	205	185	216
4750	173	191	187	207	177	196	191	211
5000	176	185	188	198	179	188	190	200
5250	168	168	184	184	173	173	187	187

Test 1 – Chev cast iron manifolds, single 2.5in exhaust and muffler

Test 2 – Chev cast iron manifolds, dual 2.25in exhaust and mufflers and 2.0in balance pipe

Test 3 – tubular 3 into 1 headers with 1.625in dia x 28in long primaries, single 2.5in exhaust and muffler

Test 4 – tubular 3 into 1 headers as above, dual 2.25in exhaust and mufflers and 2.0in balance pipe

79

Nearly all large engines over about 3.3 litres will show a 10 to 20hp increase just from fitting a good dual exhaust system. However, to avoid a loss of mid-range torque a balance pipe must be fitted to interconnect the two exhaust pipes. The best location, power wise, for the balance pipe is close to the front of the gearbox. Preferably it should be as short as possible and of the same diameter as the exhaust. If there are clearance problems use a pipe size which can be comfortably accommodated in the available space.

Because of limited space or the need to retain just one catalytic converter, it may be necessary to use a single large diameter exhaust. This can pose a problem in V6 and V8 engines as many "Y" pipes are very restrictive at the place where the two engine pipes connect. What we want is a nice smooth, free-flow "Y" connection.

By now it should be obvious that in performance/economy applications the actual exhaust system rather than just the exhaust manifold should attract our attention in the quest for more power. Naturally the system must have gentle bends and a good size bore to reduce flow restriction. Table 6.5 sets out the pipe sizes which should be aimed for. Unfortunately it is difficult to find sufficient space under many modern cars to fit such large exhausts and still maintain good ground clearance. If this is a problem remember that it is quite acceptable to "flatten" the exhaust by up to 0.25in over a 6in length, to fit it closer to crossmembers etc. Also, because exhaust gases cool and contract as they pass along the system, the pipe diameter can be reduced for the last half of the system's length. This won't have much effect on power output and it may help reduce noise, allowing the use of a less restrictive muffler.

The type and number of mufflers fitted will depend on how quiet you want your car. Personally, I prefer a quiet mellow tone which doesn't give me a headache when I drive and which doesn't attract the attention of the law. If fitted as far to the rear of the car as possible, well-designed mufflers will not reduce power by more than about 3–5%. Fitted closer to the engine, where the exhaust gases are very hot, they cause more flow restriction and power loss.

There are many muffler designs but the types most suited for performance applications are of either straight-through or reverse flow (also called "S" flow) design. Most people think of straight-through mufflers as only suitable for loud boy racer-types, but many high quality quiet mufflers are of this design. I prefer this type

When it is necessary to retain a single large diameter exhaust system in V6 and V8 applications every effort should be made to make the "Y" connection between the two engine pipes as free flowing as possible.

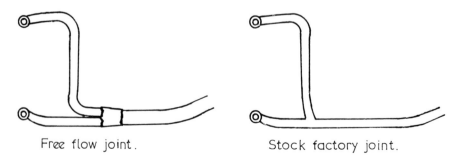

Free flow joint.   Stock factory joint.

Table 6.5   Exhaust pipe sizes for good flow

Engine sizes (litres)	Preferred size	Minimum size
1.0	1.75in	1.625in
1.3	1.875in	1.75in
1.6	2.0in	1.875in
2.0	2.25in	2.0in
2.4	2.25in	2.125in
2.8	2.5in	2.25in
3.2	1 x 2.5in	2.25in
	2 x 2.0in	
3.5	2 x 2.25in	1 x 2.5in
		2 x 2.0in
4.2	2 x 2.25in	2 x 2.0in
5.0	2 x 2.5in	2 x 2.25in

Note: all pipe diameters are outside diameters

although two mufflers are usually necessary to stop exhaust "popping" on the overrun. The quietest designs often have an open resonating chamber in the middle to further reduce popping. Many high performance mufflers are now of the reverse flow design. These generally do not contain any sound absorbing material so they are a little lighter than straight-through types. Reverse flow mufflers can be very quiet but many are noisy, and the noisy ones frequently do not make any more power. Usually, reverse flow mufflers are not prone to popping on the overrun so often only one muffler, or a muffler and a small resonator, will be all that is required to produce an acceptable exhaust tone.

Turbo cars also frequently have inefficient exhaust systems. It would appear that a number of car makers do not have much confidence in their customers as they purposely "plug-up" the exhaust to keep the boost pressure and power down. One manufacturer, for example, equips their 2 litre turbo with a 2in exhaust, yet just before the final muffler a restrictor plate with a 1 in hole is fitted! This prevents the turbo from spinning up to full boost and cuts power dramatically. Removing the restrictor results in another 1.5 psi boost. I have not been able to determine why this was done. Could it have been to meet emission standards? Or was there a reliability problem at higher boost on unleaded fuel? I do not know, and the manufacturers are not telling.

The very first modification required on nearly all turbo cars is a free flow exhaust. If the exhaust is not free flowing then all other engine modifications will be a complete waste as the back pressure will prevent the engine making good boost and turbo lag could become quite a problem. Table 6.6 shows the exhaust system size required. This table refers to pipe sizes on the downstream side of the turbo as normally in performance/economy applications an increase in pipe size between the manifold and turbo will reduce performance or increase turbo lag. In some applications the turbo outlet may be of a larger diameter than the preferred exhaust diameter. In this situation the first 20 to 24in of the exhaust should be larger than indicated and then tapered down over a length of about 6 to 8in to the size required. Cars with 2.3 to 3 litre engines may not have sufficient underbody clearance to 81

Table 6.6   Turbo exhaust size

Engine size (litres)	Preferred size	Minimum size
1.3	2.0in	1.875in
1.6	2.25in	2.0in
2.0	2.5in	2.125in
2.3	3.0in or 2 x 2.125in	2.25in
3.0–4.0	3.0in or 2 x 2.25in	2.5in

Note: all pipe diameters are outside diameters

accommodate such large diameter exhausts. If this is a problem, the exhaust should be of the size specified for the first 30 to 35in and then it may be tapered down over a length of approximately 6in to a size which can be conveniently fitted. Alternatively, the exhaust may be split into a twin system of the size indicated, not less than 15in from the turbo.

Just how much extra power you can expect with a larger exhaust is difficult to quantify. If the standard intercooler is inadequate and the turbo very restrictive, then a big exhaust will not help much. However, if the intercooler is a fair size and the standard turbo is to a "sporty" specification, then good power gains are possible. The Subaru WRX, for example, has turbo sizing which favours top end rather than mid-range power. When a hybrid exhaust 3in to the back axle, then with a 2¹/₂in tailpipe was fitted peak power rose by 19hp at 5800rpm. In the mid-range the gains were far less impressive averaging 5–11hp between 3200 and 5000rpm.

Chapter 7

Carburation

The basic requirement for any carburettor is that it meters the fuel and air in such proportions as to be easily combustible, enabling the engine to produce good power over a wide rpm range with good economy. For best power the mixture we need is around 1:12 or 1:13, ie one pound of petrol (gasoline) to every twelve or thirteen pounds of air. Such a blend is just right for full throttle operation, but for other conditions such as ordinary light load running we want an "economy blend" of around 1:14.5 to 1:16. Table 7.1 indicates the fuel air requirements for a number of operating conditions. Obviously the carburettor has to "sense" the engine's operating conditions accurately and adjust the fuel-air mix to suit. If the carburettor is not able to do this, flat spots and engine surging will result, spoiling performance and economy. For this reason we have to be very selective as to the type and size of carburettor that we choose; a carburettor which provides good performance may not give the desired economy and vice versa.

Clearly to understand more fully what we should be looking for in a carburettor, we have to go back to the basics and get to know a little about how a carburettor works. All carburettors employ a fuel inlet system, an idle system and a main running system. Many in addition also have an acceleration pump system and a power system.

The inlet system consists of the fuel bowl, the float, and the needle and seat. The

Table 7.1   Fuel/air Requirements

Running condition	Mixing ratio by weight Fuel: air
Starting	1:3–4
Idling	1:6–10
Low speed running	1:10–13
Light load economy running	1:14.5–16
Heavy load performance running	1:12–14

fuel, before passing to the metering systems, is stored in the fuel bowl, and it is maintained at the correct level by the float and the needle valve (needle and seat). If the fuel is not at the correct level in the fuel bowl, the carburettor metering systems will not mix the fuel and air in the required proportions. A high fuel level will increase fuel consumption and may cause erratic running. In extreme cases fuel spillover through the carburettor discharge nozzle and/or vent during cornering or braking could give rise to the engine faltering or stopping. Such a condition may be the result of an incorrectly adjusted float, or a needle and seat which is not seating properly and shutting off the fuel inlet when the float reaches the correct level. This is usually due to excessive wear of the needle and/or seat, but may also be due to dirt if the fuel system does not incorporate an inline fuel filter. A low fuel level on the other hand causes flat spots because of lean-out in corners and when accelerating. Very serious is the possibility of melted pistons due to reduced fuel flow capacity. Such a condition may be due to a float set too low, low fuel pressure, a restrictive or partially blocked fuel filter, or a needle and seat too small to flow sufficient fuel to keep the fuel bowl full.

The cold starting system provides mixture enrichment to allow starting when either the engine or the air temperature is cold. Most carburettors employ a choke plate which restricts air flow into the engine, thus providing a rich fuel/air mixture. As nearly all modern engines employ carburettors with an automatic choke, it is necessary to regularly check that the choke is opening fully, and in the prescribed

Electric automatic chokes are adjusted by turning the thermostat assembly to a leaner (L) or richer (R) position. A choke which does not open fully or which is slow to open increases fuel consumption.

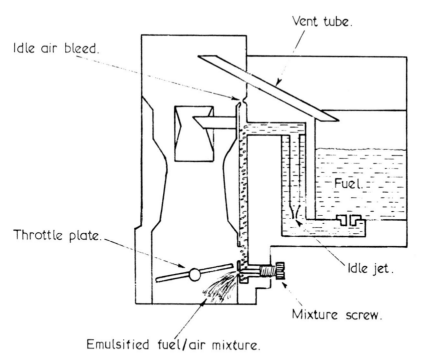

Vent tube.

Idle air bleed.

Fuel.

Throttle plate.

Idle jet.

Mixture screw.

Emulsified fuel/air mixture.

The idle system provides fuel at idle and low speeds. In the majority of carburettors turning the mixture screw in leans the mixture and turning it out richens the mixture.

time; usually about 3 minutes. A choke which is slow to open or which is not fully opening severely increases fuel consumption.

The carburettor idle system provides a relatively rich mixture at idle and low speeds, when not enough air is being drawn through the venturi to cause the main system to operate. When the throttle plate (butterfly) is nearly closed, the restriction to air flow causes a high vacuum on the engine side of the throttle plate. It is this high vacuum which causes the idle system to operate. The outside air pressure of 14.7 psi acts on the fuel in the float bowl, forcing it through the idle jet, and past the idle mixture screw into the air stream. To emulsify the fuel before it reaches the mixture screw, an air bleed is included in the system. Increasing the size of the air bleed leans the idle mixture, if the size of idle jet remains constant.

The progression or transfer holes are a part of the idle system and allow a smooth transition from the idle fuel circuit to the main fuel system without "flat spots", provided the carburettor size has been correctly matched to the engine displacement. As the throttle is opened a little wider past idle, the progression holes are uncovered by the throttle plate, and begin to flow fuel metered and emulsified by the idle jet. At this time fuel flow past the mixture screw decreases and gradually tapers off as the next progression hole is uncovered by the throttle plate.

When the throttle is opened further, the pressure differential between the idle-progression holes and the air pressure acting on the fuel in the fuel bowl decreases, causing fuel flow in the idle system to decrease. Finally, the pressure is too low to push the fuel up the full height of the idle jet and the idle system ceases to supply fuel. 85

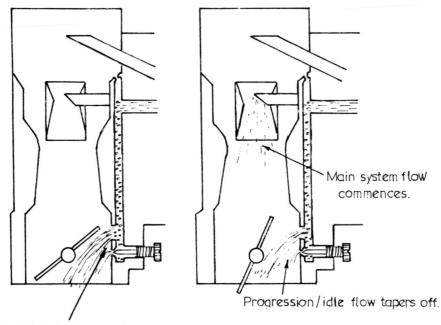

Main system flow commences.

Progression/idle flow tapers off.

Emulsified mixture flows from progression and idle holes.

The progression system is an extension of the idle system. It flows fuel when the throttle is opened a little past idle.

Fuel flow through the main metering system though will have commenced before flow in the idle circuit is reduced, providing a carburettor of the right size is fitted.

The main system meters fuel for cruising and high speed. As the throttle is opened and engine speed increases, air flow through the venturi rises, bringing the main system into operation. The heart of the carburettor is the main venturi, as it causes the pressure differential necessary to push the fuel from the fuel well, through the main jet, and up to the discharge hole in the auxiliary venturi (boost venturi).

In the internal combustion engine, a partial vacuum is created in the cylinders by the downward stroke of the pistons. Because atmospheric pressure is higher than the pressure in the cylinders, air rushes in through the carburettor to equalise the pressure difference. On its way through the carburettor the air passes through the venturi, which initially necks down the inrushing air and then allows it to widen out to the throttle bore. To get through the venturi, the air must speed up, thus reducing the pressure inside the venturi to below atmospheric. This pressure differential, commonly referred to as the "signal" of the main metering system, causes the system to discharge fuel. No fuel issues from the discharge nozzle until air flow through the venturi produces a pressure drop or signal of sufficient strength for the atmospheric pressure, acting on fuel in the fuel bowl, to push fuel through the main jet and up to the discharge nozzle. Pressure drop or vacuum within the venturi varies with engine speed and throttle opening. Wide open throttle and peak rpm

86

give the highest air flow, and consequently the highest pressure difference between the fuel bowl and discharge nozzle. This in turn gives the highest fuel flow into the engine.

To compensate for various engine displacements and engine operational speeds, a range of carburettors with a variety of venturi diameters are available to create the necessary pressure drop to bring the main fuel circuit into operation at the proper time. A small venturi will provide a higher pressure difference at any give rpm and throttle opening than a large diameter venturi. This is a very important aspect of carburation, which partly explains why the biggest is seldom the best. If the signal being applied by the venturi is too weak, due to the venturi being overly large, this could delay fuel discharge in the main system, causing a flat spot. To cover over this flat spot the idle will have to be richened up, which could spoil low speed running due to an overly rich mixture, or the acceleration-pump jet size could be increased. Increased fuel consumption will be evident as a result of either solution.

The auxiliary venturi functions as a signal amplifier for the main venturi, allowing for more precise and quicker fuel flow responses. This is important in present day engines as it allows the use of a slightly larger, less restrictive main venturi than would normally be possible, without sacrificing throttle response. The tail of the auxiliary or boost venturi discharges at the point of lowest pressure in the main venturi. Thus the air flow is accelerated through the boost venturi, and because of this,

The main system is activated by the air speed through the main venturi creating a vacuum of sufficient intensity to draw fuel up from the fuel bowl. It functions at cruise and higher speeds. The power valve is a diaphragm-type valve controlled by manifold vacuum, adding fuel to the main system at above normal cruising loads. This type of power system is found in Holley carburettors and fixed venturi downdraught Webers such as the 32DFM and 32/36 DGAV.

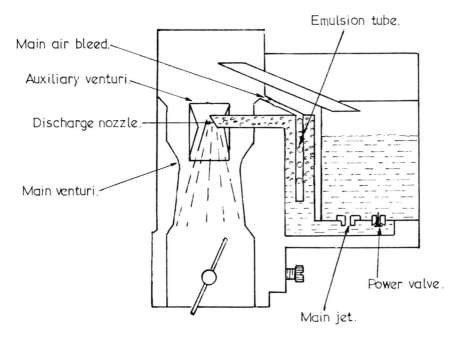

Emulsion tube.

Main air bleed.

Auxiliary venturi.

Discharge nozzle.

Main venturi.

Power valve.

Main jet.

the air and fuel emerging are travelling faster than the surrounding air passing through the main venturi. This has the effect of assisting fuel atomisation, and subsequently improves the quality of combustion.

The actual fuel metering in the main system is controlled by the main jet, the air bleed jet, and the emulsion tube. Some carburettors also feature a metering rod to control fuel flow through the main jet as part of the power system.

The main jet controls fuel flow from the fuel well. An increase in diameter richens the mixture, but more is involved as the shape of the jet entry and exit, as well as the bore finish, also affect fuel flow. Carburettor manufacturers measure the flow of every jet to ensure precise fuel flow and low exhaust emissions, and number the jet to its flow characteristics, not according to its nominal bore diameter. For this reason jets should not be drilled to change their size. The only exception would be if alternative jets are either unobtainable or difficult to obtain, and then only if the engine has a single carburettor with a single main jet.

The air bleed reduces the signal from the discharge nozzle, so that there is a less effective pressure difference to cause fuel flow through the main jet. This fine tunes the main metering system, preventing the mixture from becoming too rich at higher rpm. A larger air bleed leans the mixture, particularly at wide open throttle and high rpm. Additionally, the air bleed introduces air into the emulsion tube, to emulsify the fuel passing up to the discharge nozzle. This produces a lighter, frothy mixture of fuel and air which improves atomisation when the fuel is released from the discharge nozzle. It also serves to lower the viscosity of the fuel, making it lighter and able to respond more rapidly to changing signals from the auxiliary venturi. Thus the main system can keep more in step with the fuel requirements of the engine.

The emulsion tube has the task of emulsifying previously metered air issuing from the air bleed jet with the fuel coming from the main jet. Its influence is more marked at less than full throttle and during acceleration. The diameter of the emulsion tube and the size and location of holes to emulsify the fuel all affect and influence its operation. Usually, a change of emulsion tube will necessitate a main jet and an air bleed change.

Many carburettors also have a power system for mixture enrichment at heavy load operation. This system supplies additional fuel to complement the main metering system at above normal cruising loads. The added fuel supplied by the power system is controlled by manifold vacuum. As the load on the engine increases, the throttle must be opened wider to maintain a given speed. This lessens the restriction to air entering the engine, which in turn reduces manifold vacuum. In carburettors such as the Carter, Quadrajet and Varajet, at high vacuum the power piston is drawn down against the pressure of the power piston spring but when the vacuum level drops, as engine load increases, the spring pushes the power piston upward which in turn raises the metering rod out of the main jet. This increases fuel flow in the main system, effectively richening the mixture.

In Holley carburettors, and downdraught Webers with fixed venturis (eg 32DFM, 32/36DGAV, 38 DGAS), the power system is controlled by manifold vacuum operating on a diaphragm type valve. At high vacuum the diaphragm is drawn down against the pressure of the power valve spring, thus holding the valve closed. When the vacuum falls (usually to around 6–10in Hg), the spring overcomes manifold vacuum and the valve opens. Fuel flows from the float chamber, through the open the oil, and heat being radiated from the valley, away from the underside of the manifold.

Many cars draw in air that has been heated after passing through the radiator. This also reduces air density and performance in hot climates where the ambient temperature is usually over 25°C. The most advantageous system involves sealing the carburettor air inlet and air filter in a cold box so that hot air from around the engine cannot be drawn in. The cold box is then supplied with cool air from the front of the car by a 3in heater duct tube. The front end of the tube will require some type of deflector to prevent water and insects damaging or blocking the air filter.

An air filter also reduces the air density, particularly if it is clogged full of dust, by restricting air flow into the carburettor. Obviously the filter could be done away with, but as long engine life and effective air filtration are very closely related, this is not an acceptable option. Contrary to popular opinion, a clean air filter of good design and of sufficient size, does not reduce power output by very much at all. However, the filtration system on many cars does have a devastating effect on performance due to the use of a tiny air filter and a restrictive air box, designed to cut down induction roar and thus reduce noise inside the car.

If induction noise isn't a consideration or a remote filter mounted at the front of the car is fitted, I would recommend the use of K & N cotton gauze type filters. These filters will flow more air than any paper element or foam filter that I know of, even with a good coating of dust. As a rule K & N filters seldom reduce flow by more than about 2–3%, and in some instances they actually increase flow by nearly that amount.

When emission inspections are a consideration, the standard filter body will have to be retained. As you can see from Table 7.3, this results in the air flow being badly impeded. Just note the large jump in air flow when the standard filter body was cut down, leaving the filter element open to draw air from around its entire circumference. Obviously such a modification will not pass unnoticed by alert inspectors so a more subtle approach may be necessary. A modification which isn't easily detected is to cut away part of the air filter base. This increases flow and performance considerably, particularly if a K & N element is fitted. One disadvantage of this is that cold air induction is not possible unless a cold air box is fabricated around the air filter and carb.

Table 7.3   Air filter air flow comparison

Weber 32/36 DGAV with 26/27mm venturis tested at 1.5in Hg

Test conditions	cfm air flow
Carburettor without air filter	232
Carburettor with K & N sports air filter	229
As above with foam filter	217
Standard totally enclosed paper element with single snorkel air intake	181
As above with filter body cut down flush with base	212
Standard filter body and paper element with filter base cut away	209
As above with K & N element	223

Just how much effect a low restriction air filter has on performance can be gauged from Table 7.4. The engine, a 2 litre Ford ohc, had a head clean-up and a Phase   93

Cutting away part of the air filter base reduces air flow restriction into the engine and ups power.

IV cam, but apart from these modifications it was basically standard, even down to the cast iron exhaust manifold. Below 4000rpm the standard filter body and element didn't cut hp very much, but at 6000rpm they were knocking off 10hp or about as much as would be lost by refitting the standard camshaft.

Table 7.4   Air filter comparison test of Ford 2 litre ohc

| | Test 1 | | Test 2 | | Test 3 | |
rpm	hp	Torque	hp	Torque	hp	Torque
2000	45	119	45	119	45	118
2500	59	124	60	125	59	124
3000	77	134	75	131	76	133
3500	85	127	81	122	85	128
4000	97	128	95	125	99	130
4500	103	120	98	114	103	120
5000	110	116	106	111	109	114
5500	115	110	109	104	111	106
6000	113	99	103	90	111	97
6500	101	82	88	71	98	79

Test 1 – engine fitted with Weber 32/36 DGAV carburettor and K & N sports air filter
Test 2 – as above but with standard Ford filter body and paper element
Test 3 – as above but with standard filter base cut away and K & N element fitted

Many enthusiasts, and tuners too for that matter, are fooled into thinking that they have gained many horsepower by fitting twin 40 or 45 DCOE Webers to fairly mildly tuned engines, like the one described above. Often, the improvement in power is more the result of the removal of the standard air filter than from the larger carburettors. An engine with a mild cam could gain a similar hp increase retaining the standard carburettor and manifold, with a simple air filter body modification and replacement of the element with a free flow element such as a K & N. Usually, the carburettor will require slightly richer jetting.

The other part of the induction system which can also impede air flow is the inlet manifold. Years ago many factory manifolds were of very poor design, but now there is frequently little to be gained by replacing the standard manifold. With a few modifications the factory manifold will perform as well as high performance replacement manifolds when a mild performance/economy cam is used. Additionally, they often display superior fuel distribution characteristics in the lower and mid rpm ranges, allowing slightly leaner carburettor jetting and better economy. Changing to a different manifold could bring you problems if you have little knowledge of what to look for. Some manifolds do not work as well as the standard manifold, and many only qualify as high performance manifolds when combined with wild cams and large carburettors. Basically I've found that race manifolds, and manifolds designed to connect two or three Weber or SU sidedraught carburettors to four and six cylinder inline engines, work very well. On the other hand street manifolds for V6 and V8 engines, and manifolds manufactured to connect a single Weber, either sidedraught or downdraught, to inline engines may not work as well as the stock manifold or a modified stock manifold.

There are more manifolds available for the small block V8 Chev than any other engine; at the moment at least two dozen. However, of that number there are only two which I would consider using on a performance/economy engine, apart from the stock manifold. The 350 Chev which produced the results shown in Table 7.5 was a typical strong street motor, developed with good mid-range power and cruise economy in mind. It was bored and stroked to 383cu in, had a Phase III cam, head clean-up, cast iron exhaust manifolds and a Carter 625cfm carburettor. As can be seen, only the Edelbrock Performer and Weiand 2P-180 were superior to the standard manifold with this particular engine tune. Remember that the five manifolds tested were carefully selected from all of the inlet manifolds available as the items most likely to be superior to the standard manifold, but only two actually worked better. The obvious conclusion is that the enthusiast lacking knowledge of the subject could quite easily choose a new manifold which is inferior to the one the manufacturer fitted at the factory.

Like nearly every V8 ever manufactured, the 350 Chev is fitted with a two-plane manifold. In this type of manifold the inlet passages are arranged in an upper and lower plane, with each plane connected to half of the carburettor, if a single two or four barrel carb is used. This separates the induction pulses by 180° and allows reasonably equal cylinder filling if the manifold is a good design. Also, because the total manifold runner volume is effectively halved, there is less air mass to activate with each inlet pulse, so throttle response is usually quicker and mid-range power may be improved, as compared with a single plane manifold. The division of the manifold into two planes is, however, a mixed blessing as it causes a flow restriction at higher 95

Table 7.5   Manifold comparison test of 383cu in Chev

	Test 1		Test 2		Test 3	
rpm	hp	Torque	hp	Torque	hp	Torque
2000	135	355	133	349	134	352
2500	178	373	175	368	176	370
3000	221	387	214	375	216	379
3500	257	386	255	382	253	380
4000	269	353	268	352	263	345
4500	291	340	294	343	296	345
5000	277	291	273	287	278	292

	Test 4		Test 5		Test 6	
2000	136	358	133	350	137	361
2500	180	379	174	366	180	378
3000	225	394	214	375	225	394
3500	263	395	257	386	261	392
4000	278	365	272	357	281	369
4500	301	351	298	348	300	350
5000	283	297	281	295	282	296

Test 1 – Stock 350 Chev inlet manifold
Test 2 – Holley "Z" manifold
Test 3 – Offenhauser Dual Port manifold
Test 4 – Edelbrock Performer manifold
Test 5 – Edelbrock Torker manifold
Test 6 – Weiand 2P-180 manifold

rpm because only one half of the carburettor flow capacity is available on any induction stroke. Additionally, there may be fuel distribution problems in the upper plane at higher rpm or at small throttle openings. What happens in some manifolds at high rpm, due to the carburettor being too close to the floor of the manifold, is that the fuel/air mixture continues straight on after leaving the carburettor, then the air turns abruptly into the port runners, throwing the fuel out of suspension onto the floor of the manifold. Fuel is wasted, combustion quality and power go down as a result. At small throttle openings another problem can arise due to the directional effect imparted to the fuel/air mixture by the angle of the throttle plate. What can happen is for the mixture to flow down the partly open throttle plate and then be directed by the angle of the throttle to one end of the manifold. This restricts flow to the other end cylinders so they don't give full power. Also, there is another problem related to this which occurs when the air flow is high, but the throttle is partially open, as when cruising. Again in this situation the fuel can be thrown out of suspension, leaning the mixture entering the opposite end cylinders. To prevent detonation, less advance or richer jetting is required, reducing both power output and economy.

There are two options available to overcome these difficulties, which by the way are not unique to two-plane V8 manifolds; some inline engines also have the carburettor mounted far too close to the manifold floor. The first and easiest option, if hood clearance is not a problem, is to raise the carburettor 1–1½in using an

Eight cylinder engine

3600–4300 open manifold   400cfm four barrel
            divided manifold 500cfm four barrel
5000 plus   625cfm four barrel

Holley carburettor

Displacement (cc)

Four cylinder engine

1500–2100   [1] 280cfm model 5200 two barrel

Six cylinder engine

2000–4000 open manifold   [1] 280cfm model 5200 two barrel
3500–4100 divided manifold 450cfm model 4360 four barrel
4300 plus open manifold   450cfm model 4360 four barrel

Eight cylinder engine

3600–4300 divided manifold 450cfm model 4360 four barrel
5000 plus open manifold   450cfm model 4360 four barrel
           divided manifold [2] 585cfm model 4180 four barrel

[1]   similar carb to Weber with 32/36 throttle bores, 26/27 venturis
[2]   similar carb to model 4160, built for Ford Mustang 5 litre to give better economy than 4160.

Rochester Quadrajet carburettor

Displacement (cc)

Six cylinder engine

2500–3600   use carburettor only with divided manifold
3800–4300   carburettor may be used with either divided or open manifold

Eight cylinder engine

3500–4100   use carburettor only with divided manifold
4300 plus   carburettor may be used with either divided or open manifold

GM Strasbourg Varajet carburettor

Displacement (cc)

Four cylinder engine

1500–2300   use carburettor only with open manifold

Six cylinder engine

2000–4100   use carburettor only with open manifold

I do not like, nor do I recommend, two barrel carburettors with simultaneous opening of both throttle plates on performance/economy engines. In general such carburettors do not offer good cruise economy or acceptable low speed driveability. I   101 would much prefer to use a small two barrel with progressive opening of the secondary barrel (with this type of carb an open manifold design is required). A four barrel carburettor is also far superior providing that it has small primary throttle bores and small venturis. The small primary throttle bores and venturis ensure a high air speed through the carburettor at low speed and when cruising. Hence the fuel metering will be more accurate, which produces good economy and good low speed driveability, free of flat spots or surging.

When it comes to carburettor tuning, there is no substitute for years of experience. To make the situation even more difficult, tuning and jetting for the street is considerably harder overall than for race applications. A race carb basically has to meter the fuel accurately over only a narrow rpm range, and usually only in full throttle, high air flow conditions. A street carb, on the other hand, has to deliver satisfactory economy and deliver good performance over a broad rpm range and over a broad air flow range. Additionally, it must work satisfactorily when the air and engine are cold, and also when the weather is hot and the fuel is literally boiling in the float bowl, with the car stuck in stop-start bumper to bumper traffic. Hence do not expect to get the jetting and other adjustments right on the first attempt. Only with patience and a methodical approach can an acceptable level of carburettor tune be attained. I've been working with engines and carburettors for well over 30 years, but it can still take me a lot of time, and many attempts to get the tune to exactly what I require. In the case of my personal cars I prefer initially to get the carburettor basically right, and then over a period of weeks or even months do further fine tuning. The majority of tuners are happy enough if they can get the engine to idle fairly smoothly and accelerate without any sign of flat spots. However, this isn't good enough for a street engine, which is why it becomes necessary to extend the carb tuning session over an extended period of time. It will take time, for example, to ascertain accurately what the fuel economy is like. Also it takes time to determine just how the carburettor is performing under a multitude of differing driving conditions.

Before even attempting to tune the carburettor there are a number of basic checks to be made. Naturally the ignition system must be functioning correctly and the timing adjusted. Ensure that the fuel filter fitted in the fuel line is not clogged full of rubbish. Also check the filter located in the carburettor fuel inlet. The mixture ratio will be affected if there are any air leaks. Therefore check all vacuum hoses over their entire length for cracks. Examine all carburettor ports, solenoid ports and thermo-vacuum switch ports to ensure that all unused ports are capped or plugged. Previously, the carburettor should have been correctly sealed to the manifold, which in turn should have been correctly sealed to the head using the correct gaskets and the right type of gasket cement. Silicone rubber jointing materials such as Silastic should not be used. They are an excellent oil joint sealant, but as they are not petrol resistant they should not be used anywhere in the induction tract.

Even when the manifold and carburettor have been correctly installed, this does not guarantee that you do not have an air leak, or that a leak will not start at a later date. Some carbs have a tendency to loosen the screws that attach the body to the base, so tighten these. At the same time tighten the manifold retaining bolts, as some engines loosen these fairly rapidly. After this I test for air leaks around the carburettor throttle spindle, around the carb base, and along the face of the manifold. I've found

that the most successful method to check for leaks is to squirt a little petrol out of an oil can in these areas, with the engine running. If there is a leak the engine idle speed will change, or it may run so rich that it will stop. If you use this method of leak detection do take care and have a fire extinguisher on hand. Usually there are no problems but a backfire or a cigarette smoker arriving on the scene could start a dangerous fire with all of that fuel running around. When a leak is found this will have to be rectified by replacing the offending gaskets, or if it is around the throttle spindle the carburettor will require reconditioning or replacement.

With these checks made we can direct our attention more toward the carburettor. After stopping the engine, get someone to push the accelerator pedal down as far as it will go and hold it to the floor. There should have been a good strong shot of fuel from the accelerator pump jet, if there wasn't then it is probably blocked. The primary reason to get someone to floor the pedal is so that you can check that you are indeed getting full throttle. If that is okay next investigate to see that the float level is correct and that the needle valve isn't blocked or weeping.

With these checks and adjustments made we can set about fine tuning the carburettor. Remember that nearly all driveability problems come down to the fact that at some point in its various metering systems the carburettor is either too lean or too rich. Flooding, loading up, bogging down, or black exhaust smoke are all indications of richness, while backfiring, pinging, surging, and hesitation are signs of a lean condition.

After bringing the engine up to normal operating temperature we first set the idle mixture. As discussed earlier, this system is primarily responsible for the quality of the engine idle and also part throttle cruise and transition. The preliminary idle adjustment is to bottom the mixture screws lightly and then back them out an equal number of turns. Do not be heavy handed when seating the mixture screws as the taper on the screw and the seat could be wrecked. Additionally, a number of so called "tamper proof" carburettors now use a threaded nylon insert which is easily stripped if the screw is forced onto the seat. If the engine had previously been running reasonably well, count how many turns it takes to seat the mixture screw/s, and use this as a guide when backing the screws out. If the carb has two mixture screws they should be backed out the same amount; usually about 1 turn for Webers, $1\frac{1}{2}$ turns for Holley four barrel, $2\frac{1}{2}$–3 turns for Carters and Quadrajets. Now start the engine and turn the idle speed screw against the throttle linkage to provide a fast idle of 800–1000rpm. Next adjust the idle mixture screws to get the best idle, or if a vacuum gauge is being used adjust the mixture to obtain the highest vacuum reading. Remember that if the carb has two mixture screws both screws should be set very close to the same position. Finally, adjust the idle speed screw to give the desired idle speed.

Once the idle mixture has been adjusted, the overall driveability can be checked, and tuning adjustments made to rectify problems along the way. Remember to change only one thing at a time and do carry out the corrective action detailed for each step before moving on to the next step. If the sequence of steps is broken or changed it becomes much more difficult to isolate the cause of the problem.

Immediate off-idle hesitation and stumble is traceable to the accelerator pump. It may not be so noticeable when moving from a standstill so I carry out this check by negotiating a fairly tight, slow, U-turn. If there is a stumble as you get back on the throttle you can be sure that the accelerator pump is the problem. Usually it will be a lean condition, but do not automatically assume this as a rich pump shot will also   103 cause a hesitation. The problem could be improperly adjusted pump linkages delaying the pump action or not giving the correct pump stroke, so check this aspect first and when you are satisfied that the linkages are correctly adjusted, repeat the U-turn test. Have an observer following behind to check for smoke; a puff of black smoke indicates a pump shot too big or of too long duration, grey or brown smoke usually means all is okay, and a complete lack of smoke probably indicates that a richer pump shot is required. When this has been determined, the pump jets, pump bleeds or pump cam can be changed to rectify the problem.

Next we want to check the primary main jets and the power system. These systems have their greatest influence at cruise and when lightly accelerating. If the car feels lazy, or in extreme cases misfires, when squeezing the throttle to maintain speed over a gentle rise, then either system is probably at fault. To determine this connect a vacuum gauge and gently accelerate from 1800 to 2500rpm in top gear. If the problem occurs between about 6 to 12in Hg it is most probably the main jets, or also the metering rods and power piston spring in the case of Carter, Quadrajet and Varajet carbs. If it occurs under 5–6in Hg it indicates that, in Holleys, a different power valve is required, and in other carburettors that the main jets or metering rods are the problem. This particular aspect of carburettor tuning is possibly the most important for a performance/economy engine, but also requires the most testing to get just right. Often it will be found that the jetting which is best for economy is not entirely satisfactory for gentle acceleration, leaving the car feeling a touch lazy or dead. Conversely, jetting to accomplish that spirited feel could lead to unacceptable fuel consumption.

With that sorted out we can then tackle the secondary jetting. I prefer to do this on the dyno in conjunction with spark plug readings. The alternative is to jet for speed, again along with spark plug readings. The jetting is richened until hp or speed drops, and then leaned back one or more steps, depending on how big the power or speed jump was with each step. Obviously if a two or three step decrease is only reducing the hp by 2% then in the interests of economy the jetting will be leaned off by that amount, unless this could give rise to detonation.

Plug reading at the very best gives only a guide to mixture strength. If the heat range for the plugs is wrong, or the engine is in less than top condition with worn rings and/or worn valve guides, reading the plugs will be a waste of time. If the mixture is excessively rich or way too lean, or if the engine's detonating, the plugs will indicate this. However, there is no way that the plugs will indicate, with pinpoint accuracy, when the jetting is correct; a couple of jet sizes either way perhaps, but that is about as close as you will get from taking plug readings.

The most accurate way to get a plug reading is to use new plugs and drive them for at least 600, and preferably 1000 miles. Then when you are checking the carb jetting take the car for a good hard run of 5 or 6 miles to burn off idling and low speed deposits. If you can't get home without sitting in traffic pull the plugs while you are out along the road, so as not to distort the reading. The plugs should have insulators all about the same colour; just off white to very light tan for unleaded fuel and the same colour range, plus as dark as rust brown for leaded. The earth electrode should be straw coloured and if there are any deposits they should have a dry, fluffy appearance. Black sooty insulators and sooty plug shells indicate an extremely rich mixture. If the mixture is too lean, the insulator may be chalky white or have a satin sheen, or even be burned a blueish colour. The centre and side electrodes will possibly have a molten appearance. If there are tiny pepper specks on the insulator, or little grey balls on the end of the spark plug shell, the engine is detonating.

Only after all of the other carburettor systems have been adjusted should the secondary opening rate be altered. If you are not able to feel when the secondary barrels open, the opening rate is correct. The car bogging down when accelerating indicates that they are opening too quickly or too early. On the other hand if you can sense the car gasping for air, or feel it hesitate during acceleration, and then suddenly take off, the secondaries are opening too late.

Now that we have taken a look at carburettor tuning procedures in general, we will consider some specific problems which may arise. (If detailed tuning information is required for Weber, SU and Holley carburettors I would suggest that you refer to another of my tuning books, *Performance Tuning in Theory & Practice – Four Strokes,* available from the Haynes Publishing Group.) The most obvious problem for tuners residing in a number of lands with emission regulations is tamper-proof carburettors. These usually have seals and/or caps installed to discourage adjustment of the idle mixture screw and also the idle speed screw. Some carb makers have taken this a step further by changing the basic carburettor design and concealing some adjustments. If this latter course has been taken, the carburettor section of the workshop manual must be carefully read to discover just how to get to these hidden adjustments, and see what, if any, special tools may be required to carry out the adjustment. Where plastic or soft metal plugs or caps are used these are quite easily dislodged. Replacement plugs and caps can usually be obtained from carburettor specialists or from your local, friendly spare parts man. In some lands with emission laws, carburettors are never checked to see if they have been tampered with. However in a few places the carburettor will be given a "visual", in which case the caps and plugs must be in place.

Instead of soft plugs, hardened steel plugs are now being used in some carbs to hinder access to the idle mixture screws. Where these are used the throttle body can be quite easily broken away using a punch or chisel, allowing the plugs to be removed. On the Quadrajet, for example, the factory has even put two locator points on the manifold side of the throttle body to indicate the location and depth of the plug. By driving a punch into the body in between the locator points it is a simple matter to crack the body and remove the plug. When the carburettor is refitted to the manifold, the modification is not easily noticed, and if necessary it is a simple matter to epoxy a new plug in place once the adjustment has been completed.

When Holley redesigned their model 4160 carb for the 5 litre Mustang, calling it the 4180, they moved the mixture screws from the float bowl down to the throttle body, and hid them behind steel plugs. These plugs can be removed with a chisel as on the Quadrajet, or a part of the body can be sawed away to allow their dislodgement.

In some types of emission carbs even with access gained to the mixture screws this may not mean that you will be able to adjust the idle mixture successfully. As illustrated, an idle passage restrictor may be built into the throttle body to limit fuel flow down to the mixture screw, so if you find that many turns of the mixture screw is having no effect, this could be blocking your progress. Remove the throttle body from the carburettor and if idle circuit restrictors are evident, drill them out.

Carburettors with metering rods; Carters, Quadrajets and Varajets, appear to give   105

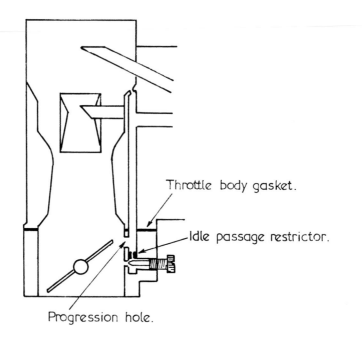

Throttle body gasket.

Idle passage restrictor.

Progression hole.

Some emissions carburettors limit idle fuel flow with a restrictor in the idle passage. If it is not possible to adjust the idle mixture successfully with the restrictor in place, it can be drilled out.

many tuners problems. Personally I like this type of carburettor for the road because it meters fuel more accurately over a broader range than the majority of carbs. Consequently it is good for economy and gives the engine a good crisp feel without bogs or hesitation; providing the adjustments are right. As discussed toward the beginning of the chapter, this type of carburettor has a combined main metering/power system, consisting of a main jet, a stepped or tapered metering rod and a power piston which is acted upon by a spring and manifold vacuum. When the engine is under a light load, vacuum in the manifold is relatively high, about 13–18in Hg. This vacuum draws the power piston down, resisting the upward force of the power spring. Thus the metering rod is shifted down in the main jet. With a thicker section of the rod within the jet, fuel flow is reduced. At increased engine load and wide throttle openings, manifold vacuum drops, allowing the power spring to push the power piston upward. In this position a thinner section of rod is within the main jet, allowing greater fuel flow.

Clearly the size of the main jet, the diameter of the various steps of the metering rod, and the strength of the power piston spring, all have an effect on fuel flow. However, it would appear that a number of tuners do not understand this fact because many think only of changing the main jet size, usually with unsatisfactory consequences. Obviously changing the main jet will increase or reduce fuel flow equally at all levels of engine load and speed. This probably is not what is required, particularly if idle and cruise vacuum is now lower than standard due to a cam change.

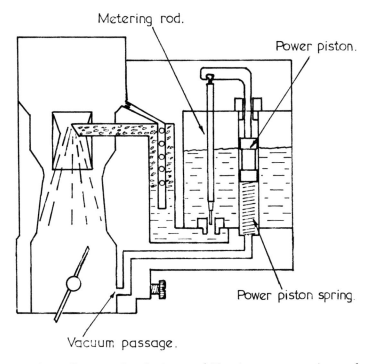

Metering rod.

Power piston.

Power piston spring.

Vacuum passage.

Carburettors such as Carters, Quadrajets and Varajets use metering rods which are raised or lowered in the main jet by manifold vacuum to control cruise and full power mixture requirements.

With less vacuum at all engine loads the metering rod will be further out of the main jet, increasing fuel flow. If we then increase the jet size the mixture will be too rich at a number of points. The engine may then bog or hesitate, and fuel consumption will most certainly increase.

I prefer to do this type of carburettor tuning on the dyno so that I can control the engine load and then check the mixture strength at various points. First off I like to get the power spring sorted. A soft spring delays the point at which enrichment commences to a lower vacuum level, and leans the mixture from that point right through the range. Conversely, a stiffer spring begins enrichment at higher vacuum and richens fuel flow right to the limit of the metering rod lift point. (Changing from a stock camshaft lowers manifold vacuum and will tend to cause the standard power spring to function as if it were stiffer.) After this, various metering rods are chosen to give the desired mixture strength at certain vacuum levels. For example, if we want to richen it up at 12in Hg vacuum, a rod a little smaller in diameter in the upper step would be chosen. If the mixture was weak under load, a rod with a smaller diameter lower section would be tested. Finally, if changing the power spring and the metering rods failed to give the required results, the main jet sizes would be fiddled, and the process repeated all over again.

Chapter 8

Fuel Injection

In a carburettor-type fuel system, the intake manifold design and carburettor size must strike a happy medium between low and high speed air flow requirements. At lower rpm air flow is very low, and in order to keep the fuel mixed with the air it is necessary to have small restrictive passages to keep the air velocity high. Conversely, when power is required, a large carburettor and larger intake passages are desirable. To accommodate these conflicting requirements a compromise must be reached which usually is optimum neither for high speed or low speed performance, but rather more suits highway cruising.

With electronic fuel injection (EFI), the elimination of the carburettor enables the induction system to be optimised more toward high speed air flow because the injector nozzles are spraying finely atomised fuel into the air stream, usually very close to the inlet valves. Hence the fuel stays in vapour as it enters the cylinders, even at low rpm when the air velocity is reduced. Because of this attribute the manifold runners can be quite long, to take advantage of pressure pulses generated by the opening and closing of the inlet valve, without fear of fuel dropping out of suspension and entering the cylinders as non-combustible raw or wet fuel. This pulse tuning of the manifold also aids performance, with the majority of manufacturers electing to use its benefits to pump up mid-range torque rather than all out power at high rpm.

I divide EFI systems into two basic camps; throttle body injection (TBI) and tuned port injection (TPI). Throttle body injection is the least desirable for a number of reasons. It is little better than a carburettor from the viewpoint of economy and frequently inferior to a carburettor as respects air flow ability. With the complications of electronics thrown in, it is not what is wanted for performance. In the TBI system a single injector, or at times two injectors, are located in the throttle body and spray atomised fuel into the air stream as air passes the throttle plate. To keep the fuel atomised, the intake manifold must be compromised with short, restrictive runners. Otherwise at lower rpm, or when the engine is cold, the fuel would drop out of suspension on the journey from the throttle body all the way to the cylinders.

metal strip warms up and bends, turning the slotted disc into a position where it closes off the port.

Fuel is supplied to the injectors by a roller-type high pressure electric fuel pump situated close to the fuel tank. In stock tune the pump delivers more fuel than the maximum requirement of the engine so that pressure in the fuel system is maintained under all engine load/rpm conditions. On leaving the pump the fuel passes into the first of two fuel dampers; the other one is located just prior to the injectors. The purpose of these dampers, as the name suggests, is to suppress fuel flow pulsations caused by the operation of the fuel pump and the injectors. Next, the fuel passes through a high flow fuel filter containing a paper element. The filter traps rubbish which may be present in the fuel, so avoiding blocked injectors. Note that to avoid high speed fuel starvation the filter must be replaced every 25,000 miles and be sure to fit it with the flow direction arrow pointing the correct way. After leaving the filter the fuel passes through the second fuel damper, and it then flows into the fuel rail and to the individual injector nozzles to be delivered, according to engine requirements, into each inlet tract as a fine mist.

To ensure precise flow through the injectors it is necessary to maintain a constant fuel pressure in the system, otherwise at higher pressures the injectors would flow more fuel than at lower pressures, even though the injector open period, the pulse width, remained the same. Hence a fuel pressure regulator is required. However, it must do more than just maintain the fuel pressure to, say, a constant 44 psi, otherwise there would still be flow differences caused by manifold vacuum variations. For example, at cruise the vacuum level in the inlet manifold may be around 15in of mercury (Hg), or stated another way, 7.4 psi below atmospheric pressure. Obviously in this situation, without compensation, the effective fuel pressure would increase from 44 psi to 51.4 psi (44 + 7.4) because the high manifold vacuum will actually draw fuel through the injectors during the open cycle. This would give rise to a rich mixture at a time when a lean mixture was required. On the other hand, at full throttle the manifold vacuum side will drop to zero, so the effective fuel pressure would remain at 44 psi. To overcome this undesirable situation of varying fuel pressures, a diaphragm operated pressure regulator is used which maintains fuel pressure at 44 psi above the depression in the inlet manifold. On one side the diaphragm senses fuel pressure, while the other side is connected to the inlet manifold to react to the prevailing vacuum level, or in the case of turbo engines to the boost level. A spring is fitted in the engine vacuum side of the regulator to establish a nominal pre-load of pressure, in this example 44 psi.

With the fuel pump flowing a constant supply of fuel to the system, a situation of too much fuel at the regulator develops. When pressure greater than 44 psi above the inlet vacuum builds up, the diaphragm moves, opening a valve which allows excess fuel through to flow back to the vehicle's fuel tank. Thus an accurately pressure-regulated supply of fuel is always available to the injectors to ensure precise metering. In practice, the regulator valve is always open to some extent, unless the fuel pump is too small or the filter is blocked or too small to supply the engine's fuel requirements. This gives a continuous flow of fuel through the system, ensuring that the fuel flowing to the injectors is cool and vapour free, which in turn improves metering accuracy. Plainly there are less energy producing molecules in 1cc of hot petrol than the same

113

volume of cold fuel. Some very sophisticated systems in fact have a fuel temperature sensor to achieve even finer accuracy.

The central brain of the fuel injection system is the electronic control unit (ECU), which is commonly referred to as the "black box". Its function is to receive information on the quantity of air drawn into the engine, the position of the throttle plate, air and coolant temperature, engine speed etc and then process this information and transmit an electric signal to the injectors, which determines when they switch on and for what duration. In many of today's cars, the ECU also processes information and transmits signals to the ignition system, the torque converter, the turbo wastegate and also some pollution devices. This information will be covered in following chapters; for the moment we want to concentrate on how it controls the fuel system.

Basically, the ECU is an information processor; that sounds less frightening than calling it a computer doesn't it? It usually functions on analog signals, but also processes some digital signals. Analog simply means an infinitely varying measurement between two points. For example, a gauge with a sweep hand such as a speedo or a tachometer gives an analog reading. To receive a signal, the ECU must first send out a constant voltage electric current to a sensor, usually of 5 volts. The sensor in turn is designed to increase or decrease electrical resistance in proportion to whatever it is measuring. Hence if the ECU sends out a constant 5 volt signal to the coolant temperature sensor which is calibrated to sense from 0°C to 80°C, and a 2.5 volt signal returns, it knows that the engine is still warming up as the coolant temperature is only 40°C. With this information it would continue to send a wide pulse to the injectors, to keep the mixture rich.

At the same time it may be receiving a digital signal, an on/off signal, from the throttle position switch, indicating that the throttle has been opened past a 40° open angle. This would indicate that the engine is under heavy load, accelerating or climbing a steep hill, and so the pulse width would be further increased to provide the needed fuel.

Just how the control unit figures out how much to increase or decrease the injector pulse width is beyond the scope of this book; however, a basic explanation is in order. During development of the engine on the dyno it is run under every possible combination of engine operating conditions to produce what is termed an engine fuel map. This process can take engineers up to 12 months, but at the end of these tests they know the engine's fuel requirements to meet performance, economy, driveability and emission requirements. From this store of data a computer programme is generated which implants in the ECU's memory just what time the injector pulse width should be for literally hundreds of engine operating conditions. For example, during the mapping tests it may have been found that at 5250rpm, with the engine at normal operating temperature, and a throttle open angle of 40°, the engine produced best power with an injector pulse width of 9.3 milliseconds. Along with anywhere from 300 to 800 other map reference points this information would be placed in memory. Later, when the engine was operating at 5250rpm with everything at normal temperature and a 40° throttle open angle, it would "look up" its information store and find what the pulse width should be for those criteria. It would then send a 9.3 millisecond pulse to the injectors in response to that input which it had received just a few milliseconds earlier.

Under normal conditions with mass air flow type systems the major portion of

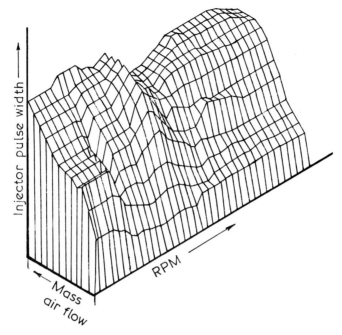

During engine development the ECU is programmed to provide precise fuel delivery for hundreds of engine operating conditions. This fuel map illustrates how the injector pulse width varies for changing engine rpm and mass air flow conditions.

The vane air flow meter is a relatively simple device which measures inlet air flow into the engine. The flow meter also contains the idle mixture screw. Turning the screw in reduces bypass air flow, causing the ECU to enrich the mixture.

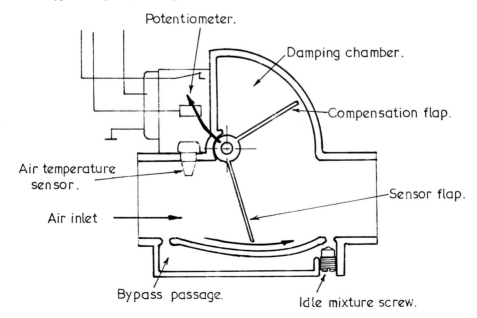

115

the control unit's input comes from the air flow sensor. There are a number of designs around, but they all measure the amount of air flowing into the engine.

The most common air flow meter, designed by Bosch a number of years ago, has been dubbed by Ford a vane air flow meter (VAF). As illustrated, this simple unit passes all of the air flowing into the engine through a passage with a spring-loaded door, or vane. As the air flows through the passage, it exerts a force on the flap, and depending on the air flow and the opposing force of the spring, it is held open to a certain angular position. Connected to the door pivot is a potentiometer, or variable resistor, which changes the control module's input voltage according to how wide the door has been blown open. An air temperature sensor is also located in the air flow meter, and from this signal, along with the air flow signal, the ECU can calculate mass air flow. Remember that air density changes with the ambient temperature, and other factors, so air flow input alone is not sufficient for accurate fuel metering. So that the flow sensor door is not disturbed by induction pulses, a compensation door is connected which works within a damping chamber. This type of air flow meter also houses an idle mixture adjusting screw and bypass passage. By varying the amount of air which is permitted to bypass the sensor flap the air flow meter signal can be changed to alter the air/fuel ratio at idle.

The other common Bosch air flow meter is a hot wire type, dubbed by General Motors a mass air flow sensor (MAF). Basically it is a tube, often with gratings to keep air flow laminar, through which flows the air entering the engine. Stretched across this tube is a very fine platinum wire which is heated by an electric current to maintain a constant temperature above ambient. A temperature sensor in the air flow meter signals the ambient temperature to the computer module so that it sends out the correct amount of power to keep the wire at the required temperature. However, air flowing into the engine flows over the wire and cools it in direct proportion to mass air flow. Consequently the ECU must increase power flow through the wire to keep the temperature constant, and then reads this signal as mass air flow. Other manufacturers use a similar air flow meter, but instead of a heated wire, they have chosen to use a heated nickel film.

A third type of air flow meter which is gaining popularity is the vortex flow sensor. This sensor uses an ultrasonic sender and receiver to measure the rate at which vortices pass through a control passage. The signal from the sensor is measured by the control unit, corrected for barometric pressure and inlet air temperature, and used to determine the injector pulse width.

The other very common type of fuel injection is called the speed density system. It does not have an air flow meter at all. Rather the ECU uses engine rpm and manifold vacuum as the central key to establishing the engine's fuel requirements. These systems are superior in that there is no air flow meter to restrict inlet flow, but they are extremely sensitive to any changes which allow the engine's breathing, it's volumetric efficiency (VE), to improve. This is bad news for tuners as most of what we do to an engine is intended to change the VE. Hence speed density systems do not allow for even a mild cam change. Most will cope with just a single improvement in other areas. Hence, a performance big bore CAT-back exhaust would be okay, but install headers and/or a high performance CAT and the system could go into convolutions unless the ECU is reprogrammed. Some tuners try to get over this by

upping the fuel pressure to increase engine richness under power (open loop) and then leaving it up to the O_2 sensor to get the mixture right at cruise (closed loop). If there is enough "latitude" programmed into the ECU this works well enough, but it is a less than ideal solution for best performance and economy.

Apart from engine rpm and manifold vacuum the other major sources for ECU input in speed density type injection are the barometric pressure sensor (BARO) and the air charge temperature sensor (ACT). The purpose of the BARO is to monitor changes in altitude. On top of a mountain, air density decreases and there is less oxygen available for combustion, consequently the ECU has to reduce the injector pulse width to keep the air/fuel ratio correct. Similarly with air charge temperature, cold air is denser so an increase in fuel delivery is required during winter and at night, but as the temperature rises the amount of fuel injected must be reduced.

Note that some manufacturers have done away with the BARO sensor and incorporated its function in with the manifold absolute pressure sensor (MAP). The MAP sensor monitors pressure (usually vacuum) in the inlet manifold. As the vacuum decreases when the throttle is cracked open to accelerate briskly or to climb a rise, the ECU assumes that the load on the engine is increasing, so it increases the injector pulse width to compensate. However, without a BARO sensor how does the computer know whether you are accelerating briskly at sea level or at 5,000ft on a mountain? The truth is that it doesn't. With this simplified (cheaper?) system, before the engine is started, but as the ignition key is turned past the ON position toward START, the ECU takes a reading from the MAP sensor. Remember, at this point the engine isn't turning over on the starter and hence the pressure in the manifold is just atmospheric pressure. The ECU stores this sample in memory and uses it as a base line or reference figure against which to compare all MAP sensor readings with the engine running. Only when the ignition is turned off is that memory sample erased.

This works fine for most people who use the car to do the shopping and get the children to school at the same altitude as their home. However, you can see the problem for the enthusiast who isn't going to switch the engine off until he has to refill the fuel tank 400 miles from home. After leaving home at say 5,000ft he may quickly descend to near sea level for say 300 miles. Clearly in open loop mode the mixture will be lean.

Speed density and mass air flow systems both use a throttle position sensor (TPS). Unlike with the Alpha-N system, which we will consider later, the ECU is not so much interested in the exact angle the throttle is open at, rather it wants to be informed when the throttle plate quickly moves from one position to another. Signals from the TPS in effect allow the ECU to pre-empt signals from the air flow sensor (for mass air flow systems) or the MAP sensor (for speed density systems). For example, when the throttle is rapidly opened from 10° open to full open the ECU immediately lengthens the injector pulse width to avoid a lean stumble in much the same manner as a carburettor accelerator pump. Then, when the MAF or MAP signal arrives the ECU sets about readjusting the injection time to sustain the engine at that power level. Mass air flow systems utilising a flap type air meter are quite slow to respond to rapid increases in air flow, as when the throttle is floored, but all systems experience some time lag which is compensated for by inputs from the TP sensor.

The third type of injection, the Alpha-N system, is reserved for competition type engines. The primary ECU inputs for this system come from the engine speed sensor and the throttle position sensor (TPS). Race engines have low and wildly fluctuating manifold vacuum and massive reversion pulses in the inlet tract caused by long duration cams. These difficulties send MAP sensors and air flow meters crazy, hence the reason for the existence of the Alpha-N system.

With this system, accurate throttle position input is important because the assumed air flow into the engine will be based on the exact throttle plate open angle and the engine rpm. The ECU isn't just interested in how quickly the throttle swings open to get the acceleration mixture taken care of, rather it must know the exact angle the throttle plate is turned to as this influences how much air is entering the cylinders. With the other two systems the TP sensor may be just a couple of sets of contacts or it may be a potentiometer. With the Alpha-N system the TP sensor is always a potentiometer which is connected to the throttle shaft and it changes the ECU input voltage according to the angle of the throttle plate.

This arrangement works well with race engines working over perhaps a 2500rpm power range, usually at half to wide open throttle and without significant concern for idle or cruise performance. However, over the first few degrees of throttle opening, which is where road cars spend most of their time, this system falls down. Just off the closed throttle position minute changes in throttle plate angle can result in huge changes in inlet air flow, which leads to resolution problems for the pot. If the pot was swinging through a radius of 300mm, a change of 15 minutes in throttle plate angle could be accurately measured and signalled to the ECU, but as the potentiometer radius is often closer to 20mm small changes in throttle position cannot be accurately sensed. Thus, when the ECU is computing injector open time based on faulty inputs, the air/fuel mixture will be incorrect. This won't stop the engine from running but it will take away the low speed and cruise smoothness and economy which we expect from fuel injection. Instead it will feel as if the engine is not up to temperature and has big carburettors supplying the fuel mixture.

Some Bosch mass air flow system TPSs contain just two sets of electric contacts. One set monitors when the throttle is closed and the other when the throttle plate is opened wider than 40°. Both sets of contacts are attached to the throttle body and are operated by the movement of the throttle shaft. Under most conditions both sets of points are open. The closed throttle points close when the throttle is closed; as when idling or decelerating. If the engine is idling and the control unit receives a signal from these points, the pulse width is changed to enrich the mixture. On the other hand if the speed sensor indicates that the engine is running at 3000rpm and the points are closed, the ECU concludes that the vehicle is coasting so it shuts off fuel to the injectors to reduce fuel consumption and lower emissions. If the engine speed continues to fall below 1800rpm the injectors are reactivated to stop the engine cutting out. Alternatively, if the throttle is opened to accelerate before the engine drops to 1800rpm, the closed throttle points would immediately open and the regular injector pulse resume. The high engine load points close when the throttle plate angle exceeds 40°. The electric signal received by the control unit causes it to send a wider pulse to the injectors which increases fuel flow by about 8%, to provide the fuel/air mix required for maximum power.

The other input signal received by the electronic control unit, and used to trim the injector pulse width which is common to all three systems, is the coolant temperature sensor (CTS). When the engine is cold, more fuel must be delivered to ensure smooth running and best engine performance. This need for additional fuel actually indicates that injectors do not in fact perfectly atomise petrol into combustible droplets; air speed and swirl and air temperature and also engine component temperature (inlet port, inlet and exhaust valve, combustion chamber, spark plug, cylinder wall and piston crown) also contribute to fuel atomisation. Thus, until the engine reaches operating temperature (usually about 70°C/158°F) additional fuel has to be injected because only a percentage will be in combustible droplet size and mixed in combustible proportions with the surrounding air at the time the spark plug fires. The remaining fuel in bigger droplets or poorly mixed will burn, but too slowly to contribute to power production.

Another type of sensor, technically known as the exhaust oxygen sensor or "Lambda Probe", but more usually called the O_2 sensor (O_2 or EGO), is common in injection systems for emissions applications. This sensor is fitted in the exhaust system, close to the engine. It is a metal-coated ceramic probe which works like a puny battery, producing about 100 millivolts when oxygen content in the exhaust is high, as when the mixture is lean. When the oxygen content falls, indicating a rich mixture, its voltage increases. If the O_2 sensor signals a rich mixture to the ECU, the pulse width is reduced under closed-loop cruise conditions.

In the closed-loop mode the ECU locks into a 14.7:1 air/fuel ratio programme because modern three-way catalytic converters increase hydrocarbon (HC) and carbon monoxide (CO) emissions if the mixture is any richer, and nitrogen oxides (NOx) go up if the mixture goes any leaner. The closed-loop mode operates when the vehicle is in a steady state cruise and the O_2 sensor has warmed up to 315°C. In this mode if the O_2 sensor reads that the mixture is either above or below the stoichiometric air/fuel mixture of 14.7:1, the control unit immediately reacts to correct the condition. In the open-loop mode the ECU ignores signals from the O_2 sensor and calculates fuel requirements according to the input from the other sensors. For example, if the throttle is floored, the control unit immediately goes open-loop to supply a richer than 14.7:1 mixture. During warm up or when decelerating, the ECU is also in the open-loop mode.

The majority of air flow measuring fuel injection systems are capable of handling the fuel and air required for about a 15% power increase without modification. Non-emissions systems may tolerate up to a 25% power rise. If you do not wish to become involved in modifying any part of the EFI system this must be kept in mind when you are planning your modifications. Stock fuel injection cannot handle big cams, so unless the manufacturer has fitted a fairly sporty cam, about what I would rate a Phase II grind, you are going to be limited to about a Phase III profile. Engines which come from the factory with a Phase II cam may be able to go a step further than I have suggested, but all air flow sensors have difficulty handling inlet tract reversion pulses, so may send the wrong signal to the ECU, thus upsetting fuelling.

There can be a number of reasons for the fuel injection system not being able to cope with our modifications. Some systems are fuel limiting, meaning that some or a number of components in the fuel supply system are not capable of flowing the required amount of fuel at the correct pressure to enable more hp to be produced. The fuel pump or injectors could be at their flow limit, or perhaps the fuel filter or fuel lines are too restrictive. With any of these problems the engine will run fine, except at peak rpm under load. At that time the engine may just feel dead, or if there is serious starvation there will be misfiring and surging.

To check if in fact it is a fuel problem, and to isolate what part of the system is deficient, a series of tests are required, preferably on a chassis dyno. First, test exhaust gas carbon monoxide (CO) level at full throttle at various engine speeds. The CO should preferably read around 5%, while anything less than 3% is too lean. When the CO is reading lean, replace the fuel filter and repeat the test. If it is still lean check how the engine responds to increased fuel pressure. This is simply a matter of disconnecting the manifold vacuum hose from the fuel pressure regulator, and then fitting a length of hose with a "T" piece. To one side of the "T" connect a pressure gauge, and to the other side connect a pump. (A 25cc medical syringe makes an inexpensive pump for low pressure tests.) Using the pump to pressurise the regulator, first test at 5 psi, and then repeat at higher pressures if necessary. If the system normally has a fuel pressure of 44 psi, adding 5 psi to the vacuum side of the regulator raises the fuel pressure at the injectors to 49 psi, which will increase fuel flow at all points by around 5%. Note that for the first test with turbo engines the regulator must be pressurised by normal turbo boost pressure, plus 5 psi. Hence, if maximum boost is 12 psi, then put 17 psi into the regulator.

If increasing the fuel pressure brings the CO back to acceptable levels it could mean that the injectors are too small, but it may also indicate the ECU is not giving the injectors sufficient pulse width. However, before you jump to either conclusion it is wise to go through the following checks to ensure that the actual fuel pressure and fuel flow volume at the injectors is within specification. Connect a vacuum gauge to the inlet manifold and a fuel pressure gauge to the fuel rail. At zero vacuum the fuel pressure should be that specified by the manufacturer. Note that if the vacuum gauge

A blocked petrol filter can cost horsepower or even a blown engine by reducing fuel pressure and flow volume at the injectors. When hidden out of sight perhaps under the vehicle, regular filter replacement is frequently overlooked.

is reading above zero this figure divided by 2, when added to the fuel pressure reading, must equal the pressure specified for zero vacuum. For example, with a Bosch system designed to work at 44 psi above manifold pressure, if the vacuum gauge reads 4in of Hg the fuel pressure should at the same time be 42 psi (44 – 4/2 = 42). Conversely, if the engine is turbocharged the fuel pressure reading minus the manifold boost pressure gauge reading must equal 44 psi. For example, if the boost gauge reads 7 psi the fuel gauge should read 51 psi (44 + 7 = 51).

If the pressure isn't up to specification there must be a flow restriction or an internal pressure leak. To check for an internal leak let the engine idle and note the pressure reading. In a Bosch system if the idle vacuum is 16in of Hg then the fuel pressure should be 36 psi (44 – 16/2 = 36). Switch off the engine and note the gauge. If the fuel pressure falls, you have an internal leak. Leaks in fuel lines or at connections should be obvious, so we start by testing the fuel pump. Start the engine to bring the system up to pressure, switch off and clamp the pump outlet hose. If the pressure ceases falling the pump is the problem, and should be replaced. However, if the pressure continues to drop the leak must be elsewhere, so loosen the pump outlet clamp and start the engine. Switch off and quickly apply a clamp to the pressure regulator to fuel tank return line and retension the pump outlet clamp. If the pressure stops falling, the regulator must be leaking, but if the pressure continues to drop some of the injectors must be leaking, so remove the fuel rail and injectors and repeat the previous test, observing which injectors are at fault. Permissible leakage is one drop per minute.

Check for flow restrictions by connecting a hose into the fuel system at the fuel rail, and have it flow into a container. Then compare the flow attained with what is specified in your workshop manual. For example, some Bosch pumps are rated at 130 litres per hour, so in 1 minute of pumping the container should collect a minimum of 2 litres of fuel. If it is less than this there is a blockage in the system. To determine if the filter is the problem, next connect the drain hose and container on the pump outlet. If the flow rate is unchanged, disconnect the pump inlet hose and connect a length of hose which is immersed in a container with at least 3 litres of fuel. Activate the pump for 1 minute and measure how much petrol it discharges. If it is less than specified, the pump requires replacement; however, if the flow rate is correct, the fuel tank pick-up is either blocked or damaged.

Even when the system flows the quantity of fuel specified by the manufacturer this may not be sufficient to meet the needs of a modified engine. To determine the approximate amount of fuel flow needed I use the following formula:

Fuel flow (cc of petrol per minute) = HP x K
where HP = maximum horsepower
K = 5.6 for turbo/supercharged engines
4.6 for naturally aspirated engines

Thus a 140hp non-turbo engine requires about 644cc, 0.65 litre, of petrol per minute to produce that 140hp. If the pump, filter and fuel lines flow less than this the engine is going to experience fuel starvation at high loads and peak hp rpm. Particularly with turbo motors this problem surfaces because the high fuel pressure which the regulator imposes on the system at high boost levels can actually cause diminishing fuel flow as the fuel pump attempts to force more fuel into a system which is already at say 65 psi. As the pressure increases then pump flow rates decrease.

If the fuel system is capable of flowing fuel at the required rate then investigate the potential flow rate of the injectors using the formula:

Total injector flow (cc per minute) = SF x N x M

where SF = injector static flow (cc of flow per minute when open continuously)

N = total number of injectors

M = injector duty cycle

Static flow data for the standard injectors can be found in the vehicle workshop manual. However, the duty cycle requires some explanation.

The injector duty cycle, or the time which it is open per minute should not exceed 80%. If the injector is open continuously, 100%, then it will overheat and either fail to accurately respond to signals from the ECU or else burn out. Some tuners reason that road cars seldom see wide open throttle and maximum rpm for more than 20–30 seconds so it does not hurt for the injectors to go to 100% in short bursts. There may be some merit in this argument but I will not run injectors past 85% in road cars which never see weekend competition. If the car does get competition use I keep below 80% duty cycle.

Let us assume now that this 140hp non-turbo motor is not used in weekend sport and that it has 4 injectors each with a static flow of 167cc/min at 2.5 bar. Working on the basis of an 85% duty cycle, total fuel flow will be 568cc per minute, which is well short of our anticipated 644cc per minute required to make 140hp. In this example it is obvious that if during the rolling road dyno test the CO reading was extremely lean, then these small 167cc/min injectors are probably the source of the problem.

To get sufficient fuel into the engine, either larger fuel injectors will have to be fitted or it may be feasible, and certainly less expensive, to increase the fuel pressure, thus increasing flow through the standard injectors. On this car the standard fuel system operates at 36 psi (2.5 bar) so it would be quite easy to get good flow gains with increased fuel pressure. However, the fuel pressure must never exceed 5 bar (72.5 psi) otherwise injector control will be lost. At any rate I have found that only a few very high capacity injectors as fitted to race engines actually show any flow increase once 65 psi fuel pressure is exceeded. This is something to watch with turbo engines as a 44 psi system pressure combined with turbo boost of say 16 psi puts the injectors close to their flow limit. Extra fuel pressure or extra boost will not see injector flow increase more than 2–3%, if at all, when the fuel pressure goes from 60 psi to 70 psi.

At lower pressures (i.e. below 60 psi) we can calculate the injector static flow with raised fuel pressure using the formula:

$$\text{Revised static flow} = \sqrt{\frac{RP}{OP}} \text{ x SF}$$

where SF = injector static flow at standard system pressure

RP = revised fuel system pressure

OP = standard fuel system pressure

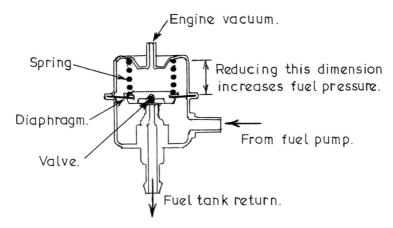

Injector flow capacity goes up with an increase in fuel pressure. The stock fuel pressure regulator can be modified to raise fuel pressure by carefully squeezing it up in a vice.

In this example, raising the fuel pressure from 36 psi to 44 psi will increase static flow of 167cc/min injectors to 185cc/min. Working on an 85% duty cycle this would be sufficient fuel for approximately 137hp which is close to what we anticipate (140hp). To raise the fuel pressure the pressure regulator will have to be replaced or modified. For this car it would be easy to obtain a 44 psi regulator off a wrecked vehicle very cheaply, or a new item could be purchased. Alternatively, the standard regulator can be modified to bring the pressure up to 44 psi or higher by sqeezing it in a vice. It sounds crude but it works. Place the regulator between two sockets (so as to protect the fuel and vacuum connections) then squeeze it up a little between the jaws of a vice. Don't squash the regulator, the idea is to compress the spring inside the regulator by reducing the length of the case. If you don't get the pressure up enough from the first try, then squeeze it up some more.

The alternative to raising the fuel pressure is to fit larger injectors. When new injectors are fitted, this becomes very expensive. A cheap alternative is to spend some time searching out injector flow data in workshop manuals for cars commonly found in breakers' yards around your area. Don't just look at fuel flow but also consider the fuel pressure of the prospective donor vehicle. Many perfectly good injectors are rotting in breakers' yards because tuners do not do their homework, and conversely many useless injectors are purchased for the same reason. For example, you might overlook 214cc/min injectors as being way too large, but if they achieve that flow rating at 44 psi they could be right on the money, flowing 195cc/min at 36 psi (using the above formula). Note that fuel pressure should not be reduced below 2 bar (29 psi) as fuel atomisation suffers.

If it is a turbo engine and the injectors are undersize I prefer to fit an additional injector, a "fifth injector", up close to the throttle body. Usually a solid aluminium block will have to be machined to mount the injector on the manifold plenum. The size of the fifth injector is easily calculated by subtracting the combined flow rate of the standard injectors from the anticipated flow required.

Whenever the fuel pressure is increased or larger injectors are fitted to get the fuelling right for maximum hp, the ECU will probably have to be reprogrammed, 123 otherwise the idle and cruise fuel requirements will be wrong.

Earlier it was stated that a high speed/high load lean condition may not be the result of small injectors or restricted fuel flow but was possibly because of insufficient injector pulse width. This function is controlled by a program within the ECU or by a program within a PROM chip which plugs into the ECU. For example, this time assume our engine which we hope will deliver 140hp started out from the factory with injectors which each flow 195cc/min. However, at 6600rpm where the standard engine produced maximum power it only required 530cc of petrol/min (132cc per injector) therefore the ECU was programmed to give the injectors a pulse width, or open period, of just 5.42 milliseconds. With the engine now modified to produce 140hp its fuel requirement rises to 644cc/min (161cc per injector). This need can be accommodated by reprogramming the ECU to send out a signal which keeps the injectors open and flowing petrol for 6.61 milliseconds. Note that with this engine producing maximum power at 7000rpm the injector pulse width must not extend beyond 6.8 milliseconds otherwise the 85% duty cycle period could be exceeded at the 7500rpm redline. The maximum permissible pulse width can be calculated using this formula:

$$\text{Maximum pulse width (milliseconds)} = \frac{60,000}{(\text{rpm} + 500)} \text{ x M}$$

$$\text{where M} = \text{injector duty cycle}$$
$$\text{rpm} = \text{maximum hp rpm* for batch fire injection}$$
$$\text{or maximum hp rpm* divided by 2 for}$$
$$\text{sequential injection.}$$
$$\text{*Use maximum engine rpm for turbo}$$
$$\text{engines.}$$

Naturally, when an engine is modified the factory ECU program will possibly be incorrect through the entire range, not just at peak hp revs. Hence the injector pulse width and the ignition timing will have to be "trimmed" at regular intervals right through the engine's operational rev range at full throttle. This process will then be repeated at half throttle, quarter throttle and cruise to obtain best performance and minimal fuel consumption.

For many popular vehicles the aftermarket can supply performance chips (or an exchange ECU with a modified program for ECU's which do not have a plug-in chip). However, this tuning route is fraught with problems. Just as it is impossible when a conventional carburettor and ignition distributor is used for some "expert" to post you exactly the correct size carb jets and exactly the right distributor advance springs from your description of engine modifications which you have given over the telephone, so likewise with performance chips. The chip (or change-over ECU) is often a "fits all sizes" type proposition – it fits all, but is tailored to no specific engine. The chip programmer often borrows a guinea pig car, let's say a Nissan Sunny from a friend/neighbour/relative for a couple of days. He phones the Hyper cam company and fits their most popular road cam. Likewise when he phones Mega exhausts and the same again with the cylinder head from Turbo heads. The computer whiz (remember many know little about engines; they are computer people, seldom are they experienced engine tuners) then sets about programming a chip to suit this modification combo just described. After he gets the car driveable he may give it a run on a wheel dyno. When he is satisfied that a reasonable level of performance has been obtained the information on the chip will be recorded, as he hopes to later transfer this to hundreds of other chips which he will market throughout the land as the "Blooper fast road chip for Nissan Sunnys". Too bad that your Sunny doesn't sport the same fast road mods as his. He is also not going to tell you that your £250 chip cost him 50 cents in Singapore.

Sometimes chips are sold as part of a head, cam and exhaust package. These generally work reasonably well but are often overpriced and you are locked into a particular level of performance. What if you have previously paid out for a decent exhaust, or what if you want a milder cam but a big valve head? If they offer to supply a different cam, beware; it probably means their chip is another "fits all sizes" variety.

Reputable chip people will only retail a performance chip as part of a dyno tuning session. They fit a chip with a baseline program and, while running the car on a rolling road, they tailor the chip, trimming the program, to make your engine work at its best. Again, beware of those who fit the chip, run the car on the dyno and say "it doesn't need any changes, that's the best power output we have seen from an engine like yours," and send you off £250 poorer. It is most unlikely that the programme is exactly right the first time, and how do they know that it's not possible to tailor in even more power or better economy?

Table 8.1 shows just how much power and economy the owner of a 3.8 Buick was missing out on because the dyno operator, who was franchised by a reputable chip supplier as an authorised agent, was slack. Apparently the agent did some adjustments

To be of any real value, a performance chip must be programmed to suit your engine. Hence, when a plug-in chip or exchange ECU is fitted, it should be "dialed in" with your car running on the dyno.

Table 8.1   Buick 3.8 chip tuning comparison

		Test 1			Test 2	
rpm	hp	Torque	BSFC	hp	Torque	BSFC
2000	82	216	.371	83	218	.380
2500	107	224	.374	106	223	.382
3000	140	245	.422	140	245	.380
3500	158	235	.503	161	242	.430
4000	180	237	.490	189	249	.420
4500	206	241	.500	216	252	.426
5000	224	235	.620	235	247	.450
5500	227	217	.850	243	232	.513
6000				241	211	.559

Test 1 – standard engine with modified cam, head, exhaust and ECU package as delivered by authorised agent

Test 2 – as above with ECU carefully tuned for best power and economy

while running on the rolling road, but just look at the results when the tuning was done properly. Incidentally, the owner wasn't too concerned that the engine seemed sluggish above 5000rpm; in fact he felt the performance was quite good, but he was most unhappy with the increased fuel consumption. This was why he went searching for answers when the chip agent assured him all was well – "You can't expect more power without increasing the fuel consumption." Prior to adjusting the fuel curve the engine was consuming 193lb of petrol per hour to produce only 227hp. After sorting the fuelling out, this decreased to 124.6lb/hr, which still isn't brilliant, and power increased by 16hp to 243hp.

Another method of getting a modified pulse signal to the injectors is to fit an auxiliary ECU which "adjusts" the pulse signal from the stock ECU. The auxiliary ECU then sends out a signal to the injectors which either increases or decreases the injector open period. These systems are usually fairly basic in that if the auxiliary computer is adjusted to give a 5% longer pulse width to correct a lean condition at 5500rpm, then the same 5% increase will be added at other points in the fuel map. This can give rise to overfueling at some locations in much the same way as an increase in fuel pressure, consequently I like to keep right away from auxiliary ECU's. The only exception is when a "fifth" injector has been added; then I like to see an auxiliary ECU installed to properly control fuel flow from this injector.

For the most part, if we haven't gone too wild with our engine tuning, the stock injection system, if it is of the air flow measuring type, will have enough built-in latitude to supply the additional fuel required. With emissions engines, most problems are directly related to cam changes. With increased valve overlap it is possible for mixture draw-through to be experienced at some point in the rev range. This fuel may then be ignited in the hot exhaust causing the O_2 probe to send a false signal to the ECU. For example, if this afterburn in the exhaust has consumed much of the oxygen, the probe will sense it as resulting from a rich mixture. The ECU then responds by reducing the injector pulse width, perhaps causing excessive leanness. As a result, at cruise speed the engine may feel unresponsive and go through a period of mild surging. To avoid this, stick to the cam designs which I have suggested.

Rather than being fuel limiting, some fuel injection systems are air flow limiting. This usually isn't a problem in performance/economy tune, but it is good to be aware of the kind of things which may be holding your engine back from making the sort of power which you desire.

The vane air flow meter causes a fair amount of restriction. Bosch rate the air flow of their air flow meters in cubic metres per hour (m^3/hr) which does not mean much to most people as they are more used to seeing cubic feet per minute air flow rates (cfm). To convert m^3/hr to cfm multiply by 0.6. Thus a 380m^3/hr item will flow 228cfm according to the way Bosch measure the air flow. In the real world this size air flow meter is suitable up to about 130–135hp, but after that it is holding the engine back from its full potential.

Actually a most important consideration with vane air flow meters is to ensure that the moving flap only swings wide open when air flow into the engine is at its peak (i.e. at maximum hp). Some tuners see this moving flap as a restriction to air flow (which it is) so they reduce the spring tension to allow the flap to easily swing wide open. This is completely wrong, in fact as the air flow potential of the modified engine is much higher than the standard item it is frequently necessary to increase spring tension on the flap so that it is wide open only when engine air flow is at its maximum. Remember that in mass air flow systems the major source of input for the ECU is the air flow meter. If the air flow flap goes wide open at less than actual peak flow into the engine, then how is the ECU going to be able to get the fuelling right? The answer is that it will not, the engine will be lean.

What if our engine has a 380m^3/hr vane air flow meter and we want 160hp? There are four choices: either we put up with the air flow restriction caused by the small meter with its tension spring wound right up to go wide open only at peak air flow; we could go to say a 500m^3/hr meter which is suitable up to about 180hp and wind the spring tension off so that it goes wide open at peak air flow; we could fit a hot wire air flow meter and reprogramme the ECU; or we could toss out the air flow meter and the ECU and fit a potentiometer to the throttle plate and a new programmable ECU which doesn't rely on air flow sensing.

The next potential point of flow restriction is the throttle plate/s. On a 4-cylinder engine a 56mm throttle plate will flow enough air to make 140hp. A 60mm butterfly (or a combination 35mm and 49mm plate) will be sufficient for 160hp. A 65mm plate will be suitable for 190hp. On a 6-cylinder engine this latter throttle plate would be allowing the engine to flow okay up around 240hp, while on a V8 the same plate would be suitable to close on 300hp. On a V8 a 75mm throttle body would be good for over 400hp.

If the standard throttle body is indeed restricting air flow then a larger body may be obtained or, if there is sufficient wall thickness in the standard body, it could be machined to a larger bore. Most will bore at least 2mm, but some will allow up to 7mm. Try to go to a size which will allow you to cannibalise a throttle plate off another throttle body. This saves time and money as it is quite time consuming and expensive getting a larger throttle plate machined with the correct angles around the edge of the plate.

Remember when you opt for a larger throttle plate that the car will not be so easy to drive around town. With a smaller throttle body, just cracking the throttle open may

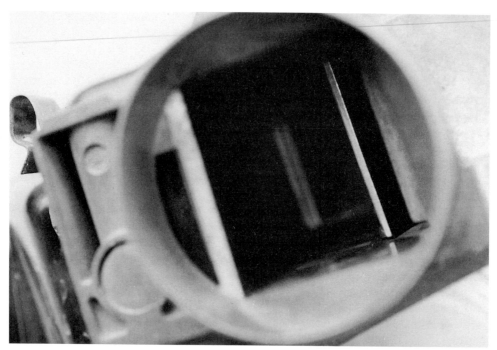

The flap in vane air flow meters do cause inlet flow restriction, but spring tension must not be reduced to allow the flap to swing open more easily. The flap must only go wide open when air flow into the engine is at its peak, i.e. at maximum hp.

have given a steady, if a little bit jerky, increase in power, but with a big throttle plate a whole lot more air rushes into the engine with just small movements of the accelerator pedal. This may make the car quite jerky and unpleasant around town and wheelspin on wet roads can also be a problem. For this reason some manufacturers have a throttle body with two throttle plates opening progressively. The small plate opens usually to about 40° before the larger butterfly begins to open.

The next part of the system (which may be cast as just one part or be several parts bolted together) is usually simply called the inlet manifold. In reality there are two distinctive parts: the manifold runners which are really an extension of the inlet port and, second, there is the plenum – an air chamber from which the individual cylinders draw air. The plenum volume is typically about 80% of the engine size in road vehicles, thus a 2 litre engine will be drawing from a plenum with a volume of about 1.6 litres.

Most fuel injected engines have quite long manifold runners to boost mid-range torque. However, long runners which are too small in diameter may restrict power at high rpm.

For example, the early TPI 305 Camaro and 350 Corvette were both tuned in the factory to work best between 2000 and 4000rpm, but by 4500rpm these engines were crying out for more air. The 350, for instance, is air flow limited to about 285–290hp. Fabricating different runners allows the engine to make another 15–25hp, with the correct cam. After that, the stock air flow sensor strangles the engine.

When we say some component is strangling the engine, don't get the idea that the engine just stops dead. What it means is that the engine is not being allowed to work to its full potential at higher speeds. Thus, in one class of racing, 5.7 litre V8 engines are required to use a Holley 2300 two barrel carb. This limits the engine to about 360hp at 5000rpm and they will still make 340hp at 6250rpm. Sticking a four barrel carb on the same engine lets more air in, allowing the engine to make 420hp at 5000rpm and up around 510hp at 6500–7000rpm, tapering off to 490hp at 7500rpm. Because such a big cam is required the engine only wants to work over a 2000rpm range with the small carb, but with the 4-barrel allowing a lot more air in the engine not only makes 40% more power but the power band improves to a 3000rpm range.

The same sort of principle applies, if in a less dramatic fashion, with road engines. Get the breathing right and you can use a lot less cam to raise bottom end and mid-range performance. On the other hand, get the breathing wrong and you can really muck up the bottom end, with only small gains at the top end. Looking at Table 8.2 you can see what occurred during testing of a 350 Chev. This engine was a bit hotter than what might be termed a performance/economy unit, but I feel this test well illustrates the point which I have just made. The cam was what I would classify as a Phase V grind, being a hydraulic roller with 112° centres, 226° inlet duration, 222° exhaust duration and 0.510in lift. The Brodix aluminium heads were midly ported and were fitted with 2.02in inlet and 1.6in exhaust valves. The compression ratio was 9.8:1 which required the use of 95 RON unleaded. With the standard Chevy manifold base and runners, which have an internal diameter of 37.5mm the engine ran very well and part throttle performance was excellent. However, note how the power shot up when bigger runners were fitted. These were the same length as standard but the port dia was increased to 42mm and the manifold base was ported out to match. Finally, an Accel Super-Ram was fitted. This features a large plenum and short large dia "D" shape runners, 10in long and equivalent to about 49mm in diameter. Note how the bottom end falls right away and it is only from 5000rpm up that this combination is working better than the longer modest bore runners. I suspect this manifold is better suited to a big 400cu in plus Chev.

Table 8.2   Chev 350 inlet runner comparison

	Test 1		Test 2		Test 3	
rpm	hp	Torque	hp	Torque	hp	Torque
2500	158	332	161	338	151	317
3000	224	393	228	400	208	365
3500	273	410	296	444	266	400
4000	303	398	351	461	321	421
4500	308	359	360	420	360	419
5000	294	309	356	374	390	410
5500	292	279	372	355	406	388
6000	270	236	376	329	389	341
6500			328	265	356	288

Test 1 – standard Chev 350 TP1 manifold base and runners

Test 2 – ported manifold base and runner bore increased 4.5mm

Test 3 – Accel Super-Ram manifold base and runners

If the standard manifold has runners which are too long and/or too small in the port diameter you may be able to purchase performance replacements for a few very popular engines. However, in general you will have to build a new manifold or modify the standard item as it is not possible to port out these manifolds using conventional grinding tips. Some companies can pump an abrasive mixture through the ports to increase the internal runner size but this is limited by the thickness of the cast walls; go too far and the manifold will fall to pieces from engine vibrations.

A better proposition is to chop up a stock manifold and fit bigger bore runners the same length as standard. Before cutting up the manifold, talk to someone well-versed in welding aluminium as this will have some bearing on where you should cut. I prefer to make just three cuts; the first just back from the injector mounting bosses, the second just off from the plenum, and the third through the plenum itself.

The first and second cuts allow a major portion of the runners to be tossed. These pieces are replaced by 3mm wall aluminium tube which is mandrel bent to the correct shape. Before welding these new runners into place, grind out the ports on the part of the manifold which bolts to the cylinder head. After welding the runners look down the manifold from the cylinder head face and, using a round hand file, clear any "dingle berries" which you can reach. The third cut is optional and is a waste of time if the runners enter the plenum very close together. However, if there is enough space the plenum can be cut through and small "trumpets" fitted to each runner to improve flow. If there is very little space, at least the runner entry can be ground out and the equivalent of a rolled entry can be added to the mouth of each runner

There are only two manual adjustments on electronic injection systems; for idle speed and idle mixture. The idle speed screw allows a variance in the amount of air flowing in the passage bypassing the throttle plate. Turning the screw out increases air flow, upping idle speed. If the bypass passage is too small to give the desired idle speed, drill a 2mm hole in the throttle plate, and increase the hole size in 0.25mm increments to get the idle rpm required. Before drilling the throttle plate check that the

The adjustment screw on the throttle body sets the engine idle speed. Turning the screw out allows more air flow into the engine which increases the idle rpm.

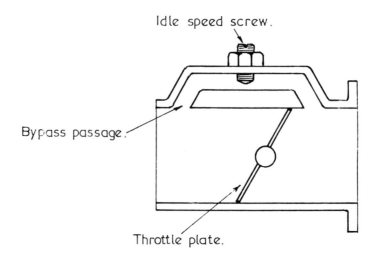

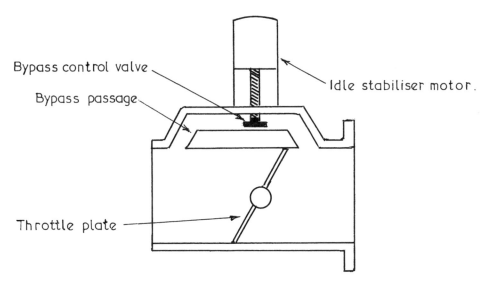

Bypass control valve

Bypass passage

Idle stabiliser motor.

Throttle plate

The idle stabliser motor regulates engine idle speed by controlling the amount of air admitted through the throttle bypass passage.

throttle body bypass passage is not partially blocked by carbon, as this will restrict the amount of idle adjustment available.

The idle mixture screw, located on the air flow meter, also varies the amount of air flow in its bypass passage. Turning the screw out increases flow in this passage and reduces air flow past the air flow door. As the computer now receives a signal that a reduced mass of air is flowing past the flap, it decreases the pulse width. However, as the actual amount of air flowing into the engine hasn't altered, the throttle body bypass controls this, the fuel/air mixture is made leaner. Alternatively, turning the mixture screw in reduces bypass flow and increases air flow past the flow meter door. The ECU senses this as increased air flow and sends a longer pulse to the injectors to enrich the mixture. Note that to discourage tampering, the mixture screw is usually out of sight, covered by a plastic cap.

Many of the most recent systems do not have any provision to adjust either the idle speed or the idle mixture, both functions being fully controlled by the computer. If the manufacturer has set the idle speed at 850rpm the ECU will try to keep the idle at that speed ±50rpm. As shown in the diagram a motor is fitted where you would normally expect to find an idle speed screw. When the computer senses the idle speed is falling, as when the air conditioning cuts in or when load on the alternator increases because of the engine cooling fan switching on, for example, then it sends a signal to this motor to back off the air passage plunger, allowing more air to bypass the throttle plate and increase the idle speed back up to 850rpm. Conversely, when the idle speed increases above 850rpm the ECU signals and the motor restricts bypass air flow to bring engine speed down to the manufacturer's set figure.

Chapter 9

The Ignition System

The ignition system has the complex duty of producing high voltage surges of up to 40,000 volts to fire the spark plugs, initiating combustion of the fuel/air charge which has been inducted into the cylinders. It must do this in the correct firing order, and at the instant necessary to properly ignite the compressed mixture. Additionally, in modern engines the spark must be of sufficient intensity and of sufficient duration to completely fire very lean, and hence less combustible mixtures, to lower emissions and improve fuel efficiency.

Few modern engines use a points-type distributor to time and distribute the spark. However, we will first consider the operation of this type of ignition system as this will enhance our understanding of the workings of the various electronic and computer-controlled systems.

The points-type system relies on a 12 volt battery to supply the initial electrical energy, a set of points to time the spark, and a coil to intensify the voltage of the electrical energy supplied by the battery so that it is capable of jumping the spark plug gap and igniting the fuel mixture.

As illustrated, the switching of the primary, or low voltage circuit, is accomplished by the contact breaker points which are opened and closed by the distributor cam. When the points are closed, electric current flows through the coil's low voltage primary winding, and then through the points to earth. This current flow through the low tension winding produces a magnetic field which surrounds the coil's secondary or high voltage winding. When movement of the distributor cam causes the points to open, the primary circuit is broken. Current flow through the coil primary winding stops, and the magnetic field collapses, causing a high voltage electric current to be inducted in the secondary winding. The high voltage current then flows from the coil to the centre of the distributor cap, and through the carbon brush to the rotor button. The turning rotor in turn directs the current back to the distributor cap and out to the individual spark plugs where it jumps the gap to start off the combustion process.

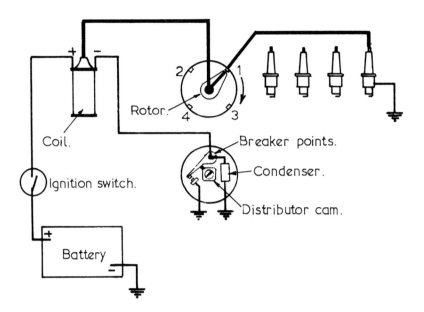

The points-type ignition system relies on a set of points to make and break the low voltage electrical circuit to produce a high voltage ignition spark at each spark plug.

Today's engines do not have ignition points to produce and time the ignition spark. The most basic modern engine distributor uses a toothed pulse generator rotor and electronic circuitry to control current flow through a high energy ignition coil.

There are two basic problems with the conventional points-type distributor which has led to the almost universal adoption of electronic ignition. In time the points wear and pit, which changes the ignition timing, upsetting performance and emissions. Pitting reduces the conductivity of the points, lessening current flow in the coil primary winding. This in turn leads to a feeble secondary voltage which may be too weak to fire the plugs. Again performance and emissions suffer.

The other problem arises at higher engine speeds. With an increase in engine speed the time that the points are closed between each opening period is decreased. This means the coil has less time to build up a full magnetic field between firings, reducing the voltage available to fire the plugs. Today's engines, with lean mixtures and wide plug gaps, require a higher voltage to get combustion started than engines in the past, so a conventional points ignition may cause misfiring at higher engine rpm.

To overcome these deficiencies the more common electronic ignition systems use magnetic pulses and electronic circuitry to open and close the low voltage circuit, rather than mechanical contact points. A number of different designs are in use, but the basic mode of operation is similar. The distributor shaft turns a pulse generator rotor inside a stationary permanent magnet. Functioning like a mini alternator this induces a signal in the pick-up coil located within the distributor. This electric signal causes the electronic circuit to switch "on" and "off". When the circuit is switched on, current flows through the primary windings of the ignition coil, and when it is then switched off, the magnetic field collapses, inducing a high voltage in the coil secondary winding. As in the points-type system the high voltage current then flows to the centre of the distributor cap, through the carbon brush and rotor button out to the individual spark plugs. Because the system does not contain tungsten contact points which pit and burn, a substantially higher primary circuit current can be utilised to ensure that the coil is fully saturated, even in the short time available at higher rpm. Thus a high intensity spark is provided at all engine speeds likely to be encountered in road use. This had led to some manufacturers calling this system high energy ignition (HEI).

Fully computerised ignition, called by some manufacturers electronic spark timing (EST), functions in a similar way to the HEI system in that it provides a high intensity spark at higher rpm. However, the major difference with this type of ignition system is that the ignition advance is adjusted electronically by the ECU for various engine speeds and engine load conditions. The ECU receives signals from a variety of sensors and then according to its programmed memory selects the appropriate ignition advance angle to meet performance and emission requirements. The distributor may include the pulse generator to send the firing reference signal to the ECU, but at times the distributor will contain only a rotor button to direct the high voltage secondary current to the spark plugs. When this is the case, the pulse trigger may be located at the rear of the engine with "firing" pins embedded in the circumference of the flywheel. As each pin passes by the magnetic pick-up a pulse is relayed to the electronic control unit (ECU) which calculates the appropriate advance angle and then switches the ignition coil primary circuit on and off. With this latter system moving the distributor body will not alter the initial ignition timing. This is determined by the location of the magnetic pick-up and the position of the firing pins.

With any type of road ignition system some arrangement is employed to alter the ignition timing to suit various engine operating conditions. For example, at idle the ignition

The majority of modern engines employ computerised spark advance. This electronic spark timing (EST) unit from a carburettored engine enhances performance by electronically adjusting the ignition firing angle in a non-linear fashion to suit various engine rpm and engine load conditions.

may be timed to fire the plugs at anything from 5° to 18° before the piston reaches top dead centre (TDC) on the compression stroke. However, at high rpm and wide open throttle the advance required for best performance may be around 25° to 35° BTDC while at cruise an additional 10° to 15° advance will be necessary to give best economy.

This extra advance is required to allow the fuel mixture the correct amount of time to burn properly. Clearly at 3000rpm the combustion flame has to have progressed the same amount as it would have at 700rpm, so that maximum energy is available to force the piston down as it passes TDC. The only way that this time deficit can be made up is to start the combustion flame burning earlier by firing the spark plugs several degrees advanced on the firing angle at idle.

Apart from this time factor there are a number of other reasons why the ignition firing angle must be varied for different engine operating modes, and why the advance angle changes from one engine to another. The fuel/air ratio influences the flame speed. Very lean and rich mixtures both burn slowly and require more spark advance. A mixture close to full power lean burns the fastest and requires less advance. At cruise, for example, the mixture is usually adjusted to be a touch lean in the interests of economy, hence more advance is needed. However, there is another reason why the spark lead must be increased in this operating mode; that is mixture density. With the throttle just cracked open the cylinders do not become crammed full of air and fuel, so even when compressed the oxygen and fuel molecules are slightly separated, which in turn slows the speed of flame travel through the combustion chamber. From this you will understand an increase in the compression ratio has the reverse effect, that of increasing mixture density, thus necessitating less advance. A cam change also influences mixture density. If the lobe duration is made longer, mixture density will be reduced at lower engine speeds, while in the mid-range and at maximum rpm it will be greater. To accommodate this circumstance more advance will be needed at lower rpm and reduced advance will be called for higher in the rev range. Changes to the exhaust system or in the exhaust gas recirculation (EGR) valve operation affect mixture density in yet another way. By lessening the amount of exhaust gas left unscavenged in the cylinder and by stopping EGR operation there is more room to pack fuel mixture into, hence mixture density increases. Additionally, because there are fewer inert exhaust gas molecules to separate oxygen and fuel molecules, flame travel through the combustion space is faster.

Engine design also figures in the amount of ignition advance needed for efficient combustion. The size of the combustion space and the position of the spark plug obviously affects the degree of advance wanted. The further the flame has to travel, as in a large combustion chamber, the longer it will take to burn the mixture completely. Conversely, the closer the spark plug to the centre of the chamber, as in a 4 valve pent-roof chamber, the quicker the combustion time. Some cylinder heads have been created with inlet ports and combustion chambers which induce a high degree of swirl to the inlet charge. This homogenises the mixture more thoroughly and speeds up flame propagation. Increasing the amount of squish has a similar effect. The stroke of the crankshaft, and the ratio of the connecting rod length to the length of the stroke, influence the degree of advance needed because these two factors affect the time it takes the piston to move to, and just past, TDC.

Obviously in a modified engine a number of the above factors will have been changed from what they were in the standard engine. Hence the amount of advance needed under various engine operating conditions could now be different to achieve

In a pent-roof 4 valve combustion chamber the spark plug is located in the centre of the combustion space so less spark advance is required.

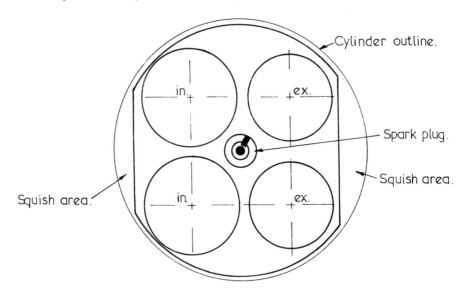

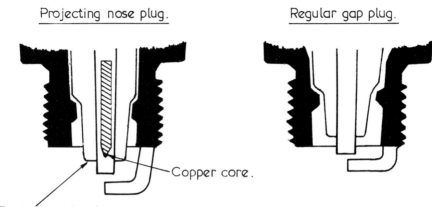

Projecting nose plug.   Regular gap plug.

Copper core.

Projecting insulator nose.

Copper-cored projecting nose plugs are preferred for non-turbo performance/economy engines. For turbo applications a regular gap plug with a copper-cored centre electrode is more resistant to plug tip burning and detonation.

electrode. The shorter nose is necessary to avoid high speed insulator glazing and electrode melt-down. Unfortunately this type of plug does not offer the low speed fouling resistance of the projecting nose design. There are a number of solutions to this problem; the first is to put up with a misfire when accelerating on fouled plugs, which I feel is less than satisfactory. Secondly, you can risk using projecting nose plugs but initially, until you accurately assess them, limit full throttle bursts to less than 60 seconds. Thirdly, you can use projecting nose plugs in the city and swap to regular short-nosed plugs for highway running.

The width of the spark plug gap for best performance depends primarily on the compression pressure of the fuel/air charge, the engine rpm and the high speed electrical intensity of the coil. Obviously increasing the first two factors without an increase in the latter calls for a decrease in the gap width. Therefore, it is fairly safe to say that many modified performance/economy engines will require a gap narrower than that recommended by the manufacturer.

Manufacturers generally stipulate a relatively wide gap of 0.040in to 0.060in as this improves performance at lower rpm and reduces the risk of the gap being bridged by whiskers of carbon, or beads of lead or petrol. As there is much less turbulence in the combustion chamber at low engine speeds, it is very easy for a blob of carbon or fuel to settle between the electrodes, shorting the plug out. With a wider gap the odds are better because the speck of carbon or fuel may not be large enough to bridge the gap. Later, when the engine is given a few more revs, the increased turbulence will blow the electrodes clean. Also, because the spark generated in a wide gap is larger than in a narrow gap, an important consideration in lean burn emissions engines which have the inlet charge diluted by exhaust gas recirculation, a more sizeable initial flame is produced. This improves flame propagation through the fuel mixture and allows for a more complete burn.

As the engine speed and compression pressures increase, the coil is not able to supply electrical energy of sufficient voltage or duration to jump a wide spark gap and keep the air between the electrodes ionised for a period long enough to initiate   153 combustion. What happens is that the coil has enough energy reserve to electrically bridge the spark plug electrodes but, before the spark generated can get a combustion flame started, turbulence within the combustion chamber will actually blow out the spark. This was a big problem with early electronic and particularly capacitor discharge ignitions, as the spark was produced for only a short duration. When a narrow gap is used, the magnetic field within the gap is much more intense, as it is confined to a much smaller space. Hence the spark holds together for long enough to effect ignition, in spite of receiving severe buffeting from the turbulent gases within the combustion chamber.

From experience, I would recommend that any modified engine using a conventional points-type ignition should not use a plug gap exceeding 0.028in. If it has breakerless high energy ignition, the gap can be as wide as 0.040in. A gap wider than this just encourages high speed misfire and crossfire particularly in V8 engines, and in many engines there are problems with high voltage flashover within the distributor cap or leakage through the rotor button to the distributor shaft. In some engines with high energy ignitions this later problem can actually wreck the advance mechanism.

In addition to using narrower plug gaps there are a number of other steps which should be taken to ensure an intense spark of long duration, even at high rpm and high cylinder pressures. The life of a spark plug is up to 20,000 miles, but it should be filed, regapped and tested every 6,000 miles. Filing the electrodes lowers the voltage required to fire the plug, firstly because electricity prefers to jump across sharp edges, and secondly because the electrical conductivity of the electrodes is improved. Combustion heat and pressure tend to break up and oxidise the electrode firing surfaces, increasing the electrical resistance. Filing removes this "dead" material and exposes new, highly-conductive metal. To avoid damaging the plugs, bend the earth electrode back just far enough to permit filing of the firing surfaces. As shown, a points file should be used to file a flat surface with sharp edges on both the centre and side electrode.

Spark plugs should never be cleaned with a wire brush, as metallic deposits will impregnate the insulator nose and short out the plug. I also do not recommend cleaning in an abrasive blast plug cleaner as some abrasive material always seems to become wedged between the insulator and plug shell. If this cannot be probed out with

Filing the side and centre electrode square to expose new metal and produce sharp corners reduces the voltage required to fire the plug.

File end of earth electrode.

File centre electrode flat.

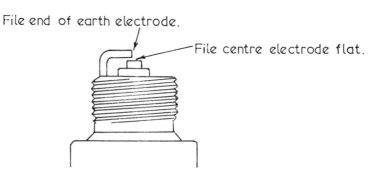

a scriber, it will later drop into the cylinder and possibly cause damage. However, if you choose to have your plugs abrasive blasted, be sure to remove all abrasive grit inside the plug nose and around the threads and gasket.

Because of their design, electronic ignition systems require some extra attention to ensure good service and high spark output. To avoid overloading any of the electronic components the engine must never be cranked over if any of the spark plug leads or the coil lead is disconnected. For example, when carrying out a compression check, the low voltage positive (+) ignition wire at the coil should be disconnected.

As with any ignition system the coil polarity must be correct for good firing performance. A coil with reversed polarity loses the equivalent of 40% energy because when connected in this manner the spark has to jump from what would normally be the earth electrode to the centre electrode. The side electrode is many hundred degrees cooler than the centre electrode, hence there is much more restrained electron activity on the metal surface. This considerably increases the voltage required to cause the electrons to leave one electrode and jump to the other, thus ionising the gap and creating a spark. Cold engines are more difficult to get started for this very reason. The plug electrodes are cold therefore a very high voltage is necessary to tear the electrons from one surface and have them jump the gap to the other electrode. As illustrated, a dished spark plug earth electrode indicates reversed polarity. The dish is caused by metal leaving the electrode each time a spark jumps across to the centre electrode.

The polarity is correct when the wire from the coil to the distributor is connected to the coil terminal with the same polarity as the earth terminal of the battery. Therefore, if the negative (−) battery terminal is earthed, the wire running between the coil and distributor should be connected to the negative coil terminal. To avoid incorrect electrical connections it is wise always to tag wires before they are disconnected. A diagram is also an aid in ensuring that all wires are reconnected to the correct terminals.

Reversed polarity increases the voltage requirement necessary to fire the plug and initiate combustion. A dished side electrode indicates reversed polarity.

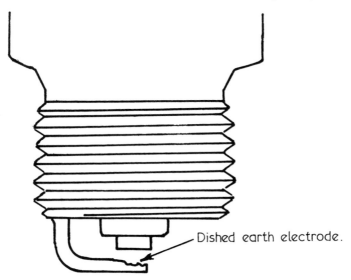

Dished earth electrode.

Most stock electronic ignition system coils work well in road engines, even at high rpm, providing the spark plug gap is not too wide. There are exceptions, however, where the standard ignition coil just isn't up to the task. For example, the ignition output of the General Motors Delco HEI system weakens at about 5000rpm in V8 engines; with the same ignition 6 cylinder engines run fine with 0.040in plug gaps to nearly 7000rpm because fewer sparks per minute are required. Hence if your GM V8 is required to make good power at engine speeds higher than 5000rpm, an ignition booster kit will be required, or alternatively the plug gaps should be reduced to 0.032in. Whenever it is necessary to uprate an electronic ignition it is necessary to use components, preferably in a kit, which have been tailored to work with the standard system. If the incorrect type of coil is fitted it could damage the electronic devices, and the replacement coil's output will probably be inferior to the stock coil anyway. Never swap coils which appear similar unless they have the same part number. It is not unusual for coils from the same manufacturer to appear similar, but to be quite different internally. Some electronic systems, while basically alike through a whole family of engines, may use coils that look to be identical; however, the internal windings and the core could be different for 4, 6 and 8 cylinder engines.

The high tension leads provide the electrical connection between the coil and distributor cap and the spark plugs. Usually in road cars radio suppression cables, with a powdered carbon impregnated rayon cord to conduct the high voltage current, are fitted. With age the electrical resistance of this type of "wire" increases, which reduces spark intensity and increases the probability of misfire under load or at higher rpm. To avoid this problem only the best quality silicone-jacketed leads should be used, and replaced every three years. Also, when removing the leads from the plugs or from the distributor cap do not jerk them off as this also can reduce their conductivity. Firmly

The ignition module (igniter) and coil are a matched set. Fitting an uprated coil with the stock igniter will probably cause the igniter to overheat and burn out.

grip the rubber boot, give it a half turn, and then while holding the boot and metal connector remove the cable. An alternative to carbon core leads is leads with a metal core. These leads have a very long life if the insulation is not damaged. Use induction-type suppression leads with an induction spiral within the lead to effectively suppress electrical "noise" which could affect inputs to the ECU or ignition module (igniter).

The ignition cables must have good boots, without any cracks or holes, fitted at each end to prevent high voltage trackover or arcing. Many misfires under load can be attributed to the spark jumping from an exposed spark plug top to a nearby earth, or from the coil tower to one of the low voltage terminals on the coil.

Apart from the plug leads, the distributor cap and rotor button and the coil tower can also be high voltage leakage areas. Obviously these parts must be free of dust, moisture, cracks and carbon tracks if a good strong ignition surge is to reach the plugs. Periodically check to ensure that none of these conditions exist. In particular, when high voltage HEI type systems are in use, attention must be paid to keeping all the insulating mediums clean, otherwise the system will actually be performing more poorly than a conventional type ignition because of electrical flashover or leakage. With these systems only the best quality distributor caps and rotors made of alkyd material should be fitted.

Unwittingly, some enthusiasts bring ignition troubles upon themselves when removing build-up on the distributor cap terminals and the rotor button contact. Quite often the knife or screwdriver being used to remove the unwanted material slips and scratches the glaze inside the cap. This drastically reduces the dielectric strength and can lead to a carbon track developing during wet conditions. Similarly, when a piece of abrasive paper is used to polish the rotor button contact, the insulating glaze is cut, allowing electrical leakage to earth through the distributor shaft. Carbon on the rotor button contact does no harm, so just wipe off the powdery stuff and leave the rest there.

In high compression V8 engines cross fire can occur whenever high voltage ignition leads are grouped closely together, or allowed to run in parallel for any distance. Cross fire causes the engine to run roughly, and in high load or high rpm situations may give rise to serious pre-ignition or detonation. The problem is not due to poor insulation, but rather is a product of magnetic induction. A magnetic field surrounds any high tension conductor, and the lead which is carrying high voltage at any instance induces voltage into an adjacent plug lead. A cross fire that will give trouble is most likely to occur between consecutive firing cylinders when these are located alongside each other in the engine. Hence if the engine has the common V8 firing order of 1–8–4–3–6–5–7–2, cylinders 5 and 7 are most likely to give trouble. With the Ford firing order of 1–5–4–2–6–3–7–8, cylinders 7 and 8 are most likely to experience cross fire problems. The easiest way around the difficulty is to route the leads in such a manner so that the offending leads cross over once. Hence with the first firing order, leads 5 and 7 would be crossed to invert the magnetic field and effectively cut out any induction. Note that one lead must pass over the other lead just once; never tape any leads together or run them through steel clips or other metal fittings.

Chapter 10

Turbocharging and Intercooling

The first wave of engines given the "hot-up" treatment by tuners simply bolting on a turbocharger were a real disappointment. When the throttle was pressed down at speeds below 3000 to 4000rpm nothing happened: it seemed as if the engine was running with all of the plugs fouled. Then, after gaining some boost, the vehicle would rocket off with an incredible surge of power which was most disconcerting and intimidating. Controlling a turbo car on a twisting slippery road was a nightmare. That was 30 years ago when turbocharging first became fashionable on race cars. Tuners didn't know much about this new technology and tried to apply what little knowledge had been gained on the race circuit to the road. It didn't work. At about the same time a number of car makers were involved in their own development projects which eventually led to the design of smaller, lighter turbos and compatible engine management systems that have virtually eliminated the dreaded "turbo lag". The majority of new generation turbo cars are pleasant to drive, but with a few ill-conceived modifications they can be quickly transformed into the volatile beasts of former times. Therefore before undertaking any modifications on a factory turbo car a thorough knowledge of the subject is an asset if driveability problems are to be avoided.

There is nothing magical or hard to comprehend about why a turbo greatly increases the potency of an internal combustion engine. Basically, the power an engine produces is a product of the amount of fuel/air mixture it is able to breathe in and then burn. A turbocharger is a type of supercharger or compressor that forcibly crams into the cylinders far more mixture than the engine could draw in in naturally-aspirated form. At 100% volumetric efficiency and a manifold vacuum level of zero, a 500cc cylinder will be filled with 500cc of fuel mixture due to the effect of normal air pressure, 14.7 psi at sea level. Theoretically, if the inlet boost is 7.4 psi above atmospheric the cylinder will fill with about 750cc of mixture, so the engine will perform as if it were 50% larger. Hence at cruise a lightweight 2 litre engine will perform with a fuel efficiency just a little less than that of an ordinary 2 litre engine, mainly due to the reduced compression ratio, but at full boost of, say, 7.4 psi, it will perform as a super-lightweight 3 litre unit.

The turbo is made up of a centrifugal compressor, which is part of the induction system, connected by a common shaft to a turbine which is joined to the exhaust system. The engine's exhaust gases thus drive the turbine, utilising energy that would otherwise go to waste. The turbine in turn spins the impeller to force fuel/air mixture into the engine. Certainly the concept is very simple, but things become a lot more complex when translated into the real world. Firstly, the turbocharger itself is an expensive, highly-engineered, precision item. On the exhaust side it has to be able to withstand enormous stresses due to operating temperatures which may exceed 1000°C, while at the same time the turbine is spinning at 100,000rpm and more. Additionally, the precise shape and dimensions of the turbine and impeller, and their separate housings, need carefully to be tailored to give the required throttle response, driveability and power.

Aside from this there are the problems arising out of a fundamental characteristic

The turbocharger turbine wheel is driven by the engine's exhaust gases. Being connected to a common shaft, the compressor impeller forces the air charge into the cylinders under pressure. When full boost is reached, the wastegate opens, bypassing some of the exhaust gas away from the turbine. Note that the turbine illustrated is a split pulse type with divided exhaust inlets, used to improve low speed boost.

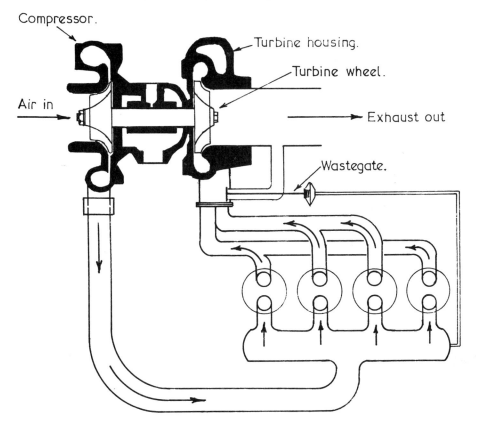

This tiny turbocharger adds about 30% to the engine's power output. The centrifugal compressor, on the right, pressurises the induction system. The turbine side of the turbo is hidden away under a heat shield. Lubricating oil is fed to the turbo bearings through the oil feed pipe visible in the centre of the turbo.

of a centrifugal type compressor; namely that flow through it rises in proportion to the square of its rotational speed. Hence at lower engine rpm there is little or no boost, and at higher rpm and full throttle, boost is excessive. It is in the resolving of this dilemma of how to get low speed performance up without unduly restricting high rpm power, and perhaps causing excessive high speed fuel consumption, in which the real science of turbocharging lies.

Looking firstly at the low speed component of this problem it should be obvious that modifications which reduce the low rpm performance of a naturally-aspirated engine will have a like effect on a turbo engine. In fact the decline in performance and economy will be greater in the turbo engine due to the compression ratio being 1 to 1.5 points lower. Therefore big ports and cams are definitely not for road turbo cars. If the engine is 2.3 litres or larger and the car isn't too heavy, a Phase III cam is about as wild as you would want to go. Personally, in engines of this size I prefer a Phase II grind if the car sees a lot of running on the highway, and a Phase I grind if the majority of driving is done in the city. For engines smaller than 2 litres a Phase I cam is a good compromise for highway/city use, but if most running is done in the city you will probably be happiest with the standard factory cam or the standard factory cam out of a non-turbo model.

The other factor in low speed performance is the actual boost of the turbo at lower rpm. Here the size of the exhaust turbine and the dimensions of its housing play a major role. Naturally a large diameter turbine, which will flow a lot of exhaust gas without causing much restriction at high rpm, is very heavy so it will need a large exhaust flow to get it spinning up to speed to create boost. Because the exhaust flow is low at lower rpm with the throttle closed, the turbine will be rotating slowly. Opening the throttle increases flow but it takes time to accelerate the heavy turbine up to speed to produce boost. It is this time lag between opening the throttle and actually getting response which is called "turbo lag". A small turbine, on the other hand, has less inertia so it spools up to speed to produce boost more quickly. However, if it is too small it plugs up the exhaust at higher rpm, and by restricting exhaust flow reduces power and increases fuel consumption. Clearly a compromise must be struck, with the majority of manufacturers choosing comparatively small turbines to enhance performance, particularly from 1800 to 4000rpm.

When it comes to the exhaust turbine housing the critical dimension is what is called the A/R ratio. As illustrated, this refers to the ratio between the area of the turbine nozzle A, and the radius from the centre of the turbine axle to the centroid of the housing throat R. The smaller the A/R, the smaller the passage and the faster the turbo spins for a given exhaust flow. This is good for low speed boost but a housing which is too small causes excessive back pressure and heat. A large turbine housing A/R flows the exhaust gas without causing so much restriction at higher rpm; however, due to the turbine speed being reduced at lower revs, low speed boost may be poor. Again a compromise is necessary, with car manufacturers generally opting to get either low speed or mid-range boost up at the expense of maximum power and economy.

The turbine housing A/R ratio is determined by dividing the area of the turbine nozzle A by the radius R from the centre of the turbine axle to the centroid of the housing throat.

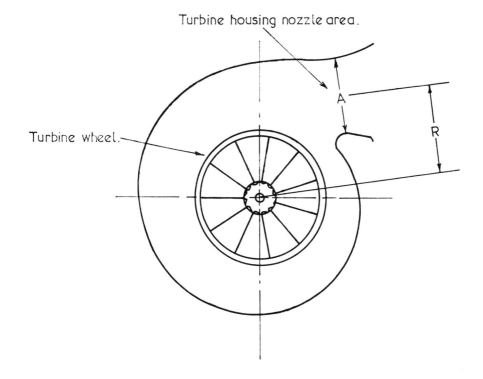

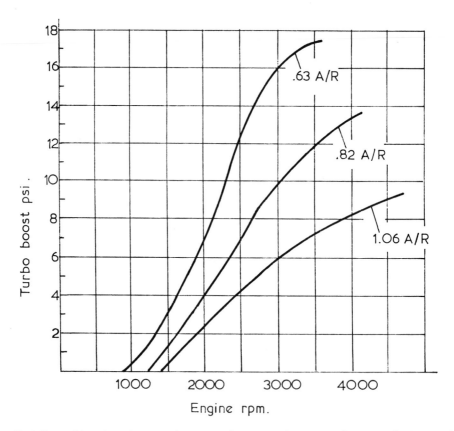

Small A/R turbine housings make more boost at lower engine speeds but reduce maximum power and economy because of exhaust flow restriction.

On the inlet or compressor side of the turbo unit selecting the correct impeller and housing is considerably easier. Manufacturers match the compressor to a given engine by calculating the anticipated inlet air flow and then plotting the flow against the pressure ratio on a series of compressor performance maps. A compressor is chosen which gives the required flow and pressure in a good efficiency zone, without running into surge.

Many enthusiasts think of improving the performance of their turbo car simply in terms of increasing the boost pressure. This should not be a primary consideration for a number of reasons. For example, if the mufflers are restrictive and the exhaust pipe is too small, bumping the boost from say 6 psi to 9 psi will not give the 15 to 20% power increase that many would expect, simply because the engine cannot breathe. Additionally, the extra boost will add heat to the inlet change temperature which by itself will reduce power as well as bringing the engine closer to detonation. In total, the power increase will be no better than about 10%.

Consider the engines used in CART races in the USA of which the Indianapolis 500 is the most famous. The purpose-built race engines are restricted to a capacity of 2.6 litres and a turbo boost of 9 psi, and yet they produce around 800hp. Why? Not because of massive boost pressures, but because the inlet and exhaust systems and cylinder heads flow efficiently thus encouraging good flow in and out of the cylinders. Therefore the very first modifications should be directed toward improving the breathing of the engine. Get the exhaust size right and the system completely free of leaks. The original Ford Pinto 2.3 turbo, for example, required nearly 10 psi exhaust pressure to make just over 5 psi boost with the standard exhaust. By re-routing the crossover pipe from the exhaust manifold to the turbo, and fitting a 2¹/₂in system down-stream of the turbo, the engine made full boost earlier and with only 6 psi exhaust back pressure. With reduced back pressure the cylinders were better scavenged of hot exhaust gases, which lowers the risk of detonation and improves fuel economy by several percent. When exhaust gases are left unscavenged, they add a considerable amount of heat to the inlet charge, raising the charge temperature and increasing the danger of detonation. Apart from causing sluggish performance, exhaust leaks are to be avoided because of their danger to personal health. I've seen minor exhaust leaks which were almost undetectable cost up to 2 psi in lost boost.

Next, clean up the cylinder head by unshrouding the valves and reprofiling their underhead shape, and rework the port bowl area on both the inlet and exhaust side. If you plan on fitting a modified cam that too should be carried out before altering the boost. After that, tune the injection and ignition systems as outlined in previous chapters. Pay a lot of attention to getting the ignition right. Turbo engines which are a bit sluggish at lower speeds can be transformed by a little more low rpm ignition advance. However, be careful to take advance off the top end otherwise piston damage is likely. Next, give consideration to lowering the gearing by changing the rear axle ratio. With lower gearing the vehicle will be much more spirited in traffic and when cruising on the highway. As discussed in a later chapter, with the proper gearing the vehicle's performance can be transformed. In particular, all 4 cylinder cars, and cars with 6 cylinder engines smaller than about 2.5 litres, require relatively low gearing.

Finally compare the boost pressure, using an accurate gauge, with what is stated in the specifications. If it is lower than specified this could be due to the modified cam or perhaps the wastegate is opening prematurely; at this point I assume that exhaust leaks ahead of the turbo have been rectified. To test the wastegate disconnect the hoses leading to it and run the engine at full load, being careful not to let the turbo overboost. If the boost comes up to specification, the wastegate should be adjusted to open at the factory boost level. On the other hand if the boost level doesn't rise, the wastegate must be leaking or jammed partly open. Note in a very few cases lack of boost could be due to an over-small turbine or small A/R housing.

If after making the above modifications you desire still more boost, some steps must be taken before changing the wastegate opening pressure. This action is not as straightforward as many enthusiasts and some tuners believe, as an increase in boost may cause the turbo to overspeed or send the compressor into surge conditions. To ascertain the probability of either situation arising we have to go through a series of calculations and plot the results on the turbo manufacturer's compressor map. This may appear to be a lot of bother, but because car makers are tending to use smaller turbos there is some risk of turbo reliability-related problems at high rpm and/or above sea level operation.

The first calculation is to determine the compressor pressure ratio, using the formula:

$$Pr = \frac{Bp + Ap}{Ap}$$

where Bp = boost pressure ps

Ap = air pressure psi (14.7 psi at sea level;
subtract 0.5 psi for each
1000ft above sea level)

For example we may want to increase the boost pressure to 11.5 psi and operate at 5000ft altitude.

$$Bp = 11.5 \text{ psi}$$

$$Ap = 14.7 - 2.5 \text{ psi}$$

$$\text{Therefore } Pr = \frac{11.5 + 12.2}{12.2}$$

$$= 1.94$$

The next step is to find the density ratio and this involves a number of calculations due to the fact that the inlet air is heated as it is compressed; the less efficient the compressor the more heat that is passed to the inlet air.

First calculate the compressor outlet air temperature rise assuming a perfect compressor using the formula:

$$It = F \times (At + 460)$$

where It = ideal temperature rise °F

At = ambient temperature °F

F = factor from Table 10.1.

Hence if the air temperature outside the car is 80°F then:

$$It = 0.208 \times (80 + 460)$$

$$= 0.208 \times 540$$

$$= 112.3°F.$$

However, because the compressor doesn't have a 100% adiabatic efficiency we then have to calculate the actual air temperature rise with the formula:

$$Rt = \frac{It \times 100}{E}$$

where Rt = real compressor temperature rise °F

E = compressor efficiency (assume 60% efficiency)

$$\text{Therefore } Rt = \frac{112.3 \times 100}{60}$$

$$= 187.2°F$$

The compressor discharge air temperature will be the outside air temperature, 80°F, plus the real compressor temperature rise:

$$Dt = At + Rt$$

$$= 80 + 187.2$$

$$= 267.2°F.$$

Having found the compressor air discharge temperature and with the pressure ratio previously calculated, the compressor density ratio can then be figured out using the formula:

$$DR = \frac{(At + 460) \times Pr}{(Dt + 460)}$$

where DR = compressor density ratio

At = ambient temperature °F

Dt = compressor discharge temperature °F

Pr = compressor pressure ratio

$$\text{Therefore } DR = \frac{(80 + 460) \times 1.94}{267.2 + 460}$$

$$= \frac{540 \times 1.94}{727.2}$$

$$= 1.44$$

The final calculation is to determine the compressor inlet flow so that this figure can be plotted on the map to find if the compressor will overspeed or surge at our desired boost of 11.5 psi and an altitude of 5000ft. The formula is:

$$CF = \frac{L \times RPM \times VE \times DR}{56.6}$$

where CF = compressor inlet flow cubic feet per minute

L = engine capacity in litres

RPM = maximum engine speed

VE = engine volumetric efficiency (usually about 0.9 for an engine with a mild cam)

DR = compressor density ratio

Assuming that the engine capacity is 2 litres and the maximum rpm is 6200, then the compressor inlet air flow will be:

$$CF = \frac{2 \times 6200 \times 0.9 \times 1.44}{56.6}$$

$$= 284 \text{ cubic feet per minute (CFM)}$$

When the compressor map is scaled in lbs/min air flow rather than CFM it is necessary to multiply the above flow figure by 0.07. Hence in this example the flow is 19.9 lbs/min.

Plotting this on the compressor map opposite the 1.94 pressure ratio we find that the compressor will be operating well away from the surge line at maximum engine rpm and the turbo speed for this type of turbo is within reliable limits at about 114,000rpm. However, to be certain that the compressor will not run into surge at other engine speeds and boost levels the above calculations would have to be repeated. For example, if this engine made full boost of 11.5 psi at 5000ft altitude and at an engine speed of 3000rpm, the compressor would be just into the surge range.

To increase the boost pressure the wastegate will require adjustment or modification. The integral wastegate on turbochargers like the AiResearch T-03 is easily adjusted as the actuator is usually connected to the wastegate via a threaded rod. Simply altering the length of the actuator rod will change the boost pressure at which the wastegate opens to bypass some exhaust flow away from the turbo. If the actuator rod isn't threaded it is a simple matter to unbolt the actuator, saw the rod in half and thread it with a suitable thread such as 1/4in NC. Using an internally threaded coupling sleeve and a jam nut the actuator then can be adjusted. When sawing and threading the actuator rod care must be taken to hold the rod securely to avoid damaging the actuator diaphragm.

Table 10.1   Factors for calculating inlet air temperature

Pr	F	Pr	F	Pr	F	Pr	F
1.35	0.089	1.8	0.181	2.25	0.258	2.7	0.325
1.4	0.100	1.85	0.192	2.3	0.266	2.75	0.331
1.45	0.110	1.9	0.199	2.35	0.274	2.8	0.338
1.50	0.120	1.95	0.208	2.4	0.281	2.85	0.345
1.55	0.130	2.0	0.217	2.45	0.289	2.9	0.352
1.6	0.142	2.05	0.225	2.5	0.296	2.95	0.358
1.65	0.152	2.1	0.234	2.55	0.303	3.0	0.365
1.7	0.162	2.15	0.242	2.6	0.311	3.1	0.377
1.75	0.172	2.2	0.250	2.65	0.318	3.2	0.390

Since this type of actuator is controlled by inlet boost pressure, an alternative method of adjusting the boost pressure is to fit a hard plastic tube in the pressure line which runs from the compressor to the wastegate and perforate it with a number of bleed holes. By bleeding off some boost pressure signal the actuator is tricked into allowing boost pressure to rise above the pre-set factory level before opening the wastegate. Since only tiny holes are needed it is best to perforate the tube using a 0.040in needle which has been heated so as to melt a hole in the plastic. Commence

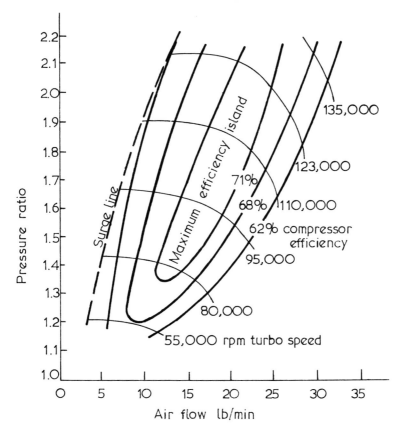

Compressor maps are used for determining compressor suitability for specific engine specifications and operating criteria.

with just one hole and add additional holes, as needed, to raise the boost level. Note that this method of boost control must not be used on engines which add fuel into the air stream ahead of the turbocharger.

When a poppet valve wastegate is utilised, the perforated tube trick can also be used, although there are a number of alternatives. Simply placing a spacer under the diaphragm pre-load spring will raise the boost pressure at which the diaphragm rises to bypass exhaust get away from the turbine. Replacing the spring with a stiffer item has the same effect. A more sophisticated control is to fit a spring pre-load seat that is attached to a threaded rod which passes through to the outside of the actuator chamber to provide pre-load adjustment. Screwing the rod down increases spring pre-load, thus raising the boost level.

Just how much power increase can be realised honestly with increased boost can be easily figured reasonably accurately using the formula:

$$PG\% = (DR - 1) \times 100$$

where PG% = percentage power gain

DR = compressor density ratio

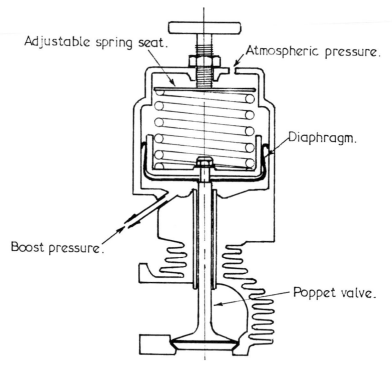

Adjustable spring seat.

Atmospheric pressure.

Diaphragm.

Boost pressure.

Poppet valve.

When a poppet valve type wastegate is used, the boost pressure can be easily changed by installing an adjustable pre-load spring seat.

I won't go through the calculations. If you refer back a few pages you will see how we arrive at the density ratio. For example, an engine operating at sea level, with 80°F ambient temperature and 7 psi boost, will have a DR of 1.23, assuming 60% compressor efficiency. Therefore its power gain over a naturally aspirated engine will be about 23%. Now if that same engine has the boost raised to 11 psi, the DR becomes 1.36; a 36% power gain over a naturally-aspirated engine but only a 13% gain over an engine boosted to 7 psi, and that is assuming the engine would handle the extra boost without running into detonation. Why so small a gain you ask? The answer is quite simple – heat. At 7 psi boost the inlet air temperature (Dt) will be 188°F and at 11 psi this rises to 235°F. Obviously anything that can be done to get rid of heat out of the inlet charge will result in significant power gains.

This is exactly what intercooling aims to achieve. As illustrated, an air-to-air intercooler is really just like a cooling system radiator through which flows the inlet charge after it leaves the turbo. It is called an air-to-air intercooler because the charge air which is within the "radiator" gives off its heat to the outside air. With an air-to-water intercooler, common in boat and truck applications, the heat exchanger is enclosed within a water jacket through which water flows to take away inlet charge heat. Because of the possibility of fuel condensation and a subsequent backfire blowing the core of the intercooler or the ducting apart, intercoolers should not be used in applications where fuel enters the inlet system ahead of it.

Basically, an intercooler's ability to reduce inlet charge air temperature will

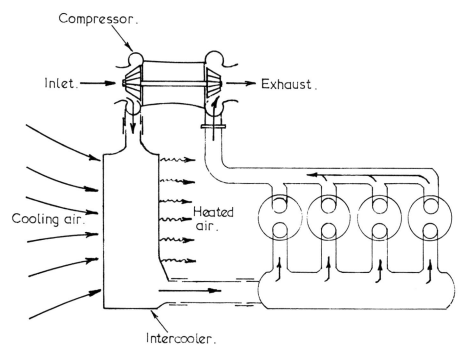

An air-to-air intercooler gives off heat from the compressed inlet charge to the cooling air passing by its core fins and tubes.

depend on the size of the heat exchanger, the ambient air temperature and the flow rate of cooling air through the heat exchanger. The actual size of the heat exchanger is obviously limited by the amount of space available to locate it and by the cost. As with coolant system radiators, the more the area of cooling tubes and fins, the greater the expense. The ambient temperature isn't something over which we have any control, but the flow rate of this air through the heat exchanger can be improved at lower vehicle speeds by the use of a good electric fan. Even so, the intercooler will be more effective at removing charge air heat at higher vehicle speeds.

Realistic intercooler efficiency, temperature-wise, is about 80%. Temperature efficiency or effectiveness is defined as the ratio between the actual charge air temperature decrease and the possible decrease. Hence a heat exchanger which is 100% effective would reduce the charge air temperature to the same level as the ambient temperature. Except in race applications, such a large intercooler would not be practical. Conversely, an intercooler which is less than about 60% efficient is basically of little value. If the intercooler is 80% effective, it will draw off 80% of the heat rise generated in the charge air by the turbo. Hence if the ambient temperature is 85°F and the charge leaving the compressor is at 235°F, a heat rise of 150° (235 – 85 = 150), it will remove 120° of the heat rise (150 x 0.8 = 120), resulting in a charge air temperature of 115°F (150 – 120 + 85 = 115) leaving the intercooler.

There are drawbacks which make intercooling of limited value in turbo systems operating at boost levels lower than about 5 psi. Obviously there is some flow resistance due to turbulence in the intercooler and ducting. In a poorly-designed 169 cooling system with a number of tight bends, this alone can reduce the boost pressure actually entering the engine by 2 psi. Additionally, there is a natural pressure drop due to the charge air being cooled. In a well-designed intercooler system the total pressure drop should not be more than 10% of the boost pressure as measured at the compressor outlet. Hence a system that is regulated to 13 psi should deliver 11.7 psi at the inlet manifold. Of course this boost loss could be compensated for by adjusting the wastegate to a higher boost. If the wastegate is a solenoid-operated unit controlled by the vehicle's computer, and hence not easily adjustable, the pressure loss can be overcome by relocating the pressure sensor from the compressor outlet to the inlet manifold.

Just how effective intercooling can be purely from the performance viewpoint can be seen by referring to our previous example, where raising the boost from 7 psi to 11 psi resulted in a power increase of only 13% at the very most. With an 80% efficient intercooler and an overall boost loss of 1 psi, the charge air temperature will fall from 235°F to 111°F and the power will rise by 46% over the stock 7 psi boost level and by 23% over the non-intercooled 11 psi boost. Clearly, very efficient intercooling is an effective means of obtaining large performance increases without adding additional stress to the engine.

However, to realise this potential increase the intercooler must actually work as efficiently as it does on paper. Consequently it is necessary to carefully check out your potential intercooler supplier. Ask him to produce test figures to prove how much temperature drop occurs across the intercooler. Then get him to calculate how efficient the intercooler is at your proposed boost pressure. If he can't work it out he probably doesn't know very much about intercooling, so shop elsewhere. If he does the calculation go home and check if his figures tally. This caution is necessary because there are not too many people who actually test their intercoolers to find out how efficient they really are. The more common approach is to build an intercooler to fit a particular vehicle and then draw some numbers out of the air to persuade potential customers that the product works marvellously.

Finding a home for the intercooler is quite a challenge. The common solution is to mount the unit in front of the radiator, but in hot climates, particularly if the vehicle is air conditioned, this is less than successful because of reduced engine cooling efficiency. Additionally, the length of ducting required increases turbo lag and sluggishness at lower rpm. An alternative is to mount the intercooler at the side of the radiator. This may not be possible because of space limitations in which case a narrower custom-built radiator with an extra row or two of tubes can be used with space left for a narrow intercooler alongside. The position chosen by Ford for the Mustang SVO was to mount the intercooler up high alongside the engine, with cooling air being admitted through a bonnet-scoop. This in many ways is an excellent location as the amount of ducting is greatly reduced, so turbo lag isn't affected and because of the intercooler location engine cooling is not impaired. However, at lower speeds the intercooler will not be very effective, due to lack of cooling air flow, unless a small electric fan is mounted beneath the core.

Where direct intercooling is not desirable some intercooling effect can be achieved by directing cool air onto the inlet duct which carries the air charge to the inlet manifold. Preferably the duct should be cast with fins on the external surface to increase the heat radiating area, and it should be left rough cast and painted matt black.

170

A finned inlet duct will help reduce the charge air temperature. For maximum efficiency the duct should be finned over its entire length. Leave the fins rough cast and paint the duct matt black to increase radiating efficiency. Cooling air is directed over the inlet duct via a bonnet scoop or trunking.

The cooling air could be admitted through a bonnet-scoop or it may be ducted from the front of the vehicle through a flexible pipe about 4in in diameter. Whatever method is used, the cooling air must be diffused over as much area of the charge air duct as possible to gain the maximum cooling effect. Shield the duct from engine and exhaust heat. Also ensure that cooling air doesn't blow over the exhaust manifold or the turbine side of the turbo as this could take too much heat out of the exhaust gases and reduce boost.

Apart from the performance aspect there is another beneficial side to intercooling; namely reliability of the engine and turbocharger. A rule of thumb is that for every 100 degrees the intake charge temperature is reduced there is a 100 degree drop in exhaust temperature. This makes life easier for the exhaust valves and seats, the turbine and housing, the exhaust manifold, and the engine cooling system. As you should appreciate by now, turbocharging puts a lot of heat into the inlet air and increasing the boost just worsens the situation. Many tuners shrug this off; in fact I know of some who have doubled the standard boost pressure from 8 psi to 17 psi with the only engine modifications being the addition of forged pistons and a lowering of the compression ratio by 0.5. They figured that the engine won't detonate due to electronic controls, and as high boost pressures are good for business from the aspect of advertising and it is what the customer wants, go ahead and use high boost. It is true that many turbo engines have a knock sensor to detect detonation. The system which I prefer has the wastegate controlled to open when detonation is detected. Thus boost is 171 always kept below detonation level. The more common system retards the ignition timing at the onset of detonation, and this is less than satisfactory. In effect it is the easy way around the problem, without really getting right to the problem itself. Retarding the spark severely increases the turbine and housing temperature, so much so that at sustained high boost the housing warps and eventually the turbine wheel contacts it and the turbo blows. The other possibility occurs because the retarded timing greatly increases the temperature of the piston crown, combustion chamber and in particular the exhaust valve. With all of this additional heat being added to an already overheated inlet charge, the engine pre-ignites. If initially this is not intense enough to melt the pistons, the knock sensor reads the shock as detonation and further retards the ignition timing. With more retard more heat is added to the turbo, combustion chambers, pistons and exhaust valves, until eventually either the turbo lets go or the pistons are holed by pre-ignition. Not a good scenario at all; obviously only more restrained levels of boost, together with an intercooler of sufficient capacity, can avoid this type of outcome.

Of course intercooling and/or higher boost levels only result in more power if there is a corresponding increase in fuel flow to keep step with the additional inlet air flow. Some injection and electronic engine management systems will compensate for the extra flow resulting from a boost increase of about 4psi and 80% effective intercooling, while others have just enough reserve capacity to cope with either intercooling alone or a boost increase of 3 to 4 psi. If the fuel system cannot maintain flow at the desired level, action as outlined in the earlier chapter on fuel injection will be necessary. The problem is not always insufficient flow, but lack of fuel pressure to give the required flow at the injectors at elevated boost pressure. This can be overcome by the use of a high pressure, high flow fuel pump.

For example, when a Ford Cosworth Sierra was modified, the fuel system was found to be just adequate for the standard engine. As shown in Table 10.2 the standard engine produced 200hp without any bother at 6000rpm, although the mixture leaned at higher rpm. It was reasoned that this was probably due to the electronics interrupting fuel flow 500rpm prematurely. Because the management system was going to be modified to raise the boost 40% to 13 psi it was decided to carry out some additional electronic trickery to change the fuel curve and allow full power up to 6800rpm. Out of regard for the increased turbo boost the intercooler size was doubled. Test 2 shows what effect these changes had on power output. Maximum power was up 10% which wasn't too impressive considering the work involved. The next step was to fit an auxiliary injector nozzle to get more fuel into the engine at higher rpm. In addition, the turbine housing was changed to free up exhaust flow. As can be seen in Test 3, these modifications really paid off. The engine was now more responsive at all engine speeds and it ran easily to 6800rpm, where it now produced 242hp. With the bottom end strengthened to allow 7500rpm in safety, the output would probably have climbed to in excess of 250hp at 7000 to 7250rpm.

Another approach to more power and better fuel economy is to use a turbine housing with a larger A/R ratio than stock. In general, manufacturers fit small A/R turbine housings to their engines to get good low speed boost. The small nozzle increases turbine speed so that even at lower engine speeds there is sufficient exhaust gas flow to spin the compressor fast enough to make boost. The trade-off is that as the engine speed increases, the small turbine housing nozzle restricts exhaust flow out of

Table 10.2   Comparison testing of Cosworth Sierra 2 litre turbo

rpm	Test 1		Test 2		Test 3	
	hp	Torque	hp	Torque	hp	Torque
2000	46	121	51	135	51	133
2500	85	179	93	196	95	200
3000	110	193	118	206	122	214
3500	127	191	139	208	141	212
4000	143	188	163	214	167	219
4500	171	199	190	222	196	229
5000	188	197	202	212	211	222
5500	195	186	213	203	219	209
6000	200	175	220	193	227	199
6500			216	175	235	190
6800					242	187

Test 1 – standard engine

Test 2 – electronics modified to give 13 psi boost and richen fuel curve, intercooler size doubled

Test 3 – as above plus auxiliary injector added and turbine housing changed

the engine in the same way as would a small diameter exhaust pipe. Maximum power is thus limited by restricted exhaust flow and fuel consumption increases because the pistons consume power, forcing the exhaust gas out of the cylinders and through the turbo. Even at cruise many turbos cost up around 5% to 8% fuel economy loss due to increased back pressure.

In the most mildly tuned turbo engines the turbine housing chosen should give full boost on wide open throttle at the engine's peak torque rpm. Fitting a housing smaller than this usually does very little to improve low rpm performance and it will, as a rule, result in excessive higher rpm power losses and a significant drop in economy at cruise and on boost. Ideally, the exhaust back pressure, as measured at the turbine inlet and with a 2ft long open exhaust connected to the outlet, should not be more than about 25% higher than the boost pressure at maximum hp rpm. Therefore if maximum boost is 10 psi, the exhaust pressure at the turbine inlet should not be more than 12.5 psi at maximum power revs.

With performance/economy engines a higher level of performance and reduced fuel consumption is desired so in this instance a turbine housing is selected which achieves peak boost at about 500 to 700rpm higher than the stock turbo engine's peak torque revs. A turbine housing of this A/R ratio will reduce considerably the exhaust back pressure so that at maximum power rpm the exhaust pressure at the turbine inlet will be about the same as the maximum boost pressure. Thus when a full exhaust is added, the total exhaust pressure should not be more than about 3 to 4 psi higher than the boost pressure at maximum revs. Table 10.3 shows a comparison of the inlet and exhaust pressures for a full emissions Porche 911 turbo with the stock exhaust system in place. At peak power rpm back pressure in the standard exhaust is 4.7 psi higher than the boost pressure, but with an open exhaust the exhaust pressure was just over 1 psi higher than the boost.

Table 10.3   Comparison of inlet and exhaust pressures in Porsche 911 Turbo

rpm	Boost pressure	Exhaust back pressure
1500	1.5 psi	1.1 psi
2000	4.0 psi	2.6 psi
2500	9.6 psi	6.0 psi
3000	10.9 psi	7.6 psi
3500	11.0 psi	8.7 psi
4000	11.0 psi	10.3 psi
4500	11.2 psi	13.0 psi
5000	11.4 psi	14.7 psi
5500	11.6 psi	16.3 psi
6000	11.6 psi	17.2 psi

Note: peak power occurs at 5500rpm; peak torque at 3000rpm.

When a larger A/R housing is used, the effect is similar to fitting a warm cam. The engine makes less power at lower rpm because the turbine spins the compressor more slowly, hence the boost level is reduced. However, at higher engine speeds the engine makes more power, not because of more boost, but because the energy which was previously being consumed forcing the exhaust gases out past the turbine wheel is now doing the more useful work of increasing the twisting force being applied to the engine's crankshaft. Therefore more maximum power can be produced at lower maximum boost pressures, as shown in Table 10.4.

Table 10.4 also shows clearly the massive increase in fuel consumption which occurred when a smaller turbine housing was tried on this twin cam 2.8 litre Toyota in an attempt to improve the performance below 3500rpm. BSFC stands for brake specific fuel consumption. This figure is assessed during engine development work on the dyno as one of the factors to indicate just how well the engine is performing. It is

Table 10.4   Comparison testing of turbine housing on Toyota 2.8 litre

rpm	Test 1			Test 2		
	hp	Torque	BSFC	hp	Torque	BSFC
1500	52	182	0.502	57	199	0.512
2000	73	192	0.496	81	212	0.514
2500	104	219	0.498	127	266	0.514
3000	150	263	0.493	159	278	0.511
3500	190	285	0.496	179	269	0.519
4000	225	295	0.500	208	273	0.525
4500	248	289	0.502	237	277	0.537
5000	264	277	0.511	255	268	0.552
5500	274	262	0.516	265	253	0.556
6000	283	248	0.529	260	228	0.599
6500	268	217	0.554	231	187	0.631

Test 1 – large A/R ratio turbine housing, 11.5 psi boost with intercooling

Test 2 – smaller A/R ratio turbine housing, 13 psi boost with intercooling calculated by dividing the engine's fuel flow, lb of fuel per hour, by the power output. If the engine was consuming 100lb of fuel per hour to make 200hp at 5500rpm, then the BSFC would be 0.500lb/hp hr (100 ÷ 200 = 0.500). Obviously the less fuel the engine is using for each hp produced, the more efficiently it must be working. With the large turbine housing the engine made 283hp and showed a fuel flow of 149.7lb per hour, but when the smaller housing was tested, power fell to 265hp and the fuel flow was 147.4lb per hour. This means that the small A/R housing cost 18hp and from 4500rpm to 6500rpm it cost 7 to 14% in economy at full throttle.

It was apparent from these initial tests that the larger A/R turbine housing should be retained to give the best economy. During subsequent testing a final package was developed to overcome the lack of performance below 3500rpm. It included an exhaust cam with shorter duration, increased compression ratio and a reduction in boost to 10 psi, and a further refinement of the ignition and fuel curves. Maximum power fell by only 7hp and the engine picked up just over 20hp at 2500rpm, and 12 to 15hp more from 3000 to 4000rpm. Also the BSFC fell to around 0.485, indicating an improvement in efficiency.

The use of larger A/R turbine housings should not generally be considered for engines smaller than about 2.0 litres, and then only if the vehicle is correctly geared, has a manual gearbox, and is not overweight, otherwise around town performance may be a little sluggish unless extensive developmental work is undertaken. To some extent intercooling will help because even though the boost pressure with a larger A/R housing will be reduced at lower rpm with intercooling added, the compression ratio may be raised, providing the stock boost pressure is maintained, and this will pick up low speed performance quite considerably.

When power increases 15% over stock are desired some turbo engines may require an extensive rework to maintain reliability. The areas where problems can occur vary from engine to engine. It could be blown head gaskets. For some engines this may be simply overcome by fitting a different head gasket of better design and/or materials; others may require stronger head studs which do not stretch at higher pressures. The problem could be with the pistons. Perhaps they need to be stronger forgings, with wider areas between the ring lands, or with thicker crowns to increase their durability at elevated temperature. Maybe the ring placement is wrong, allowing the top ring to overheat and lose its tension after a minute or two of full boost. For some engines the problem area could be with the exhaust valves and seats. Some valve seat materials become as soft as putty at high temperature, allowing them to pound out or perhaps drop out of the head. Naturally these potential difficulties must be given due consideration when higher power levels are desired.

Everyone who has much to do with turbochargers regularly hears horror stories of turbo failures. Mostly the enthusiast blames his turbo or his oil for such early failure, often at less than 10,000 miles service. More often than not the driver is to blame, although there is some truth to oil-related failures which is why I recommend only the use of oils which are produced to provide turbo protection. Using a 100% synthetic oil and changing it along with the filter at the intervals outlined in a later chapter is good insurance, but in essence this is just the start of turbo care.

Today, many turbos have a water-cooled bearing arrangement to increase the reliability and life of the bearings. Unfortunately this has lulled many into a false sense of security as they feel the turbo no longer needs to "idle down" before the engine is stopped. This just isn't so; after a run which has put a fair amount of heat into the turbo it must be allowed time to cool for a period of about 3 minutes. Actually I don't advocate allowing the engine to idle for that period. I would rather see it run at about 1500rpm or a little higher to promote a good flow of oil through the turbo bearings. At idle the oil flow will not be sufficient, which could allow the heat in the turbine to carbonise the oil. If the oil becomes carbonised it blocks the minute clearance between the shaft and bearings. When the engine is next operated oil flow through the bearings is reduced: without adequate lubrication the bearings soon fail. However, this may not be the limit of the problem as the shaft may also be wrecked; the turbine and impeller wheels may touch their respective housings, damaging the turbo beyond economical repair.

Some enthusiasts do the right thing in allowing the turbo to cool before stopping the engine, but just before switch-off they give the throttle a few quick jabs to, in their words, "clear the plugs!". Such action may spin the turbo up to 30,000rpm and then with oil flow cut, when the engine is stopped, the bearings soon run dry and suffer premature wear.

A similar problem occurs right after starting the engine. It can take up to 30 seconds for oil to flow to the turbo so don't quickly rev the engine as this spins the turbine to high speed at a time when the bearings have only minimal lubricant in reserve. In similar vein when a turbo is refitted after being off the engine for any time, or if a reconditioned unit is being fitted, do prime it with engine oil before attaching the oil feed line. When this isn't done the bearings are damaged from the time the engine is fired up. Likewise, if the engine has not been started for some time, as during winter, it is wise if the turbo or oil line can be reached easily to prime it with oil before starting the engine.

Whenever a turbocharger is removed from the engine place it in a plastic bag so as to prevent foreign matter entering the turbine or compressor, or the oilway. Also cover the inlet and exhaust ducts on the engine so that no nuts or washers etc. can get into them and later find their way into the turbo. By following these simple precautions expensive damage is easily avoided.

In normal usage a turbocharger should require servicing only about every 30,000 to 50,000 miles. If the vehicle spends a good deal of time idling at lights or at high speed, the service interval could be more frequent. Usually, a service kit is available containing the necessary bearings, seals, bolts etc. Turbos are of very simple construction and quite easy to service if approached with proper consideration for cleanliness of oilways and bearing surfaces, and if it is remembered that the rotating assembly has to spin at speeds in excess of 100,000rpm. Some manufacturers do not recommend that servicing be done except by authorised agents with the necessary, expensive, service equipment to rebalance the turbine/impeller assembly as imbalance may cause undue noise. However, I have never experienced any problems when the compressor wheel and turbine wheel/shaft is undamaged, and thus reusable. Simply marking the position of the impeller on the shaft with a dab of paint during disassembly and then on reassembly accurately lining up the paint mark on the impeller with the paint mark on the end of the shaft overcomes any imbalance/noise problems. Obviously if either the impeller or the turbine wheel/shaft are replaced because of damage or wear, the complete assembly will require balancing.

During disassembly carefully hold the centre housing/bearing assembly in a vice by the irregularly-shaped nut on the turbine end of the shaft. By the way, the nut is ground that shape to balance the assembly. Because there isn't much area for the vice to grip onto be very careful when removing the other nut which holds the impeller onto the shaft. If the assembly slips you will wreck the turbine blades. When the blades are bent don't attempt to straighten them otherwise they will eventually break off. If it is an impeller blade that goes it could finish up inside the engine and do damage, or the impeller may explode and come through the compressor housing. Expert opinion should be sought when the blades are bent. When minor, the assembly may be reusable, but it is best to have this determined by someone experienced.

There are two other points of which to be mindful. Before dismantling the turbo, mark the positions of the compressor housing and the turbine housing on the centre core assembly. This will save you a lot of assembly hassles later. Also, take care to follow carefully the torque settings recommended by the manufacturer when reassembling the unit. If the manufacturer says that a particular nut is to be tensioned to what may appear to be a small value, such as 10ft/lb, follow the instructions and do not rely upon your own judgement. Possibly you will not have a tension wrench which is accurate at anything less than about 30ft/lb, so borrow or buy a suitable wrench.

Chapter 11

The Bottom End

In the main, modern engines are quite robust and will give reliable service with very little attention to the bottom end when tuned for performance and economy. Unless the engine is regularly worked at high rpm or is turbocharged, the stock crankshaft, connecting rods, pistons and bearings should be up to the task and the manufacturer's recommended rebuild clearances and procedure will be satisfactory.

The weak link in many engines is the pistons. Unless the stock piston is an unslotted semi-competition type it will not take sustained high engine speeds or constant turbo boost. The problem isn't that manufacturers can't make better pistons, but as in all other areas of engine design a compromise is necessary to accommodate a number of conflicting requirements. The majority of drivers demand that an engine be quiet at idle and cruise, and consume a minimum of oil at ordinary speeds. A piston with two long slots cut in the oil ring groove best meets those requirements, at the expense of sustained high rpm reliability. The long slots effectively divide the piston crown from the skirt. This keeps the high temperature prevalent in the crown isolated from the piston skirt, thus allowing tight piston to cylinder clearances of 0.001 to 0.0015in. Such tight clearances reduce the tendency of the pistons to rock in the bore and emit noise. Also the skirt does much to scrape oil from the cylinder walls, reducing the load on the rings to control oil consumption. Hence even when the engine has seen a long service life and the rings are shot, oil consumption will still be reasonable at normal engine speeds.

These benefits come at a price; reduced reliability. When the engine is new there should not be any problems providing the manufacturer's rpm limit is observed. However, as the pistons age constant flexing of the skirt causes cracks to appear. A piece of the skirt may break away or the entire skirt may part company with the crown. Needless to say an expensive blow up could result.

To avoid this type of problem, high performance engines usually come from the factory with unslotted pistons. Speciality piston manufacturers can supply this type of piston to suit just about any engine. With this design the piston is solid with just a few small holes drilled in the oil ring groove to provide oil drain-back. The disadvantage is that these pistons need three to five times as much clearance as slotted pistons, because a lot of heat will transfer to the skirt at high engine loads. However, at idle and cruise, when the piston crown is relatively cool, there won't be much heat getting to the skirt to expand it out to the cylinder wall. Hence the pistons rock about more and produce noise. Additionally, this rocking increases ring and groove wear, necessitating more frequent overhauls.

There has been a good deal of discussion among engine tuners as to whether forged or cast pistons are better. For road engines I have no personal preference; if the piston manufacturer produces a good product either type will work equally well. Therefore if forged pistons are more expensive and heavier I would not hesitate to use a good cast piston. The exception would be in high output road turbo engines where the higher material density of forged pistons may give an added margin of reliability. Being denser, thermal conductivity from the piston crown is superior, reducing crown temperature by about 100°F. Also forged pistons are capable of withstanding higher pressures and heat loads.

Care is necessary whenever pistons are being handled. Accidentally dropping a piston could distort the skirt and eventually lead to seizure. Belting the piston pin out with a hammer and drift can also push the skirt out of shape. If the pin will not push out easily, heat the piston in boiling water or oil and then gently tap it out. Where the pin is a press fit in the connecting rod it must be removed and installed using special tools to avoid piston damage.

No matter how carefully pistons are handled they can still be easily wrecked in service if the connecting rod is misaligned. Therefore when the engine is being reconditioned the rod alignment should be checked to ensure that the rods are not bent, twisted or incorrectly offset.

If it is decided that stronger unslotted pistons are necessary because sustained high rpm usage is contemplated, a decision has then to be made whether the bore will remain within the range of the manufacturer's standard rebore sizes or whether a

Pistons are ground tapered and oval to allow for expansion caused by additional heat in the piston crown and around the pin boss areas.

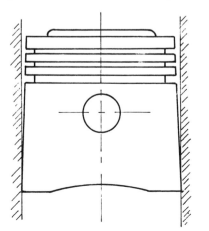
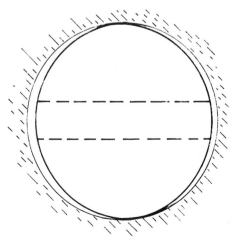

massive overbore will be sought. Many modern engines use light thin-wall castings which will not successfully rebore more than 0.030in over stock. Quite frankly I do not like to see road engines which are expected to see a long and reliable life taken to the limit. I usually do not recommend more than 0.060 to 0.080in oversize, even for very thick-wall blocks, which are frequently taken 0.120in oversize. I'm not prepared to trade long term reliability for a few extra cc.

When an engine is taken 0.060 to 0.080 oversize have the boring bar operator take the metal out in two cuts. It will cost more because of the time involved but the cylinders will be easier to hone accurately because the boring tool marks will not be so deep and rough. Finely machined cylinders with parallel walls are a necessity. Any leakage past the rings reduces performance, wastes fuel and increases oil consumption. Hence only reputable operators with the best equipment should be given the job. The hone must leave the cylinders perfectly round and parallel with a 45° cross-hatch pattern and a surface finish of 10 to 12 micro-inches. A finish like this makes it necessary to run the rings in, but they will last for a long time and not leak. After honing, the bores must be thoroughly scrubbed out with hot, soapy water to remove all honing grit.

For ease of bedding in I prefer moly-filled nodular cast iron piston rings. Nodular iron has almost three times the strength of conventional grey cast iron and because it is ductile rather than brittle, it can be bent without breaking. Molybdenum belongs to the same family as chrome but is superior as it has a lower coefficient of friction and higher resistance to abrasion. Its thermal conductivity is several times greater than chrome plated cast iron and because of its porous nature it acts like an oil reservoir, reducing ring wear and cylinder scuffing and wear.

Chrome plated rings are harder to bed-in than any other type of ring, but they offer a long service life and seem to be less affected by detonation then moly-filled rings. I have never experienced any problems with moly rings although a few reputable tuners maintain that they will not hold up under heavy detonation as well as chrome plated rings.

Apart from a perfect seal being necessary between the ring face and cylinder wall an equally important consideration is a perfect seal between the bottom of the ring and the piston ring groove. If the bottom of the groove is worn or scratched, leakage will occur. I like very tight groove to ring clearances of 0.001 to 0.0015in. Certainly with new pistons and rings the clearance should not be more than 0.002in. The wider the clearance the more the rings can flop about and accelerate groove and ring wear. Eventually the ring will move about so savagely that it breaks. If the clearance is over 0.0045in with new rings fitted, the pistons should be replaced or reconditioned.

Another cause of ring breakage is insufficient ring gap, allowing the ring ends to crash together. The minimum gap per inch of bore is as follows: turbo engines 0.005in for the top ring and 0.0035in for the second ring, naturally-aspirated 0.004in for the top ring and 0.003in for the second ring.

When rings are being fitted, care is needed to avoid fitting them the wrong way up and to prevent damage by incorrect installation practices. Compression rings can be permanently twisted or distorted out of round if they are stretched open too far or if they are fitted in the piston ring groove at one end and then screwed around until the ring is in place. Rings should only be expanded sufficiently to just fit over the piston,

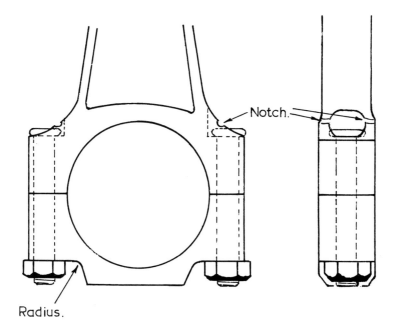

Radius.

Connecting rods which are regularly worked hard may crack through at the corners of the flats machined for the rod bolt and nut seat. To relieve the stress concentration the rod cap is radiused in the corners and the rod is notched, as shown. Note that rods which use bolts without nuts do not require relief notching.

applications is to lightly radius the sharp corners which are formed by the flat machined for the rod bolt and nut seat. These sharp corners can cause stress concentration and eventual cracking.

Whenever an engine is dismantled, new connecting rod bolts must always be fitted; the old bolts should never be reused. Apart from piston breakages, rod bolt stretch or breakage is probably the most common cause of serious internal damage in modern engines. Where special bolts of higher grade steel are available these should be utilised in preference to the standard item.

Unless the engine is going to be operated at sustained engine speeds significantly higher than the manufacturers recommended rpm limit, don't waste your time and money polishing the rods. The tough skin formed on the rod by forging actually gives the rod much of its strength and fatigue resistance. Therefore rods should never be polished unless this is followed up with shot peening to form a new work-toughened and compressed skin. It is quite pointless polishing the entire rod because the main area of weakness is, in fact, along the edges of the rod. If you take time to inspect a rod you will see a rough ridge of metal along the edges where the metal appears to have been sawn away. This is where excess metal called flash was squeezed from the forging dies when the rod was being made. Later, most of the flash is trimmed off, leaving behind a rough ridge. There is no hard forging skin along this ridge; actually its roughness is a stress raiser. If it is decided that the rods are to be polished it is this ridge which has to be removed, using a belt sander. After rough sanding the entire beam should be polished using fine emery cloth and then buffed. Finally the polished 185 areas should be shot peened to add strength to the rod and increase its fatigue resistance.

The shot peening process has a very useful place in the preparation of connecting rods which are to be fitted in fast revving engines. Fatigue failure most often starts at the surface because under usual forms of loading maximum stress is at the surface and it is here that surface imperfections and irregularities, which are in actuality stress raisers, are to be found. By bombarding the part with steel shot the surface layer is compressed and unified. Consequently when the component is under load any tensile stresses at the surface will be lessened, while compressive stresses will be increased. Because shot peening can seal over surface cracks, all crack testing must be carried out prior to peening. Additionally, any straightening or aligning should be done before peening, as either operation will diminish the effect of shot peening. After being peened, the part should be checked dimensionally as there will be some growth, and also check for bending as this may occur if the peening has been done incorrectly.

Cylinder block preparation is very basic and simple. First knock out all the welch plugs (freeze or core plugs) and inspect the coolant passages for rust or scale. Any sediment or flaky material can be dislodged with a screwdriver and then flushed out. If an inhibitor has not been used and advanced corrosion is evident, it will be necessary to boil the block in a chemical bath. When this is done the oil gallery plugs must be removed and all oilways carefully cleaned and flushed to ensure that any rubbish present in the boiling tank which could have found its way into the oilways is expelled. Next, all stud holes should be cleaned, with particular attention being paid to the head stud holes and the main bearing cap stud holes. The standard two bolt cast iron main bearing caps will be quite adequate for mildly tuned performance/economy engines so don't throw away any money on steel caps.

After being bored, or any other machining work has been done, the block must again be thoroughly cleaned. Initially, scrub it out using a bristle scrubbing brush and plenty of hot soapy water. Scrub inside every cylinder and every place within the crankcase. Then give the block a blast of high pressure hot water to remove every trace of machining dust or honing grit. Give the oilways a final flush with hot water, quickly dry the block using compressed air and immediately spray all machined surfaces with a water dispersant such as WD-40 to stop rust. After this oil the cylinder walls and in the case of pushrod engines also the lifter bores. If the engine is not to be immediately assembled place the block in a heavy duty plastic bag (a garbage bag is excellent), force as much air out of the bag as possible, and then seal it.

The manufacturer's standard engine bearings can be used, or if preferred trimetal bearings may be fitted for the mains and big ends in engines which leave the factory with bi-metal copper lead or aluminium tin bearings. Both F770 specification and F77 specification tri-metal bearing have a higher load endurance factor and fatigue strength than either bi-metal bearings which makes them the favoured bearing types for performance engines. The F770 and F77 bearings use a 24% lead,75% copper intermediate layer that imparts the superior characteristics of good fatigue strength and load carrying capacity, as well as resistance to hydraulic break out. The running surface is a 0.001in thick lead-based overlay which imparts good embedability characteristics. All engines have some dirt circulating in the lubrication oil no matter how carefully the engine has been cleaned and assembled. Bi-metal bearings lack this soft overlay so any minute dirt particles act as a grinding agent between the bearing and crankshaft journals, wearing away at the bearing. Tri-metal bearings on the other hand allow this dirt or wear debris to embed in the soft overlay. In effect the lead alloy overlay absorbs or digests the foreign material, without undue damage to the bearing itself. Of course as the overlay wears thinner after, say, 50,000 to 70,000 miles of driving, its ability to digest dirt particles is reduced. Naturally when dirt is embedded in the bearing surface some additional abrasive wear of the crank journals does occur.

F770 and F77 specification bearings have identical bearing materials; their differences lie in the manner that they are manufactured. With F770 bearings a copper lead alloy powder is sintered onto the steel backing whereas the F77 bearings have the copper lead alloy cast onto the steel backing strip. At this stage of development cast copper lead F77 bearings offer a slight advantage over the cheaper to produce F770 type. In race engines I wouldn't use anything but F77 bearings made by such companies as Vandervell, TRW (Clevite CL-77) and Sealed Power, but for road engines F770 bearings are more than adequate.

Correct bearing clearance is an obvious necessity. Excessive clearance promotes knocking and pounding, and causes excessive oil throw off into the cylinders. This produces higher frictional losses and increases fuel consumption as the pistons and rings drag the surplus oil off the bore walls. In addition, oil control past the rings is reduced. Oil consumption increases, as does the risk of detonation because oil in the combustion chamber dramatically lowers the fuel's effective octane rating. Excessive clearance at the big end bearings starves the main bearings of needed lubricant and gives rise to rapid wear, or even bearing failure. In a similar vein excessive con rod side clearance or float on the crankpin is to be avoided for the same reasons. This problem most frequently occurs when the crankpin is accidently widened during crankshaft reconditioning work. Insufficient bearing clearance leads to rapid bearing deterioration as a result of the elevated temperatures that come about due to reduced oil flow or a thin oil film. To avoid this type of problem I prefer to see performance/economy engines assembled with bearing clearances close to the manufacturer's specified upper limit. Hence if the specifications called for clearances of 0.0008 to 0.0018in I would try to keep the clearance up around 0.0015 to 0.002in.

Bearing clearance is checked by accurately measuring the inside diameter of every main bearing and big end bearing housing, correctly tensioned and without the bearing shells fitted. Measurements should be made perpendicular to the joint line of the bearing housings taking care to keep the micrometer square to the housing bore. From these measurements subtract the respective crank journal diameters and then subtract the bearing insert thickness multiplied by two. The final figures give the bearing clearances.

Before being fitted, the bearings should be carefully washed in clean solvent to remove the protective film, and then dried and covered so that they do not collect any dust. The bearing housings need to be cleaned with a kitchen scouring pad like Scotchbrite which has been moistened with solvent. This is done to remove any varnish deposits which could retard heat transfer from the bearing shell. After being scoured, the housings must be wiped clean and then washed with solvent. It should be noted that careful cleaning of the bearing shells and housings is essential. The presence of oil or varnish either on the back of the bearing shell or on the bore of the housing will cut heat transfer. The presence of any dirt particles on either surface will reduce bearing clearances, and in severe cases leads to early bearing failure. 187

After ensuring that the shells and housings are perfectly clean and dry, the main bearing shells may be fitted. This sounds simple enough but I have seen engines damaged because someone got it wrong. Some bearings have identical oil grooves and oil holes in both halves, allowing them to be fitted in either the upper or lower position. However, many engines require that the big end bearing shells and sometimes also the main bearing shells only be installed in one position otherwise oil flow will be cut off. Hence when bearing inserts are being fitted take care to ensure that the insert with the oil hole is matched to the oil hole in the cylinder block or connecting rod. Also check that the oil holes correctly align; if they do not, rectify the misalignment using a small round key file. After filing, carefully dress the back of the bearing shell to remove any metal fraze. Once fitted in their respective housings give the bearing surfaces a liberal coating of straight engine oil: don't add anything to the oil. Lower the crankshaft into the block and fit the main bearing caps in their correct numbered locations and with the arrows facing the front of the block. Tighten the caps to about 30ft lb and then with the aid of a lever force the crank backward and forward a couple of times to make the flanges of the thrust bearing line up. After this tap the crankshaft from side to side with a soft hammer and in turn tap the main bearing caps to improve the alignment of the bearings. Finally, progressively tighten each cap bolt to its specified tension. At this point the crankshaft end float can be measured. With a cast iron block preferably it should be within 0.004 to 0.006in. If it is more than this, thicker thrust bearings will be required.

Big end bearings are fitted following the same basic steps. The main exception is that the bolts should initially be tensioned to about 15ft lb before tapping the caps to align the bearing inserts. Also I like to use Loctite on the bolt threads to avoid engine damage from the bolts later loosening off. Note that when piston/rod assemblies are being installed, protruding connecting rod bolts must be covered with plastic or rubber sleeves to prevent the threads digging into the crankpin.

Most enthusiasts pay little attention to the pulley or harmonic balancer attached to the nose of the crankshaft. However, they have their part to play in the durability of the engine and in keeping the under-bonnet environment safe. A number of engines use a pressed metal drive pulley which is spot welded or riveted. When the manufacturer's recommended rev limit is regularly exceeded, a pulley of this construction is liable to fly apart, wrecking anything in its path. If the engine is to be extended above the recommended engine speed either a cast pulley, or a pulley machined from solid stock, should be used.

Five, six and eight cylinder engines and a few four cylinder engines are fitted with a harmonic balancer to dampen crankshaft torsional vibrations which if not controlled could wreck the crankshaft and bearings. Harmonic balancers are made of three parts bonded together. A rubber belt is bonded between the hub and the outer inertia ring which in some engines also serves as a pulley. Failure is caused by this outer ring losing its bond with the rubber. When this takes place it can fly off at any time, often with spectacular and expensive results. The only way to avoid that from occurring is to inspect the harmonic dampener on a regular basis. To assist in your inspection paint a common line across the face of the harmonic balancer from the outer ring across to the hub. If the line moves apart it indicates that the rubber bond has broken, allowing the inertia ring to move around on the hub. Fit a new or reconditioned harmonic balancer, do not try to repair it by screwing the outer ring to the hub. The inertia ring has to be able to move, within limits, to dampen crank vibration. Locking it up solid will eventually wreck the bearings and the crankshaft.

Before fitting the crankshaft pulley to the engine paint it black and then after fitting it accurately find top dead centre (TDC) and file a good groove into it to align with the TDC mark on the engine timing case. Paint the filed groove and the timing marks on the timing case either white or silver. Taking the time to do this will make it easier to adjust the ignition timing accurately. Stock timing marks are notoriously inaccurate, and they are often difficult to see clearly so anything that you can do to rectify these problems will help.

The stock flywheel gives little trouble in the majority of road engines. If the crank flange and flywheel mating surfaces are clean and the flywheel is correctly mounted with the retaining bolts coated with Loctite and properly torqued, there should be few problems at normal engine speeds. However, at higher rpm some engines do display a tendency to loosen the flywheel bolts. If your engine type is prone to this sort of trouble it can be overcome either by fitting two $^3/_8$in dowels and/or additional retaining bolts.

From the aspect of performance the flywheel does have an effect. Removing metal from the outer edges of the flywheel improves acceleration. Because the amount of power required to overcome the flywheel's inertia is reduced, this power is then available to accelerate the vehicle more rapidly. Lightening should only be done near the outside as weight close to the centre has virtually no inertia effect. Actually it is a very dangerous practice to remove metal from the centre. Flywheels are none too strong and taking metal from the centre could lead to an explosion. Taking a lot of weight off the flywheel is undesirable for a road car as it can give rise to a lumpy engine idle and jerky slow speed driving. Manufacturers fit a relatively heavy flywheel to absorb the uneven torsional pulses coming through the crankshaft, and to keep the engine turning fairly smoothly at lower engine speeds.

Chapter 12

Lubrication

Because modern engines are so reliable and maintenance-free, lubrication tends basically to be forgotten. Hence the oil is changed only when it turns to a black goo or perhaps an oil company advertisement prods us to act. On the other hand there are still a few who suffer "lubrication paranoia", changing the lubricant frequently and fortifying it with expensive additives which supposedly make engines last forever. As is usually the case, the prudent course is somewhere between these extremes. Obviously to obtain the best service life from an engine the correct oil must be used and it must be replaced regularly.

Engine oil has to perform a number of basic tasks: lubricate and prevent wear by minimising friction, seal combustion pressure, cool vital engine parts, permit easy starting, keep the engine clean of sludge, minimise combustion chamber deposits, provide rust and corrosion protection and resist foaming. To indicate just how well an oil performs, the American Petroleum Institute (API) assigns oil a service rating such as SD, SE and SF. Currently the toughest API rating is SJ, and to carry that rating an oil must, in theory, pass a series of dyno tests. One test monitors the oil's ability to prevent valve train wear in an overhead cam 2.3 litre American Ford. Like its 2 litre European cousin this engine is notorious for valve train problems, in its early life being subject to a recall for abnormal cam lobe wear. Another test monitors the oil's capacity to prevent wear and resist oxidation in a 350cu in Oldsmobile run for 64 hours with the oil at 149°C sump temperature. The big oil companies do test their oils honestly according to the prescribed API test schedule but it is not unknown for some unscrupulous businesses to fudge the test results or even rate their oils without carrying out any of the API tests. I will only recommend the use of SJ-rated oil from reputable oil companies, and for turbo engines I use only those oils which are actually rated by the oil company as suitable for use in turbo engines as I have found that ordinary SJ-rated oils can cause excessive varnish and carbon deposits in the turbo bearings.

The viscosity of oil is a measure of its ability to flow through a graduated hole at an established temperature; −18°C for W (winter) rating and 99°C for SAE rating. High viscosity oils are thicker and offer more resistance to flow while low viscosity oils flow more easily. Obviously in a highly stressed performance engine we need a high viscosity oil to keep metal parts from contacting one another at higher temperatures. However, such a thick oil would fail to get between closely fitting parts in sufficient quantities after engine start up when the oil is cold. Additionally, the starter motor would not be able to turn the engine over in winter due to the friction caused by the thick oil. The solution is to use a multi-grade oil suitable for your climate as indicated in Table 12.1.

Table 12.1 Recommended oil viscosity

Temperature °C	Temperature °F	Oil Viscosity
0 to 45	32 to 113	20W–50
0 to 30	32 to 86	20W–40, 20W–50
−8 to 30	18 to 86	15W–40
−18 to 15	0 to 60	10W–40
−18 to 3	0 to 37	10W–30
−38 to −6	−36 to 21	5W–20

An oil with a rating of 20W–50 is basically made of 20W refined stock with viscosity index (VI) improvers added to give it a 50 SAE rating at 99°C. The VI improvers, polymers, are long-chain plastic molecules which expand to thicken the oil as the oil temperature increases, and reduce in size as the oil cools. Unfortunately these polymers are not completely shear stable so under certain conditions they will be chopped up, allowing the oil to thin. The prime chopping agent is transmission gears, but as very few cars (unlike motorcycles) have a common engine/transmission oil supply this is usually not a great problem. Age will weather these long-chain plastic molecules so that in time a 20W–50 oil will break down to a 20W–30. You have probably noticed that with fresh oil in the engine, oil consumption may be only a half pint in a thousand miles but after a couple of thousand miles the consumption dramatically increases to two pints per thousand miles. The reason is that the polymers shear with age, allowing the oil to thin and increase consumption.

Adding polymers is not the only way to improve the viscosity index of an oil. Another way is to blend synthetic base stocks with petroleum base stocks to produce a blended synthetic, or to use only synthetic base stocks to produce a so-called one hundred per cent synthetic.

What makes synthetics different from normal mineral oils is the refining process that produces the oil. Everyone knows that ordinary mineral oils are distilled from crude oil. Such things as tars, petrol, diesel, kerosene are removed to leave an engine oil base stock. To produce a synthetic, the refining process continues much further until very basic components of the crude are separated. These basic substances are then combined into new molecular structures to form synthetic base stock. Some synthetics use only petroleum derived base stock, but other hydrocarbon molecules from refined coal, natural gas, animal fat and bone marrow may also be added to produce specific characteristics.

All synthetics have two benefits over ordinary mineral oils. They have excellent 191 low temperature characteristics with a winter rating often as low as 5W and with the addition of polymers, the 99°C rating is usually 50 SAE, so the oil can be used in extreme climatic conditions. Because it is so thin, cold start engine wear is considerably reduced. Additionally, synthetics are more oxidation resistant and so in theory, less frequent oil changes are required. However, as a number of synthetics contain polymers which shear and break down with age, this is open to debate. I strongly recommend the use of a 100% synthetic, particularly in a cooler climate where the temperature is regularly below 5°C (41°F) or where the engine is turbocharged or is subjected to frequent short drives of less than 15 minutes duration a couple of times each day.

Any oil gets contaminated with combustion by-products and the various additives eventually stop working, so the oil must be changed. For a few years now oil companies and some car makers have been advocating very long oil change periods but I am not at all in favour of this practice. After all about the cheapest maintenance is an oil change. Table 12.2 sets out my recommended oil change periods to keep combustion chamber deposits to a minimum and reduce engine wear. To make the oil change really effective, take your car for a good run to bring it to normal operating temperature. This ensures that any sediment and sludge will be well stirred and will drain out with the oil. Take care though to avoid burns as the oil will be quite hot.

Table 12.2   Recommended oil change periods

Driving Conditions	Temperature conditions during daytime	
	Below 10°C/50°F	Above 15°C/59°F
Regularly driven less than 15 min from cold start	2000 miles/60 days	3000 miles/90 days
Stop-start city driving	2000 miles/60 days	3000 miles/90 days
Regular high speed above 80mph	4000 miles/90 days	5000 miles/120 days
Regular high speed above 80mph turbo or common engine/gearbox sump	3000 miles/90 days	3000 miles/90 days
Regularly driven at least 1 hour from cold start usually at less than 70mph	4000 miles/120 days	6000 miles/180 days

Note: change oil at mileage stated or number of days, whichever comes first. The recommended change periods are for engines in good condition – engines with excessive blow-by will require more frequent oil changes. Only mineral oils which meet the highest API rating should be used. When a full synthetic is used, the above periods can be doubled, but the oil change period must not exceed 240 days and the filter must be replaced at least every 7500 miles.

Some feel that there is something to be gained by the use of oil additives or oil produced for diesel engines. I do not use additives and I do not recommend their use. Today's road oils are well able to cope with the stresses imposed by race engines so additives are completely unnecessary. In fact some additives are reputed to cause turbo problems due to oil orifice blockages. Many manufacturer's warranties are nullified by the use of additives. Diesel engine oil is formulated to combat the combustion by-products of diesel fuel. Most oil companies have diesel oil with a petrol engine SH rating, but these oils do not provide the protection of high performance oils which usually far exceed the minimum requirements for an SH classification.

Some enthusiasts also wonder if the use of racing oils would afford some additional engine protection benefits. The answer is no and yes. No, oils like Castrol R30 and R40 (castor bean vegetable oil) and BP Corse 30, 40 or 50 (mineral oil) should not be used as they do not contain additives necessary to combat sludge build-up and resist oxidation. While being excellent for competition they are definitely not to be used in road engines. However, there are some so-called race oils which may be suitable. Look for the API service rating on the container. If it is rated SJ and is produced by a well-known oil company there should not be any problem. Some American oil companies call their high performance oils "race oil". This usually means that the oil contains more detergent and more zinc anti-wear additives than the company's more humble standard road oils.

Another question which I am frequently asked is "Is there a difference between the cheapest SJ oil at a discount parts shop and the most expensive SJ oil?". Perhaps the most expensive oil may be better but a high price is no guarantee of quality. Obviously there is a cost difference between a very good oil which far exceeds the SJ tests and one that just passes. Better additives and a larger total volume of additives, plus the best high quality shear-resistant polymers add to the cost of producing a good oil. On the other hand not all costs are related to producing a high quality product. Making a small quantity of oil dramatically increases its cost per litre which is why some oils made by small companies are so expensive.

No matter how good the oil it must be maintained at the correct temperature to lubricate effectively. A good deal of engine wear takes place when engines are

Maximum engine protection is afforded by the use of the correct grade premium SJ rated engine oil and a large capacity oil filter. Change both oil and filter regularly.

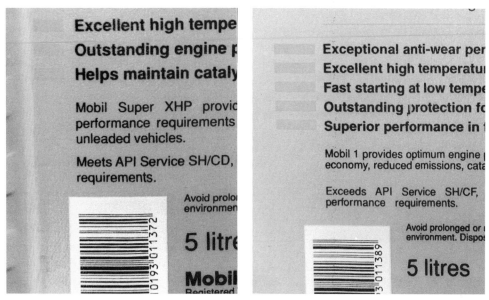

Both these oils meet API specification SH rating, but note that while one "meets" API SH the other "exceeds" API SH. This may be because one oil has a better additive package or a larger volume of additives, or more shear-resistant polymers in a higher quality base stock.

operated with cold oil. An engine should never be driven hard until the oil reaches 50°C. The ideal oil temperature is 90°C–110°C. It can go as high as 150°C but oil breakdown and excessive oxidation will take place at this temperature.

Years ago, an early modification was to fit an oil cooler but with advances in oil technology this usually is no longer necessary. During full throttle 24 hour track endurance testing, manufacturers regularly record sump oil temperatures of 150°C and as high as 180°C for the entire test period with SE and SF oil. Subsequent engine teardowns revealed that such high temperatures were not presenting any problems. This is not to say that such high oil temperatures are acceptable indefinitely but these tests do indicate that a new engine with little blow-by past the rings can be operated at 120–130°C sump oil temperature and as high as 150°C for short periods when SF oil or the latest SJ oil changed as recommended in Table 12.2 is used. I would only recommend an oil cooler if under normal driving conditions the oil temperature is regularly in excess of 120°C.

If an oil cooler is necessary there are several "musts" which should be kept in mind. Cold oil wrecks engines and deteriorates quickly so either an oil thermostat will be required or else the oil cooler should have a shutter or blind fitted in front of it which can be opened or removed when driving at constant high speed. The oil lines connecting the cooler into the system should be of at least 1/2in bore so as not to restrict flow. Additionally, the take-off sandwich block which usually fits between the oil pump and filter, or between the engine block and filter, must be of good design. Many cause severe restriction to flow by requiring the oil to travel through two 90° bends. In good designs oil passages are cast into the sandwich block, not machined, as this latter practice results in 90° bends. Oil coolers are impossible to clean out so do not purchase a used oil cooler as it could be full of dirt or bearing material. Also, if your engine or turbo suffers a bearing failure, the cooler will require replacement, otherwise this material will eventually cause another bearing failure.

The next requirement of an efficient lubrication system is adequately filtered oil. Any solid material in the oil acts as an abrasive, wearing bearings, turbo shafts and crank journals, tappets and cam lobes. Also it can quickly block turbo oilways and cause bearing failure. Most engines have an oil filter, but some are less than adequate, being only about the size of a tea cup. In almost all cases, the oil systems on modern cars are of the full-flow type. This means that all the engine oil is supposed to pass through the filter. The truth is that small filters are incapable of handling full oil flow at anything over about 2000rpm, and then only when the oil is at full operating temperature. The rest of the time the bypass opens, allowing unfiltered oil to circulate through the engine. Worse still, a lot of sediment material collects below where the bypass is located so that when it opens much of this rubbish is flushed through the engine.

The simplest way around the problem, if there is sufficient clearance, is to fit a large filter preferably 5in long by 3¹/₂in diameter. Do carefully check that the gasket size and depth is correct to effect a good seal. If such a larger filter cannot physically be accommodated on the engine it should be possible to find room to mount a remote filter somewhere under the bonnet (hood). Adapters are available that can be installed in place of the stock filter which will route oil lines to the new remote filter. As with oil coolers, these lines should be ¹/₂in minimum bore, and keep away from 90° fittings or adapter blocks with 90° passages.

Just how often the filter should be changed will depend on its size and on driving conditions/style. Any filter smaller than 5in by 3¹/₄in should be replaced at least every

Unless the oil filter is of sufficient size, the bypass will be open when the oil is cold or the engine is operating at higher rpm. Unfiltered oil is allowed through to the bearings, causing premature wear and possibly failure.

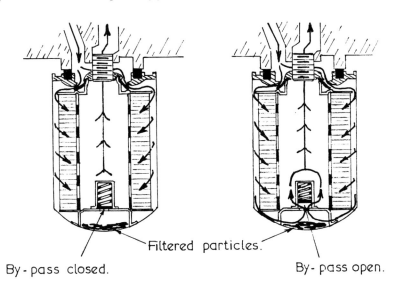

Filtered particles.

By-pass closed.   By-pass open.

time the oil is changed. If it is of a good size it should be replaced at least every second oil change or 6000 miles, whichever comes first. In the case of turbo engines and those regularly driven above 80mph, the filter should be replaced at every oil change.

For engines tuned for performance and economy the standard oil pump will usually suffice, providing gear clearances etc. are within the manufacturer's specifications. Oil pumps do wear out so do not assume that the pump is in good condition because it looks to be all right. Many pumps are none too efficient at idle so do check clearances to ensure good oil flow through the engine at lower rpm. This is most important in turbo engines. Most standard pumps can flow sufficient oil at higher rpm. Usually a relief valve is incorporated within the pump to bleed-off some flow at higher engine speeds. Hence if more flow is needed at high rpm it is a simple matter to increase flow either by fitting a stiffer relief valve spring, or inserting a spacer to increase spring tension. Instead of breaking open at, say, 30 psi the relief valve will not open until oil pressure reaches 40 psi, thus increasing oil flow through the engine. Remember that it takes power and consumes fuel pushing oil through an engine so unless the engine is known to suffer an oil flow problem be content to run with stock oil pressure and flow. Most engines have 40–50 psi oil pressure standard, few require more than 70 psi in full race trim. For road cars I would advise against anything over 60 psi, unless it is higher than this stock, as such high pressures can rupture the oil filter element when the oil is cold as well as unnecessarily consuming power. Even manufacturers have on occasions used oil pumps with excessive pressure. The Pontiac 455-SD engine, for example, has 75–80 psi; most tuners replace this with a 455-HO engine oil pump which has less flow and 60 psi.

As road tyres become more grippy and road suspension designs advance, today's cars are generating higher cornering G-forces which causes oil surge problems. Any vehicle with a wet sump (i.e. oil reservoir in the sump) will be a candidate for oil surge unless the manufacturer has taken measures with the standard oil pan to prevent surge. Oil surge can occur during violent braking, cornering and acceleration, when the oil can be forced away from the oil pickup, allowing air to be pumped to the engine and turbo bearings. If allowed to go unchecked, bearing failure will result.

Some sump pans are made with vertical baffles, but these have little effect as the oil will rise over them, particularly under hard braking and cornering. For example, at 1 G the oil will be almost vertical, pushing up the side of the sump pan and into the crankcase. A simple solution is to fit a flat, horizontal baffle, as illustrated. It should be no more than a 1/2in and preferably closer to a 1/4in above the full oil level. Ensure that the rods and crank counterweights have sufficient clearance. The baffle should cover the entire oil reservoir area of the oil pan, without any gaps around the edges or in the corners. A hole large enough for the oil pickup to fit through should be cut as close to the centre of the baffle as possible. This, however, will to some extent be determined by the location and shape of the pickup suction pipe. Around this hole, which also takes care of oil drain back into the reservoir, a 3/4in turned down lip is required to discourage oil surging up through the hole. As well, make another small hole large enough for the dipstick to fit through.

To help eliminate oil surge in some engines the oil pickup may also require modification. The actual pickup should be in the centre of the oil reservoir and exactly 1/4in off the floor of the pan, taking into consideration the thickness of the sump pan

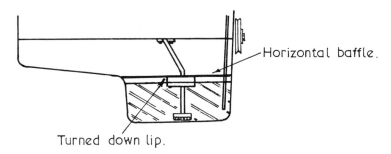

Horizontal baffle.

Turned down lip.

A horizontal baffle will prevent oil starvation during vigorous cornering, braking and acceleration manoeuvres. The pickup must be in the centre of the oil reservoir and 1/4in off the floor.

gaskets. If the pickup is closer than 1/4in, oil flow into the engine will be restricted, and if it is more than 3/8in air will be sucked in during hard driving with G forces approaching 0.8.

Some people advocate adding on an extra litre of oil to eliminate oil surge, but this is quite wrong. With an overfull sump you are sure to have the crank and rods dipping into the oil every revolution. This consumes power and aerates the oil which can also lead to bearing failure in extreme cases. As well, a lot of oil is thrown up into the cylinders. The rings have to drag it off the bore walls consuming more power and fuel. Then if the rings can't cope with the additional oil it ends up in the combustion chamber, so you will have combustion problems as oil effectively lowers the fuel octane rating. Additionally, the plugs may oil and misfire.

Remember, no matter how good your lubrication most engine wear occurs in the first few minutes after start up so keep the revs down and your foot off the power until the engine is up to operating temperature. Fuel injected engines run very smoothly, even when cold, and unfortunately this can encourage spirited driving at a time when lubrication is quite marginal. If the engine has a carburettor with a manual choke, use as little choke as possible once the vehicle is moving, otherwise a lot of raw fuel will end up down the cylinders, washing away critically needed lubricant. Carburettors with an automatic choke require careful adjustment to ensure that the minimum of choke is used and that it opens fully within about 2 to 3 minutes after starting.

Chapter 13

Cooling

The water, or more correctly called liquid cooling system, is very simple; a radiator, a water pump and a couple of hoses along with a thermostat comprise the system's components. However, the efficiency of the cooling system is dependent on much more than these basic bits. The major deterrent to effective engine cooling is poor heat transfer from the combustion chamber and cylinder due to deposits or air in the cooling system.

Metallic oxides twelve thousandths of an inch thick formed in the water passages will cut heat transfer by up to 40%. In order to maintain optimum heat transfer, the cooling system must contain an inhibitor that will stop corrosion of the water jacket surfaces and the radiator cooling tubes. If the engine has been run for any time without an inhibitor, the cooling system may require chemical cleaning and a high pressure flush to remove deposits.

There are two basic families of inhibitors; chromates and non-chromates. Sodium chromate and potassium dichromate are two of the best and most commonly used water-cooling system inhibitors. Both are highly toxic so handle them with care. Non-chromate inhibitors (borates, nitrates, nitrites) provide anti-corrosion protection in either straight water or water/anti-freeze mixtures. Chromates must not be used in a system containing anti-freeze. Mixed in the correct proportions inhibitors will protect the system for up to one year.

When freeze protection is required, a permanent type anti-freeze must be used. Ethylene glycol is preferred as methyl alcohol-based anti-freeze has a very low boiling point, and it has an adverse effect on radiator hoses and the water pump seals. A 10% glycol/90% water mixture gives freeze protection down to –3°C (27°F), a 25% concentration down to –12°C (10°F), and a 50% glycol mix down to –34°C (–29°F). Cooling solutions composed of more than two-thirds ethylene glycol should not be used as heat transfer is adversely affected. When ethylene glycol anti-freeze is used in concentrations above 30%, additional inhibitor protection against corrosion is not required. To maintain the correct level of corrosion resistance the cooling solution should be replaced annually.

In colder climates an anti-freeze must be added to the coolant to avoid ruptured radiators and cracked heads and blocks. Concentrations of above 30% anti-freeze also provide cooling system corrosion protection. When anti-freeze isn't used, or if the concentration is lower than 30%, an inhibitor must be added to the coolant to prevent corrosion.

Anti-freeze containing cooling system sealer additives should not be used, as the sealer may plug the radiator core tubes and possibly even narrow coolant passages in the engine. Stop leak or sealer of any description is not to be recommended, except in an emergency to get you home. Then, as soon as possible, have it cleaned out by a cooling system specialist with a high pressure air and water flusher.

Petroleum-derived products such as soluble oil, often used as a water pump lubricant and corrosion inhibitor, must never be used. A 2% concentration of soluble oil can raise the cylinder head deck temperature by up to 10%, due to reduced heat transfer efficiency of the coolant. Present day engines already run close to detonation, so do not increase this risk by using soluble oil. One popular radiator stop leak contains a high proportion of soluble oil, which is an added reason for staying clear of radiator sealers. Soluble oil turns water milky when added.

The presence of air bubbles in the coolant reduces the heat transfer capacity of the coolant by acting as an insulator. Water pump pumping efficiency is also reduced. Air can be sucked into the cooling system through a leaking hose and gas bubbles can form due to localised boiling around the combustion chamber. In the first case, air can be kept out of the cooling system by ensuring that there are no air or water leaks, and by keeping the coolant at the proper level. When fitted for the first time, new radiator hoses seldom leak at the connections. However, with subsequent re-use there is often some weepage, with the possibility of water loss or air being introduced into the system. To prevent this, thoroughly dry the hoses and clean the internal connecting surface of scale or corrosion particles. Then coat the connecting surface with Permatex No. 3 sealer and leave to dry a little for 15 minutes. In the meantime carefully scrape all scale from off the water pump, thermostat and radiator tank hose connection areas. This done, the hoses can be fitted and the clamps tensioned.

Remember that whenever the cooling system is disturbed it must be carefully bled to ensure that there are no pockets of air trapped in the cylinder head and block, or in the car's interior heater. Not all cars have a clearly visible bleed nipple. Some have a nipple or nipples tucked away out of sight; others, such as the Family II Opel, are bled of air by removing the coolant temperature gauge sender unit. Also, some engines will self bleed if the cooling system is slowly refilled, so these don't have a bleed nipple either.

After bleeding do not assume there are no air pockets remaining; there probably will be, so take the car for a run for at least 15 minutes with the heater full on. The combination of water surging through the coolant passages and the vibration should ensure that most air is purged from the system. After this, rebleed the system, and after the engine has been allowed to cool check the coolant level and top up if necessary.

Gas bubbles or steam pockets are prevented by pressurising the system to the degree necessary to prevent the coolant boiling. Many wonder why it is necessary to pressurise the cooling system at all as the boiling point of water, at sea level, is 100°C and most cars operate at about 88–95°C. Firstly, the system is pressurised to prevent boiling after the engine is switched off. Once the coolant stops circulating its temperature climbs rapidly to something like 110°C, way past the boiling point of water at normal sea level air pressure of 14.7 psi. If the water boiled each time the engine of every car was stopped we would all be driven crazy by the noise, and cars

The cooling system must be thoroughly bled of all trapped air to avoid overheating around the combustion chambers. The system may incorporate one or more bleed nipples, or, as in the case of this engine, air may be bled by removing the temperature sender unit.

without a coolant overflow/recovery system would suffer considerable coolant loss.

Secondly, regardless of what the temperature gauge is reading, the coolant temperature is very high in the water passage around the combustion chamber and in particular close to the exhaust valve. The temperature gauge is only giving a reading of the circulating water temperature, which is an average reading. The spot temperature around the exhaust valve seat is well above the boiling point of water, so to prevent this water from boiling and forming a steam pocket, the cooling system has to be pressurised. If the coolant were allowed to boil here, no coolant would contact the combustion chamber and carry heat away. Localised heating would occur, creating thermal stress points that would lead to cracking of the metal. Worse still, the overheated combustion chamber could induce detonation and wreck the pistons. By pressurising the system to 15 psi (105 kPa) the boiling point is raised to approximately 122°C at sea level. Normally, the coolant around the combustion chamber should not reach this temperature, but this allows a margin of safety to permit operation at altitudes above sea level, where the boiling point is reduced. Obviously to maintain the cooling system at the required pressure it will be necessary regularly to inspect the radiator pressure cap for deterioration of the seal and also check the "blow-off" pressure.

As the actual heat exchange between the cooling medium and the air takes place at the radiator, it is important that it is free of bugs or other debris that would restrict air flow, and hence reduce cooling efficiency.

Another deterrent to good air flow through the radiator is a flow path blocked by such things as the licence plate and auxiliary lights. A number of modern cars have only a relatively small under-bumper air inlet so do not restrict air flow to the radiator by partially blocking that air inlet with a pair of fog lights. The radiating efficiency will be maintained if the radiator is regularly re-painted with matt black paint. This will serve to increase the life of the core as well, by reducing external corrosion.

A high temperature thermostat which maintains coolant temperature at 88–95°C is usually fitted to production cars. Such a thermostat is fine if you want good heater efficiency in winter, but a thermostat rated at about 74–82°C (165–180°F) will at times improve power output. This is best determined on the dyno, as we run into a conflict here. One theory says that, within reason, lower coolant temperature means a lower inlet port temperature, hence the inlet charge is cooler and more dense so more air/fuel mixture crams into the cylinder during the inlet cycle to produce more power. The lower charge temperature will also permit a little more compression and/or spark advance before running into detonation. The other theory says that high coolant temperature in the range of 95–100°C (203–212°F) is the way to go, as lowering the coolant temperature "drains off" heat energy to the cooling system when we should be using that energy to force the pistons down to produce more power. What I am finding is that there is a degree of truth in both camps. Many engines do produce best power in full throttle high load situations with lower coolant temperatures around 75°C (167°F). However, there is usually a trade-off under part throttle/light load as when cruising. Here, throttle response is less crisp and there is a slight increase in fuel consumption, and I suspect also in exhaust emissions.

Actually it is becoming more difficult to consistently reduce the coolant temperature by simply fitting a cooler thermostat. This is because the manufacturer often fits a radiator just large enough to maintain the coolant at 95°C (203°F) in summer, and as car bonnet lines become lower the radiator air intake opening is becoming smaller. Fitting a larger radiator with more cooling tubes may provide a solution. However, improving air flow through the standard radiator may also solve the problem. Ideally, electric cooling fans should be mounted behind the radiator to avoid blocking air flow into the radiator core. Every effort must be made to ensure that all the air entering the radiator air intake opening actually passes through the radiator. We don't want any air bypassing through openings behind the headlights, the horns or at the sides and top and bottom of the radiator. Any openings can be blocked off, but I often find it more effective to fabricate a duct with a rubber seal which mounts up hard against the edges of the radiator. Use very light metal or plastic and mount the duct such that in a minor shunt it crumples, rather than wrecking the radiator.

Remember that we must not only consider air flow *into* the radiator. There is also the matter of *exhausting* the cooling air as any pressure in the engine bay will restrict air flow through the radiator. Reducing air flow under the front of the car with a 2–3in deep air dam or bib will help create a low pressure zone for the radiator to exhaust reasonably effectively. In this regard bonnet air scoops can be a double-edged sword. While directing a flow of cool air to an air filter or over the inlet manifold or turbocharger, if they are too large or incorrectly positioned they can increase engine bay air pressure close to the radiator.

When replacing a thermostat be sure to use the correct type. Many modern engines use a dual function bypass design thermostat which, when open to allow coolant flow through the radiator, also features a valve which closes the engine bypass port. If an ordinary thermostat is fitted, this port is left open allowing a large volume of extremely hot coolant to circulate in a closed loop within the engine, bypassing the radiator. This will cause hot spots near combustion chambers, internal overheating and

This plastic duct ensures that all air entering the air intake actually passes through the radiator. Ensuring that no cooling air bypasses the radiator improves radiator efficiency.

An air dam 2in or 3in deep under the car helps create a low pressure area which encourages hot air to exhaust from the engine bay and improves air flow through the radiator.

The thermostat on the right is a bypass type. As this type opens, the "hat" closes the engine bypass port ensuring that all coolant actually passes through the radiator. Never replace a bypass thermostat with an ordinary thermostat.

possible damage from detonation within the combustion chamber.

Never run an engine without a thermostat. The engine will take too long to warm up and will probably never reach normal operating temperature. This results in greatly accelerated engine wear and oil dilution as well as reduced power at lighter engine load. At heavy engine loads, as at high speed or when accelerating rapidly, power will also be down because of excessive heat around the combustion chambers and at the top of the cylinders giving rise to detonation. Even many race engine builders do not understand that, regardless of the radiator cap pressure, a water pump spinning in its maximum efficiency range of 4000–6000rpm produces a pressure head of around 30–40 psi in the block and head when a restriction such as a thermostat is placed in the cylinder head water outlet. This pressure packs coolant in tight around the top of the cylinders and around the combustion chambers to carry away combustion heat. Without a thermostat restricting water flow out of the head, water pressure within the water jacket falls, allowing the formation of numerous air pockets. The end result is overheated combustion chambers and detonation – and reduced power.

The cooling fan consumes a good deal of power which can be used beneficially to reduce fuel consumption and improve performance. At 2500rpm a big fan, even a flex blade or silicone slip clutch type, can drain up to 10hp. Unless the engine is working under a heavy load, a road speed of about 30mph will provide sufficient moving air to cool the engine without the aid of a fan. Naturally if you engage in peak hour city driving, a cooling fan will be required. Preferably, in the interests of power and economy, an electric fan should be fitted. Alternatively, if the car is equipped with an air conditioner it may already have a small auxiliary fan fitted which is large enough to cool the engine in traffic. Usually these fans are preset to switch on when the coolant reaches 100°C, but if the thermostatically-controlled switch is bypassed by a dash-mounted toggle switch, the fan can be manually activated at any time. I've used this system on my cars for years without any problems. At times in very heavy traffic in hot weather I've had to switch off the air conditioner for short periods otherwise the engine would overheat. This could be rectified by fitting another small electric fan, but I never seem to get around to doing it.

If you wish to retain a standard slip clutch-type fan, in spite of the power which it consumes and the noise which it makes, do ensure that it is working correctly. This type of fan will not function correctly for ever; the clutch unit and bearings wear, allowing the fan to lock up at higher rpm when it should be slipping to reduce power loss. Usually, if this type of fan is still roaring at 2500rpm and higher, the clutch assembly is locked up due to an internal failure. This is not a positive test, but it usually indicates that further investigation should be made, so consult the workshop manual.

One problem which I see from time to time is that of head gaskets with enlarged water passages. I've seen gaskets with larger holes punched into them by tuners who should know better and I've also seen high performance and race head gaskets which have been manufactured with water passages much larger than stock. Apparently these people reasoned that as there is, say, a $1/2$in coolant hole in the block and a corresponding $1/2$in hole in the head then you must get better water flow, and hence better cooling, by enlarging the coolant passage in the head gasket to $1/2$in also. This is totally wrong reasoning; with the exception of the coolant holes at the extreme rear of the engine, all of the holes in the block deck and the head are made large to make it easier to get the core sand out at the end of the casting process. To vent air which would

A big clutch type fan can consume up to 10hp and reduce fuel economy. Such a fan is best replaced by one or two electric fans, preferably located behind the radiator. Fans located in front of the radiator, like this, disrupt air flow through the radiator and reduce its efficiency.

otherwise be trapped in the block small vent holes, usually 0.060 to 0.125in diameter, are punched in the head gasket to correspond with these large core holes. Note that these small holes are primarily intended to vent air trapped in the top of the block; they are not coolant flow holes, although naturally there is some coolant flow through them.

Enlarging these head gasket vent holes just upsets the flow path of coolant   205

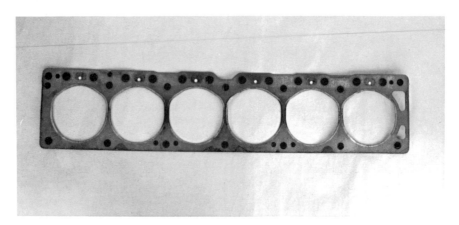

The six small white holes in this head gasket are vent holes. Opening them out to the size of the corresponding large holes in the head and block upsets coolant flow and reduces cooling efficiency.

through the engine with the result that the front cylinders run too cool and the rear cylinders run too hot, with the risk of detonation. The flow path of water through the engine is simple enough to follow. Coolant from the radiator is fed to the water pump and is forced into the front of the cylinder block. Then the coolant flows toward the rear of the block, picking up heat as it goes. When it reaches the rear of the block, the water moves up into the head through the large water passages interconnecting the block and head. From here it flows forward past the combustion chambers and ports, out through the thermostat and into the top of the radiator. From this description you will understand that any coolant passages at the front of the block just upset the flow path by allowing water to flow up into the head before it reaches the rear of the block. With reduced flow past the rear cylinders and combustion chambers these run too hot; the compression ratio and spark timing have to be cut back to avoid detonation. Conversely, the front cylinders are overcooled and lose power. Hence it should be obvious that we want only minimal water flow from the front of the block into the head if we are aiming for performance and economy.

Unfortunately some car manufacturers don't care too much about the coolant flow path with the result that their head gaskets are all stamped with large vent holes right from the front to the rear. There are two ways around this problem; the solution which I prefer is to tap the large core holes in the block, except at the rear, and screw in aluminium pipe plugs into which I have drilled a 2mm vent hole. The other solution is quite effective, in fact it can be used in conjunction with the first solution, but can only be applied to cars with a continuous flow heater system i.e. a heater system which has water flowing through it even when the heater is turned off. In this case the rear of the cylinder head is tapped to accept a heater hose fitting. By connecting the heater inlet to this fitting a constant flow of coolant passes over the rear combustion chambers, bringing their temperature closer to those at the front of the engine.

To some people all of this concern over coolant flow may appear to be a lot of effort, but if you are really serious about economy and power you have to be able to equalise, as much as practicable, combustion chamber temperatures so as to run maximum compression ratio and spark advance.

Chapter 14

Pollution Control
and the Law

Many enthusiasts feel that the motor car has been singled out, perhaps unjustly, as a major contributor to the pollution problem of our industrialised world. Because this is perceived to be discriminatory, car enthusiasts and a number of motoring journalists have adopted an anti-establishment attitude toward pollution laws. They figure that anything which the government has to force upon us is no good, and as a consequence all pollution controls tend to be viewed in the same light. To back up their conviction they point to the nasty engines which the people of the USA had to put up with during the 1970s. Emissions engines have come a long way since then so it is foolish to develop opinions based on outmoded data. Good performance and economy can be realised working within the constraints imposed by pollution laws. In some localities these laws are rigidly enforced; in other places there is virtually no enforcement. Whatever the situation locally, enthusiasts have an obligation to modify their vehicles with due regard to the spirit of the law so as to not unnecessarily foul our environment.

The major pollutants are: carbon monoxide (CO), hydrocarbons (HC), nitrogen oxides (NOx), ozone (O_3), sulphur dioxide (SO_2), lead and particulates. Petrol fueled engines emit CO, HC and NOx primarily, plus some particulate matter, and lead if leaded fuel is used. Diesels produce CO and HC at lower levels, but emit much more particulate matter and NOx. In certain sizes particulates, tiny solid particles of soot, can lodge in the lungs and cause long-term damage. They also discolour the sky. Coal-fired furnaces are primarily responsible for SO_2 emissions, which appear to cause acid rain, plus the release of NOx.

Hydrocarbons are any of a number of compounds containing hydrogen and carbon, usually derived from petroleum. Just the vapours released when tanks are being refilled with petrol releases a large amount of HC into the atmosphere. Carbon monoxide is a poisonous gas that is both odourless and colourless. This is the gas which kills if the engine is run for a period in a closed up garage so obviously we don't want much of it in the air we breathe. The nitrogen oxides are composed of 207 about 10% nitrogen dioxide (NO_2) and the rest is nitric oxide (NO). NO_2 is a toxic gas with a pungent smell and brown colour that is a by-product of any combustion process. In the air it may combine with hydroxyl (OH) to produce nitric acid (HNO_3). Obviously in either form it is not good for us or the environment. Nitric oxide on the other hand is non-toxic, colourless and odourless. However, it too has an undesirable side. The initial reaction in the atmosphere is for NO to reduce ozone (O_3) into oxygen (O_2) and the spare O atom combines with the NO to form NO_2, nitrogen dioxide. The reaction continues beyond this under the influence of sunlight which breaks the NO_2 down into NO and O. The O combines with oxygen in the atmosphere to make more ozone. Ozone is the stuff which makes your lungs hurt on smoggy days and it kills crops. It also wrecks the exterior of cars, in particular chrome and rubber.

To reduce these pollutants governments around the world have enacted, or are in the process of enacting, clean air regulations which require vehicle emissions to be below a certain maximum level. The standard varies from country to country and even from state to state according to the perceived degree of the problem. In some cities in California, for example, the smog problem is very serious. Accordingly, that state has much tougher emissions laws than the rest of the USA, and the laws are more rigidly enforced.

The actual test procedures vary in different countries and as it is the manufacturer that certifies new models before they are released onto the market I won't describe in detail exactly what is involved in obtaining certification. The basic test takes place with the vehicle on a chassis dyno which is loaded to a prescribed schedule to simulate certain city driving conditions. The test usually involves one cold start and a hot start, plus a number of idle, acceleration, cruise and deceleration phases over a 20 to 30 minute drive. The test fuel type is specified for uniformity.

During the dyno "drive" the exhaust gas is mixed with atmospheric air and routed through a constant volume pump which mixes and measures the flow. A specified proportion of the mixture is collected in a bag and after the test the contents are analysed for HC, CO and NOx concentrations. To avoid errors, air in the test cell is constantly sampled in a "background" bag so that pollutants in the atmospheric air can be ascertained and subtracted from the tailpipe sample.

The test to which enthusiasts' cars may be subjected is much simpler. It is often referred to as a "sniff" test. In the few places where this test is carried out to determine the legality or otherwise of a car, it may be performed at random by the roadside or at specified intervals of 1 or 2 years as part of the vehicle licence registration inspection. For the sniffer test a probe is placed in the tailpipe and a CO and HC reading is taken with the engine idling. The test instrument is of the non-dispersive infra red type which considering its relative low cost gives fairly accurate readings. Note that with this type of testing NOx levels are not checked, so it is not too difficult to get a modified engine to pass if it is in good mechanical condition and correctly tuned.

A much more difficult inspection for enthusiasts is the "visual" which in some places complements the sniff test. The problem for a number of enthusiasts is that their cars can have the appearance of being illegal. If the vehicle looks like a street racer with excessively wide wheels, gaudy decorations and loud exhaust, it will be given "special" treatment come inspection time. Engine/chassis numbers will be checked and charts consulted to find what size engine should be fitted; what number of carby venturis there should be; what transmission should be fitted etc. In addition, a careful

When a vehicle fails the sniff test or if a fail is probable, there are a number of steps which can be taken to get through. Obviously a full tune-up is a necessity. Fit new spark plugs at least one grade hotter than standard and open the gap up to the manufacturer's specifications. Remove these "test" plugs as soon as the inspection is over, and don't be tempted to do any hard driving either to or from the test station. Before the plugs are packed away, oil their threads. If the air filter element is dirty now is the time to replace it. Check the carburettor float level and ensure that the needle and seat is not weeping. Remember that it only takes a little excess fuel to push the HC and CO readings way up. To get extra heat into the exhaust for an afterburn of HC and CO, insert a ball bearing into the distributor vacuum hose. This will take out anything from 10° to 20° advance at idle so the engine idle speed will drop right back. Turn the idle speed screw in a half turn or more to bring the idle speed up around 850 to 950rpm. Now lean the mixture by adjusting the mixture screws about a quarter turn. Ensure that the choke is opening right off. Getting the coolant temperature up will improve fuel vaporisation and distribution at idle as well as raising the exhaust temperature, so place the piece of cardboard in front of the radiator which is large enough to bring the coolant up around 95 to 100°C. Table 14.3 sets out a few things to check for according to the HC and CO test readings.

Table 14.3   Check list for failed sniff test

Meter Reading	Check for
High HC and high CO	Rich fuel/air mixture, incorrect float setting or leaky needle valve, leaky power valve or gasket, restricted PCV valve, choke not fully off.
High HC and low CO	Air leak in induction system, cracked vacuum hoses, worn throttle spindles, broken manifold gasket or carb base gasket.
High HC and normal CO	Low compression because of worn rings or valves, fouled spark plugs, pitted points, faulty condenser, cracked distributor cap, advanced timing or sometimes excessively retarded timing.

Correctly-tuned engines which have been modified with economy in mind as well as performance should not normally have too much difficulty passing either the idle or high speed (2500rpm) sniff test in ordinary tune. If you have to resort to the standard tricks mentioned above, the engine probably has some of the problems listed in Table 14.3. Naturally if the engine has been radically modified, even more radical tricks may be called for. Inline 6 cylinder engines can easily have more heat put into both the inlet and exhaust system by switching the EFE system vacuum lines at the thermo-vacuum valve. The switch must be made just prior to testing, when the engine is still cold, otherwise the actuator will not lock into the heat-on position. With more heat in the inlet system, fuel vaporisation and cylinder to cylinder distribution is better, thus reducing both HC and CO readings. The EFE butterfly blocking off one manifold outlet increases exhaust flow resistance, decreases exhaust heat loss and improves exhaust afterburn to further reduce emission levels.

Another approach is to run a special "test" fuel. Alcohol, either ethanol or methanol, burns significantly lower emissions of both HC and CO than petrol. The NOx levels are higher but at present only the manufacturers are subjected to NOx   221 testing. By blending 15 to 25% alcohol into your petrol, the tailpipe readings will go down because the alcohol will lean out the mixture as well as burn cleaner. When purchasing the alcohol, buy a sealed 5 gallon drum from a distributor who has a high turnover of racing fuel. This should ensure that it hasn't absorbed any moisture from the atmosphere. Any water contamination makes it very difficult to blend. If you are going to use a 20/80 mix, pour 1 gallon of alcohol into a 5 gallon drum containing 4 gallons of petrol and give it a good shake. Pour a sample into a clear glass jar and check for separation or layering after a couple of hours. If it's okay, drain your fuel tank and refill with the blend. Some carb adjustment may be necessary to bring the idle speed to that required. When there is a problem with fuel separation due to water in the alcohol, 3 to 4% acetone added will assist in blending. Note that alcohol is a very effective paint stripper so if any spillage occurs; wash it off, don't wipe, immediately.

Some people no doubt feel that performance tuning and/or the modification of emissions equipment is not compatible with our need for clean air. However, a closer look will show that this is generally not the case. There are many, many cars running on our roads today which if sniff tested would fail simply because of poor maintenance. Just one misfiring plug or a bad ignition lead will push up HC emissions 500%, yet how many people do you know who drive cars with a misfire. Enthusiasts tune their cars often and replace parts as required so they do not contribute to pollution in this way. The same principle applies with regard to engine wear. Worn rings and valves significantly increase HC concentrations, but as enthusiasts are seeking performance they keep the engines in their cars "freshened up". Irregular oil change periods allow the oil to breakdown, increasing blow-by. This too raises tailpipe emissions, but few enthusiasts are guilty because they care about engines and know how important is new oil.

It may be true that the ordinary motorist has left the pollution gear on his car. However, again due to lack of maintenance and/or care, a lot of it isn't working anyway and to compound the problem the automatic choke is probably sticking half on. No doubt you have followed many cars in the city through a number of sets of lights, belching black smoke because the choke is still on. All that smoke shows that the HC and CO is very high.

When an engine is modified, a number of changes actually lower, rather than increase emissions. Increasing the compression ratio, for example, pushes the NOx levels up. However, if the increase has been achieved by milling the block to reduce the piston deck clearance, HC concentrations will fall because there is less area between the piston and head squish areas for the fuel to hide and escape combustion. Fitting a camshaft with more duration and overlap lowers NOx emissions in two ways. First, there is less trapped inlet charge at lower rpm so there is less compression which in turn keeps peak combustion pressures lower. Secondly, a modified cam will allow more exhaust reversion back into the cylinder. This dilutes the inlet charge, slows combustion and reduces peak pressures. In effect it does the same thing as EGR. Additionally, because of the increased overlap, some fuel/air mixture will pass from the inlet tract straight into the exhaust, giving an afterburn effect that lowers both HC and CO levels. Naturally both of these outcomes are more pronounced when the standard cast iron exhaust manifold is retained, as tubular headers stop a lot of reversion and they permit the gases to flow quickly from the hottest area so afterburn is significantly decreased.

To give you some idea of just how clean modified engines can be without trick tuning we will look at a couple of examples. The first is a Corvette 350 with TPI injection. It was being tuned for good power and good driveability, but economy and expense was of little concern to the owner. Basically, the modifications are as follows: Phase III cam and budget roller tip rockers, Brodix aluminium heads left unported, 9.5:1 compression ratio, 400 Chev crank to raise capacity to 383cu in, enlarged throttle body and revised manifold runners, modified electronics for fuel injection and ignition, stock exhaust manifolds with modified CAT and big bore free flow exhausts and mufflers. Table 14.4 sets out the test results. Clearly the car passed easily, in fact if a "visual" had not been necessary the CAT could have been left off and it would still have got through.

Table 14.4   Tailpipe emissions for a modified Corvette

		Standard requirement	Modified
Idle test	HC	150ppm	51ppm
	CO	1.2%	0.02%
High test	HC	220ppm	34ppm
(2500rpm)	CO	1.2%	0.01%

At the other end of the spectrum is the 4.1 litre Buick developed for good power, but without any regard for the law or expense. In its tested form the engine ultimately produced almost 350hp, so it was far from mildly tuned. However, it produced the tailpipe readings shown in Table 14.5. The engine was extensively modified: Dyer Roots type supercharger with 7 psi boost, Phase III cam, ported heads, 8.5:1 compression ratio, tubular headers and twin 2$1/2$in exhaust without CAT converter, Holley 600 cfm four barrel carb. The PCV system and charcoal canister were the only emissions equipment retained. In spite of all of these modifications the engine easily passed the sniff test. Of course a "visual" would soon put an end to this enthusiast's disregard for the law.

Table 14.5   Tailpipe emissions for a supercharged Buick

		Standard requirement	Modified
Idle test	HC	150ppm	63ppm
	CO	1.2%	0.1%
High test	HC	220ppm	29ppm
(2500rpm)	CO	1.2%	0.07%

These examples are cited not to encourage disdain for the law, but to illustrate that pollution control and performance can co-exist. We all have to breathe the air on this planet so we must concern ourselves with the pollution problem and take steps so as not to contribute to it. By taking a conservative approach with our modifications and by keeping our vehicles properly tuned, good performance and economy, along with reduced emissions, can be realised.

Chapter 15

Dyno Tuning

$\mathbf{W}$e can very easily expend a good deal of time and money in search of power and economy, and then miss out on attaining this objective simply because we have overlooked a comprehensive dyno tuning session. There is no way an engine can deliver power and economy tuned by ear, particularly with all of the engine management controls and emissions gear common to today's engines. For sure dyno tuning isn't the "be all and end all" of engine tuning, for a number of reasons. You can't really check how crisply an engine will accelerate or what its throttle response will be like, for example, due to the nature of the load applied to the engine. Also, the usefulness of dyno tuning is largely determined by the integrity and experience of the dyno operator. In all areas of life there are "sharp" and/or inexperienced operators looking for easy money; the dyno tune business is no exception. Many dyno operators know very little about power tuning and nothing about economy tuning. In my experience they are frequently just everyday motor mechanics doing tune-ups; they replace spark plugs and ignition points, set the timing and valve clearances and then produce a dyno readout to prove to the customer that the tune-up was successful. The naive customer pays his money and drives off happy in the knowledge that his car is running at peak efficiency; it must be, he now has a piece of paper which shows the car to be 6hp, or whatever, more powerful than when he drove it into the workshop. Used in this manner a dyno is just a propaganda tool, contrived to provide the unwary motorist with tangible proof, in the form of a dyno readout, that the tune-up was a success, so the mechanic is obviously a good fellow who knows his stuff.

Due to ignorance many motorists are "caught" in this manner. Obviously to avoid the same pitfall you have to be able to identify the real operator from the fellow faking it. The knowledge that you have gleaned from reading this and other books should assist you to be able to have an in depth discussion with dyno operators to see who knows what they are talking about. Have a look at the kind of cars they have in the workshop, see who their customers are etc. Only after doing some investigating can you be sure that a dyno session will be really worthwhile.

224

There are two basic types of dynamometers, the engine dynamometer and the rolling road or chassis dynamometer. The rolling road is usually employed for tuning and minor developmental work on road cars. It is very convenient as you just drive the car on to a set of rollers and run the engine to determine the power and torque output. The engine dyno is used for major or very sensitive engine development. You can keep track of many things apart from horsepower and torque outputs; inlet air flow, fuel flow and exhaust gas temperature of each cylinder, for example. The chassis dyno is not so sensitive, but even so it is a useful tuning tool when in the hands of an experienced operator. You can find, for example, that carburation changes give a little more power whereas comparison of the fuel flow figures could indicate that there has been a disproportionate increase in fuel consumption which may not be acceptable. An increase in turbo boost may seem like a good idea but on the dyno there may not be very much power increase indicating restrictive manifolds or cylinder head. The power may suddenly fall off at higher rpm and at the same point fuel flow reads the same as it did 500rpm lower in the range. This could indicate the drop off was due to a lean-out. Perhaps the injectors, the fuel pump or the fuel filters have reached their flow limit. On the other hand there could be a "bug" in the electronics which is limiting fuel flow.

There are several types of dynos in use and while they will do a good job in helping a dependable dyno operator to set up an engine properly, do not take a lot of notice of the power figures. Even among so-called "calibrated" dynos variations of up to 10% from one dyno to another are not uncommon. The reason for this can be that various dyno manufacturers calibrate their units a little differently. Also, many tuning companies do not have the money to outlay on the latest, most sophisticated dynos. Instead, they use older units, or perhaps new less sophisticated types. This in itself is not such a bad thing providing the operator knows his business and the dyno will give consistent figures from day to day. The main thing is not to try to compare the power figures from one dyno to another; do your tuning on the same dyno. Otherwise you may try out some new modification and find that it gives you 10hp more, when in fact you had lost power. It was simply that this dyno was reading higher than the one on which the engine was first tested. Table 15.1 shows the result of tests on two dynos with a 350 Chev race engine.

When an engine is run on the dyno, a record is made of its output each 250 or

Table 15.1   Dyno comparison of 350 Chev

rpm	Dyno A		Dyno B	
	hp	Torque	hp	Torque
5500	472	451	478	456
6000	505	442	533	466
6500	568	459	561	453
7000	601	451	582	437
7250	606	439	583	422
7500	612	428	585	410
7750	622	422	551	374

Note: this engine was not altered in any way between tests. The hp and torque figures have been corrected to compensate for changes in air density.

500rpm over its operating range. These output figures are then converted to tell us what the hp and torque are, as only newer dynos are interfaced with a computer to give a direct reading. At the time these calculations are being made a "correction factor" is also introduced, to keep the output figures standard. If this was not done we would have no way of accurately comparing the engine's power level on another occasion when the atmospheric conditions are likely to be quite different. Throughout the test session a check is made of the barometer reading and at frequent intervals wet and dry bulb air temperature readings are taken, as these factors influence the air density. Obviously, the cooler the air and the higher the air pressure, the more oxygen and fuel you can cram into the engine, which in turn produces more power. Conversely, if the temperature is high and the barometric pressure low, the power will fall. To compensate for this factor during the dyno session, and to give a true comparison with earlier and also possibly subsequent tests, a correction factor is added to the conversion formula.

The conversion formula to calculate the torque on one particular type of dyno is this:

$$\text{Torque} = \frac{\text{W x 26.26 x C/F}}{2}$$

where W = readout indicated by dyno needle

C/F = correction factor.

For example, if the dyno indicated the twisting force (W) to be 7.31, and the barometric pressure was 30.06ins, with a wet and dry bulb temperature of 48°F and 68°F respectively, the engine would be producing the following torque:

$$\text{W} = 7.31$$

C/F = 1.016 (found from tables using the atmospheric figures above)

$$\text{Torque} = \frac{7.31 \text{ x } 26.26 \text{ x } 1.016}{2}$$

$$= 97.52 \text{ ft/lbs.}$$

Torque is a measure of the twisting force at the crankshaft expressed as pounds-foot force (commonly called just foot pounds). For example, if an engine is producing torque of 100lbf ft it means that it will lift a load of 100lb with a lever 1ft long connected to the crankshaft. If the engine moves this 100lb load through one revolution, work is being done; in this example 628ft/lbs (twisting force x revolutions x lever length x π). Power is the rate at which this work is being done, hence,

$$\text{Power} = \frac{\text{work}}{\text{time}} \text{ (torque x revolutions)}$$

In the Imperial system, power is measured in pounds/feet per minute. However, since these units are very small, the unit we know as horsepower is used today. One horsepower equals 33,000lb/ft per minute. James Watt worked this out as a result of his experiment using strong dray horses. Obviously, because power is the rate at which work is done, two motors both producing 100lb/ft torque could have vastly different power outputs. For example, if one engine lifted its 100lb load twice as quickly as the other it must have double the horsepower. Engine speed is measured in revolutions per minute, so this is the time factor we use in calculating horsepower.

$$HP = \frac{\text{torque x rpm}}{5252}$$

Another unit which I regularly use is called brake mean effective pressure (BMEP). This figure gives a true indication of how effectively an engine is operating, regardless of its capacity or its operating rpm. It is, in fact, a measure of the average cylinder pressures generated during all four engine strokes, and is calculated using the formula:

$$BMEP = \frac{\text{HP x 13000}}{\text{L x rpm}} \quad \text{or} \quad \frac{\text{torque x 13000}}{\text{L x 5252}}$$

where L = engine capacity in litres

The average engine runs at a BMEP of about 140–165 psi, while a good street engine should run at 170–190 psi. By comparison the exceptional 3.2 litre M3 BMW is nudging 200 psi while providing excellent driveability.

Another measure used to analyse combustion efficiency is called brake specific fuel (BSF). This is worked out by dividing the engine's fuel flow (lbs of fuel per hour) by its horsepower output. If the engine was consuming 100lb of fuel per hour at 4500rpm and the power output at that rpm was 250hp, the BSF would be 0.400 (100 ÷ 250 = 0.400). Obviously the less fuel the engine is using for each horsepower produced, the more efficient combustion must be, because more energy is being extracted from every lb of fuel. As the numerical value of the BSF decreases, the combustion efficiency improves, up to the point where subsequent reductions in the BSF causes reductions in horsepower.

During any test session, whether it be on the dyno or out on the road, you should make only one change at a time. This is the sole way that you are going to find out to what the engine is responding. With just one variable introduced for each test it is often difficult to know just what step to take next, so you will understand that the introduction of two or three changes will make it virtually impossible to know where you are heading with your tuning. At times, tuning can be extremely frustrating, because you seem to keep going up so many dead end streets. However, if you stick with it, and go about your tuning in a systematic manner, you are sure to have the engine responding better and using less fuel than before you started. The thing you must remember is to make just one change at a time, and keep accurate notes of any changes. Do not let over-enthusiasm cause you to rush; take your time and make absolutely certain to think everything through.

227

Chapter 16

Gearing

One area where I am frequently at variance with car makers is in regard to gearing. Not so many years back when we had three- and four-speed manual and three-speed auto gearboxes, we had to put up with cars which were noisy and thirsty at freeway speeds in order to achieve sparkling acceleration through the twisty bits. Nowadays as the majority of transmissions are either four- and five-speed manual, or four-speed auto, there is no reason to sacrifice quiet, effortless cruising and good fuel economy in the quest for brisk acceleration. However, a number of manufacturers have gone too far with overdrive top gears, so much so that many cars actually attain maximum speed in the next lower gear. Worse, such a high top gear brings an increase in fuel consumption due to a lot of throttle being necessary to maintain speed over hills. Additionally, with manual transmissions driver fatigue and also gearbox and clutch wear are increased, due to all the extra gear shifting required.

At one time I owned a factory high-performance vehicle which I personally considered was badly over-geared. Cruising at 75–80mph on twisty roads the fuel consumption was around 22mpg; driven hard this dropped still further to 18mpg! Not too good considering the car's light weight and small 1.6 litre engine. The gearbox ratios were quite suitable so the manufacturer's parts lists were consulted to find an alternative suitable crown wheel and pinion option. They did not list any but I found that other types of vehicle from the same manufacturer used similar differentials with lower (numerically higher) gearing. My axle had a 3.8:1 ratio but there was also a 3.95:1 and 4.15:1 ratio in other models and a commercial vehicle was listed as having a 4.4:1 axle.

Next I did my sums to determine which ratio would be most suitable considering the type of roads on which I would spend most of my time. The engine really got going at 4000rpm and began to run out of puff at 6000. I wanted the engine well into the power band at my desired cruising speed of 75–80mph. The 4.15:1 crown wheel and pinion would have the engine spinning at about 4400–4500rpm at this speed so it was chosen. The car was transformed; hill climbing improved dramatically and fuel economy went to 28mpg. Top speed was now 112mph compared with 107mph previously. Apart from the diff the only other changes made to achieve these results were a slight richening of the carburettor accelerator pump jets and main jets. The speedo drive gears were also changed to keep it reading correctly.

Usually a change of axle ratio would not bring such a big improvement but this example does illustrate just how much performance and economy can be gained by a simple crown wheel and pinion swap. Also it is a modification which the law and other peering eyes can not detect easily. Manufacturers claim that they gear their cars to achieve the quietest possible running and best economy at freeway cruising speeds. However, many cars are seldom, if ever, driven on freeways, hence the need to take a careful look at the gearing to determine if it could be robbing you of performance and economy. In truth, many cars are geared to help the manufacturer pass emission tests and achieve high fuel economy figures while running on a wheel dyno without the effects of wind resistance etc. These "economy" figures are then used for advertising purposes and to pass government-legislated corporate fuel consumption laws. For these reasons in some lands it is illegal to change the axle ratio as the vehicle technically would no longer pass these tests. Also for some models auto transmissions only are available as manually shifted vehicles tend to pollute more in certain operating modes, so you can appreciate what the makers are up against in attempting to satisfy the various, usually conflicting, requirements imposed upon them.

At times though, a simple crown wheel and pinion change alone will not give the desired results, especially if the engine has been treated to a fairly warm cam. In this example the owner had spent one third of his new car's purchase price modifying it before he had even taken delivery. It was a performance auto only model which he had had modified by fitting a heavy duty five-speeder, a head job and cam, plus extensive suspension parts. The end result was a car which was undriveable in top gear at anything less than freeway speeds and which guzzled fuel at the rate of 17.5mpg. The top speed was only 6mph better than the standard auto transmission model because top gear was far too high.

The first task was to track down a suitable crown wheel and pinion but the car makers didn't list any options. However, another manufacturer who used this same differential assembly had two other ratios available, 3.7:1 and 4.1:1. The 4.1:1 would have been desirable in view of the 0.76 overdrive top gear in the five speed box but first gear with a 3.58 ratio would then have become useless. Reluctantly, the 3.7:1 crown wheel and pinion was fitted in place of the standard 3.15:1 set. The car was much more pleasant to drive, which was encouraging, fuel economy improved to just over 20mpg and top gear speed rose by 6mph. Encouraged by the results, the gearbox manufacturer was consulted to find if a different overdrive ratio was available. A 0.84:1 ratio gear was selected and fitted. Again the car improved in every respect. Fuel economy was now almost 22mpg, top gear speed increased by another 5mph and top gear was completely useable.

By now you are probably thinking "how do I determine if my car is overgeared?" Well, there are no written rules; often it is as much a matter of driving conditions, driving style and personal preference. Also, remember that some cars have 229

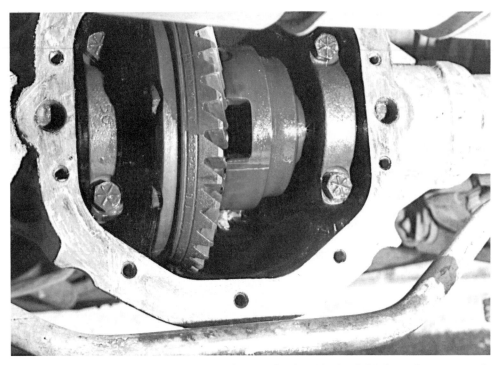

The owner of this car was smart enough to order it with the 3.36:1 performance axle and LSD instead of the standard 3.08:1 gears. Note also the large diameter rear stabiliser bar fitted to reduce body roll and balance the handling.

gearing which is just right, particularly if someone has been smart enough to order it with a performance ratio option, and some will be actually undergeared. Keep in mind too that low profile tyres change the gearing unless there has been a corresponding increase in wheel diameter to compensate. For example, a change from a 175/75 profile to a 195/60 profile will lower the gearing by about 5%, so a 3.5 axle becomes equivalent to 3.68:1.

A car which spends the major part of its time on two lane twisting roads with a speed limit of 60–70mph will naturally require lower gearing to one running on freeways without any speed restrictions. A car which is very aerodynamic can be geared much higher than a car similar in size and weight but shaped like a barge. A car with a wide power range will tolerate high gearing much better than a car with a similar engine size but having a narrower power band.

Personally I prefer gearing which allows the car to get about 500rpm into the power band at my chosen cruise speed and which attains maximum speed at peak power rpm or maybe up to 300rpm lower. Such gearing will usually yield the best fuel efficiency and reduce gear changes. For outright performance the gearing would normally be lower than this to allow the engine to run up to or within a couple of hundred rpm of the manufacturer's maximum recommended engine speed.

Table 16.1 indicates the road speed per 1000rpm which would usually give the best performance/economy compromise for a variety of engine/gearbox combinations

on good two lane unrestricted speed roads.

Table 16.1   Gearing for performance and economy

Engine capacity (litres)	Road speed mph per 1000rpm			
	4 speed (m)	5 speed (m)	6 speed (m)	4 speed (a)
1.2–1.4	15–16.5	17–18		
1.6–1.8	17–18	18–19	20–22	
1.9–2.2	18–20	19–21.5	22–24	
2.5–2.8	20–22	21–23	23–25	21.5–24
3.0–3.4	22–23	23–25.5	25–27	24.5–27
3.8–4.2	23–25	24–27	27–29	25–28
5.0–5.8	24.5–26	25–28	29–32	26–28.5

The formula used to calculate road speed in mph is as follows:

$$mph = \frac{rpm \times Td \times \pi}{GR \times 1050}$$

where Td = tyre diameter in inches

GR = overall gear ratio (gearbox ratio x axle ratio)

$\pi = 3.1416$

By transposing the formula we can find with the aid of Table 16.1 possible suitable rear axle ratios to attain a relaxed cruising speed along with peak economy and good performance.

$$GR = \frac{rpm \times Td \times \pi}{mph \times 1050}$$

where rpm = 1000

mph = speed from Table 16.1

To find the axle ratio required we must then divide GR by the gearbox gear ratio in top gear.

Fitting the correct axle ratio to increase the usefulness of top gear and improve economy also generally brings a marked improvement in acceleration. The gearbox and axle are really just torque multipliers. Hence an overall gear ratio (gearbox ratio x axle ratio) of 3:1 multiplies the engine torque by three, giving three times as much twisting force at the wheels as compared with what is available at the flywheel. Lowering the gearing to 4:1 would increase the twisting force by one third and enhance acceleration significantly. Table 16.2 reveals the effect correct gearing can have on acceleration and general performance. In this example if the original gearing had been retained, probably another 20hp would have been required to achieve the acceleration times of the car with revised gearing. A bigger cam would be necessary to pick up 20hp and as a consequence the original fuel consumption and general driveability problem referred to earlier would have been further aggravated. Selecting suitable gearing is as important as selecting any performance part or modification. The   231

Table 16.2   Effect of correct gearing on performance/economy

Engine capacity 3.0 litres
hp 175 @ 5300rpm
Torque 192 @ 3600rpm

		Performance with 3.15:1 axle and 0.76 overdrive top gear.	Performance with 3.7:1 axle and 0.84 overdrive top gear.
Maximum speed	1st	38mph @ 5800rpm	32mph @ 5800rpm
	2nd	65mph @ 5800rpm	56mph @ 5800rpm
	3rd	100mph @ 5800rpm	85mph @ 5800rpm
	4th	136mph @ 5800rpm	116mph @ 5800rpm
	5th	127mph @ 4100rpm	138mph @ 5800rpm
Acceleration	0–60	9.1 sec	8.4 sec
	0–80	14.9 sec	14.0 sec
	standing 1/4 mile	16.6 sec	15.8 sec
Fuel economy		17.5mpg	21.9mpg

wrong choice can spoil a fine car; the correct choice can transform a sluggish car into a real performer.

At times, manufacturers also get the gearbox ratios all wrong, with gaps which are unacceptably large between gears. This reduces driver pleasure and performance, and can seriously limit tuning modifications aimed at increasing engine horsepower. When BMW released the new M3 and replaced the 5-speeder with a 6-speed box I had hoped that they would have closed the gap between 2nd and 3rd gears. It is a minor thing which isn't evident most of the time, but when covering slow and twisting stuff fairly briskly it is quite a distraction. Unfortunately, instead of giving us a nice set of cogs like in the 968 Porsche they just stuck a big overdrive top gear in and retained the old 5-speed ratios (see Table 16.3).

Table 16.3   BMW M3, Porsche 968 and Ferrari F355 gearbox comparison

	BMW M3		Porsche 968		Ferrari F355	
	gear ratio	gear step	gear ratio	gear step	gear ratio	gear step
1st	4.23		3.18		3.07	
		+40.7%		+37.1%		+29.6%
2nd	2.51		2.00		2.16	
		+33.5%		+28%		+25.5%
3rd	1.67		1.44		1.61	
		+26.3%		+22.9%		+21.1%
4th	1.23		1.11		1.27	
		+18.7%		+18%		+18.9%
5th	1.00		0.91		1.03	
		+17%		+14.3%		+18.4%
6th	0.83		0.78		0.84	

Sometimes the manufacturer gets the gearbox ratios completely wrong on some models and close to what is wanted on others, so it is then a simple and inexpensive

Table 16.4   Opel/Holden/Vauxhall gearbox comparison

	4-speed		5-speed wide		5-speed semi-close	
	gear ratio	gear step	gear ratio	gear step	gear ratio	gear step
1st	3.42		3.42		3.42	
		+43%		+43%		+36.8%
2nd	1.95		1.95		2.16	
		+34.4%		+34.4%		+31.5%
3rd	1.28		1.28		1.48	
		+30.5%		+30.5%		+24.3%
4th	0.89		0.89		1.12	
				+20.2%		+20.5%
5th			0.71		0.89	

thing to obtain a desirable set of cogs from a vehicle which has been wrecked. Most people who have driven any of the front wheel drive Opel/Holden/Vauxhall cars complain of them being a slug and underpowered. However, the real problem is often the big gaps between gears combined with massive overgearing in the case of the wide ratio 5-speeder. As can be gleaned from Table 16.4, there is a semi-close 5-speed box fitted to some models which has 5 cogs spread over the same range as the old 4-speeder. The 2nd to 3rd gap is still a touch wide but otherwise this box really brings OHV front wheel drivers alive, and should be the first change made before any engine modifications are even planned. The gear step is calculated as follows:

$$\frac{\text{lower gear ratio} - \text{higher gear ratio}}{\text{lower gear ratio}} \times 100$$

Just how large a gap is tolerable between gears is dependent on many things. Engine size, power spread, vehicle weight, terrain and driver preferences all enter the equation. For example, some drivers are lazy and don't like a lot of gear changing at normal driving speeds, so they find close ratio gears a problem. Personally, I want gears which allow the engine to keep in the power band at all times and with such a close gear set I can skip gears both up and down the box when I'm not in a hurry or just feeling lazy. For me, I invariably find that if the engine has a sensible power band, then on the road I will be happy with a 6-speeder with the following gear steps going up the box: 30 to 40%, 25 to 28%, 20 to 23%, 17 to 20%, 12 to 20%. With a 5-speeder the steps would be: 35 to 40%, 25 to 28%, 22 to 25%, 19 to 21%.

Chapter 17

Suspension and Brakes

Y ou are probably questioning why a book about economy and performance has a
few pages devoted to suspension and brakes? Well, a little money spent in these
areas can contribute as much to performance in particular, and to a lesser extent to
economy, as a large amount of money expended solely on the engine. To illustrate the
point, consider the outcome of race circuit testing to determine the best
power/handling/cost compromise for a popular family sedan. Three cars were used for
the test; one was stock standard and two had a variety of engine and suspension
modifications. The standard car had a good strong 150hp 3 litre engine and safe
handling. The standard tyres were average "grocery getting" type 185/75 on 6in wide
wheels. These tyres were probably the weakest link in the package but even so the
standard car was quicker around the circuit than sporty sedans with good grippy tyres
and 125hp engines and a lot less weight. The second car had the factory performance
suspension package and the engine had been modified to develop 196hp. The factory
suspension pack included stiffer dampers, stiffer springs 1in lower than stock and
205/65 performance tyres. Additionally, this car had optional rear disc brakes fitted in
line with its 135mph top speed (18mph faster than standard). The car should have been
clearly superior to the stock version, and it was, to the tune of 2.5 seconds per lap.

The third car had been lightly modified to put out 171hp. Most of this power
increase was the result of modifications to the exhaust system and 6hp came from mild
head work. A good deal of time was spent getting the suspension right. Firstly, high
quality Koni dampers were fitted all around and then the biggest diameter stabiliser
bars that could be found were added. The front bar was 2mm thicker than stock and
the rear bar 6mm bigger. Next, the front springs were changed for springs 40% stiffer
than stock and a half inch shorter. The rear springs were left stock, as they were
designed to carry a good load of people and luggage. I don't like stiff rear springs on a
road car as they tend to cause the back of the car to skip around a good deal on second
class roads. Besides, the large rear stabiliser bar had been chosen to stiffen up the rear
and balance out the understeer which would have resulted from fitting the heavy

springs and thicker bar at the front. A limited slip diff (LSD) was also fitted and while this work was in operation the standard 3.45:1 crown wheel and pinion was changed to a 3.8:1 to improve acceleration and make fifth gear more useful. Top speed was 129mph, 6mph slower than the 196hp car but with the changed gearing its acceleration was almost the same as the more powerful car. The next change was to fit 7in wheels and high performance tyres, grippy BF Goodrich T/A 11's, size 205/60. To improve braking semi-metallic disc pads were fitted. The rear drums were left unchanged. In this form the car was only fractionally more expensive than the second car but on the circuit it was a full 2.2 seconds per lap faster in spite of having substantially less power. On the road it was more economical and far easier to drive due to the more flexible engine and the changed gearing. Also, because the car looked and sounded little different to stock, it could be cruised at high speed without attracting undue attention.

The order of changes required to the suspension will to some extent depend on personal preference and the specifications of the stock suspension. In the main today's cars have ample wheel width so that is not the place to start. Also, wide super high performance tyres are not practical for day to day driving, and they are far too expensive. To my mind a more functional place to begin suspension changes is with the dampers, frequently incorrectly called shock absorbers. Very few cars, except some expensive European jobs, have anything like adequate and reliable dampers. Without good dampers the tyres cannot maintain proper contact with the road surface so adhesion is reduced, even if the tyres are sticky Pirelli P700s or BF Goodrich T/A 11s. My personal choice is for Koni dampers, not the gas type but the standard heavy duty "Special D". These are quite expensive when compared with the standard dampers which car manufacturers fit. However, they are adjustable and repairable, so in the long run they are good value. The main disadvantage with Koni dampers is their slightly rougher ride at low speeds compared with gas dampers like Bilstein and de Carbon. On the open road they handle and ride every bit as well as these usually more expensive gas dampers.

For most cars the next place I would make a change is with the stabiliser bars. Stabiliser bars reduce roll without much increase in ride harshness, and they are usually quite inexpensive. The disadvantage of a thicker front stabiliser bar is that like stiffer front springs, it causes more understeer, so more steering lock will be required to get around corners at higher speeds. To offset this a thicker rear bar can be fitted but this move can create another problem; in front wheel drive cars a bigger rear bar can get you into an instant oversteer tail slide if you lift-off the throttle mid-corner at high speed; with rear wheel drive a bigger rear bar can cause the inside rear wheel to lift off the road so you lose drive out of tight corners at high speed unless a limited slip diff is fitted. This is not intended to scare you off heavy stabiliser bars as few people ever drive hard enough for either problem to surface. However, it is good to be aware of what can happen so as to avoid, or be prepared for, such problems.

Personally I like big stabiliser bars so that I can get good handling with smoother riding soft springs. Just how big you can go will depend on what is available from the suspension suppliers and how rugged the stabiliser bar mountings are. On small 1.6–1.8 litre front wheel drive cars I would be looking to fit 22mm bars front and rear, and possibly up to 24mm either at the front or the rear, to get the handling balance that I want. For rear wheel drive cars of the same size the bars would be 24mm front and 235 about 16–18mm rear. Mid-size rear wheel drive with 2.8–3.5 litre six cylinder engines require 26–28mm front stabiliser bars and 18–21mm rear bars. With a heavy 5 litre V8 in the front the bar size increases to 33–36mm front and 21–24mm rear.

Before you pay a lot of money for a bar from a suspension manufacturer, check to determine if the car manufacturer has optional stabiliser bars available, or bars of the same shape off another model, because the original manufacturer's bars will, as a rule, be much cheaper. For example, one car which I frequently modify has a 24mm front bar and a 14mm rear. The suspension people make 27mm and 18mm replacement bars at what I consider to be outrageous prices. On checking the car manufacturer's parts listings I found that they fit 26mm front and 18mm rear bars on vehicles built for the Police. Further investigation revealed that on one particular station wagon model they fit a 20mm rear bar. The 26mm stabiliser is less than one third the cost of a 27mm bar from the various suspension parts manufacturers, and the 18mm Police and 20mm wagon rear bar is one fifth the price of their 18mm bar!

With good dampers and heavier stabiliser bars in place I turn my attention next to tyres and wheels. If the standard wheels are a suitable width and diameter to suit the tyres I wish to use, these are retained. I like the look of wide alloy wheels, but they are not good value for money. I'm not too keen on all the effort necessary to keep them clean and looking good either. I know a lot is written about how much light alloy wheels reduce upsprung weight and how this factor improves the handling, also the cooling slots are designed to improve brake cooling, but it is only on the race track where these advantages are really noticeable. A steel wheel is heavier, but it supports the tyre just the same as an alloy wheel, it is easier to keep clean, and it can be nudged into kerbs without cracking. Also, for little expense many wheel specialists will remove the standard width rim and weld a wider one-piece rim onto the standard steel centre. In this way you can gain the advantage of extra rim width for better tyre support.

With the money saved on fancy wheels you will be able to afford better quality tyres, but here again be sure to buy only as much tyre as you need and can regularly use. Wide, sticky tyres work fine on the race track but they can be an expensive nuisance, and quite dangerous, on the road. If you think that your car's suspension is as sophisticated as, say, a Porsche 944 Turbo or a BMW M3, go ahead and fit wide and expensive tyres. Remember, however, that once the tyres are half worn the fellow with skinny tyres will overtake you if the road is wet. If there is a hint of snow leave the car at home. Even in the dry on public roads a fairly even mannered car can be transformed into a twitchy beast with excessively wide tyres, no matter how good their quality. Few rear suspensions are well enough located to cope with rough tarmac and wide rubber. When the Opel Manta 400 was released with 225/50 Pirelli P7 tyres, the journalists raved about how well it handled. They must have done their testing at the race track or on smooth freeways because on ordinary twisty roads at high speed the car was a pig, switching from understeer to vicious oversteer in an instant. Changing to 205/60 tyres changed it markedly. I think anyone who has followed a well-driven Mercedes 560 would marvel at how quickly it can be pushed along for a big, heavy car with a suspension compromised to give a luxury class ride. Yet it rides on comparatively skinny 205 section tyres with a 65 profile height. Clearly there is more to handling than merely fitting big, wide, and expensive tyres.

Table 17.1 sets out what I consider to be the best tyre compromise for a number

Table 17.1   Recommended tyre sizes

Engine size	Car weight	Minimum tyre	Handling/ride tyre	Handling tyre
1.2–1.4 litre	1700–1900lb	155/70	165/70	175/70, 175/65
1.6–1.8 litre	2000–2200lb	175/70	185/65	185/60
2.0–2.3 litre	2100–2400lb	185/70	185/65, 195/60	195/55
2.0–2.3 litre	2500–2800lb	185/70	195/65	195/60, 205/55
2.8–3.3 litre	2800–3200lb	195/65	205/60	205/55, 215/55
3.6–4.2 litre	3100–3300lb	205/65	215/60, 225/60	215/55, 225/50
5.0–6.0 litre	3200–3500lb	215/65	215/60, 225/60	225/60, 245/50

of applications. The tyres are probably much narrower and of a higher profile than you thought you needed. I don't consider that low profile tyres are necessary in the smaller widths as small tyres are stable enough if the pressures are right, without reducing the wall height. Low profile tyres are more expensive and the ride rougher. To overcome the rough ride many people use less pressure, which in turn just reduces the tyres' responsiveness to that of a higher profile tyre running more pressure. Keep in mind that changing the tyre size, either section width or profile, can alter the gearing. A standard rule is that for each size you go up in width the profile height must come down one number to retain approximately the same gearing e.g. changing from a 185/65 tyre to a 195/60 tyre will keep the gearing the same as standard.

The construction of the tyre, the rubber compound, and the tread pattern is far more important than the actual size. Unfortunately there is no way of grading these things, so often it is a matter of listening to someone else's advice when it comes to making a tyre choice. The first thing that you can look for is a good open tread with at least two wide water channels running all the way around the tyre. Additionally, there should be good, full depth, drainage grooves running from these channels to both the inner and outer edge of the tyre. Some so-called performance tyres leave a lot to be desired in this respect. To give stability to the tread blocks some tyre makers do not mould these drains more than half tread depth. Then, when the tyre is half worn, there is no water drainage away from the large channels. Other tyre companies, in an effort to increase the area of rubber in contact with the road, leave the outer third of the tyre a semi-slick. This is fine while the road is dry, but as the tyre wears and the rain comes you will wish for better drainage.

Most cars are not capable of more than 130mph so "HR" speed rated tyres are suitable. "VR" rated tyres are much more expensive so unless you need a tyre which is VR rated you will generally be wasting your money. To obtain a VR rating the tyre construction and also the rubber compound is changed to enable the tyre to run at over 130mph without flying apart. Some companies offer their high performance tyres in both HR and VR ratings. The VR tyre doesn't grip any better, it's designed not to fracture at higher speeds. Unfortunately though, some manufacturers only supply their best handling tyres with a VR or ZR rating, so if you want that additional grip there is no alternative but to pay the extra in this instance.

Of course not to be neglected when discussing tyres is tyre pressure. Generally, if you want sharp high speed handling you will have to use considerably more pressure than the manufacturer of the vehicle recommends. Personally I have found with front engine cars that I prefer pressures of about 33–36 psi front and 27–28 psi   237

Michelin MXF Fizzarrows exhibit the sort of tread pattern to look for; good water channels running all the way around the tyre and drainage grooves to both the inner and outer edges from these channels.

rear. The high front pressures give sharp steering, a secondary benefit is reduced steering effort so power steering isn't needed on most cars with 4 and 6 cylinder engines. This means that there is reduced power wastage and reduced fuel consumption. The lower rear pressures reduce the tendency of the rear end to jump about on rough surfaces and give a more comfortable ride. Also, the tyres wear more evenly, contributing to a longer life which saves you some money.

To help the tread maintain proper contact with the road, wheels of the correct width are required. If the wheels are narrow, the tread will squirm, reducing grip and increasing tread wear. If the wheels are too wide, the ride will become harsh and the aerodynamics of the car will be spoiled, increasing fuel consumption at higher speeds. Table 17.2 indicates the rim widths which should be aimed for. Remember that tyres of the same size can vary greatly in tread width. For example, a 205/60 tyre can have a tread width of 6.1 to 6.7in. Naturally this influences the rim width required. Unless the tyre has very low walls I normally like to see the rim width at least equal to the tread width to ensure good stability. Do take care if you decide to change the wheel width or the wheel offset of front wheel drive vehicles as the handling could finish up a disaster. In some lands it is now illegal to change the rim width or offset on all front wheel drive cars for this very reason.

The next modification would be to fit stiffer, but not necessarily lower, springs. Many cars have front springs which are far too soft. This permits plenty of body roll and allows the car to gently drift when cornering at normal speeds, so the tyres lose adhesion gradually rather than savagely. At the front I like the springs to be 20–50% stiffer than stock and give a ride height about a half to one inch lower than standard. With the nose dropped a little, the car becomes more aerodynamic. High speed stability is improved and fuel consumption shows a decrease. The stiffer springs

Table 17.2   Recommended rim widths

Tyre size	Minimum width (in)	Preferred width (in)	Maximum width (in)
155/70	4.5	5.0	5.5
165/70	5.0	5.5	5.5
175/70	5.0	5.5	6.0
175/65	5.0	5.5	6.0
185/70, 185/60	5.5	6.0	6.5
185/65	5.0	6.0	6.5
195/65, 195/50	6.0	6.5	7.0
195/60, 195/55	5.5	6.0	6.5
205/65, 205/50	6.5	7.0	7.5
205/60, 205/55	6.0	6.5	7.0
215/65	6.5	7.0	7.5
215/60, 215/55	6.5	7.0	7.5
225/60, 225/50	7.0	7.5	8.0
245/50	7.5	8.0	8.5

reduce roll and increase steadiness under heavy braking. Because very few cars today have any camber adjustment, the front must not be dropped very much otherwise the front tyres will have too much negative camber, which will scrub the inside of the tyre tread in no time. For good tyre wear the front end should have no more than about 0.75° negative camber unladen. Reducing the toe-in to 0 or even up to about 2mm toe-out will increase front end grip in turns, but straight ahead stability could suffer with the car showing a tendency to wander about under brakes and follow grooves in the road.

At the rear I seldom change the ride height, otherwise very stiff, rough riding springs will be necessary to keep the car off the bump rubbers on anything but smooth roads. If the car is designed to carry a good load of luggage and people, the standard springs are probably heavy enough for fast driving with just a couple of people on board and a little light luggage. Fitting stiffer springs will give the rear dampers a lot more work and if the rear axle isn't too well located, most are not, then the dampers will have a lot of trouble keeping the back tyres in contact with the road. On rough corners the rear end will become very skittish and prone to sliding out (oversteer).

Some cars have what are called "progressive rate" springs, meaning that the springs are soft at their normal ride height and stiffen non-linearly as they compress. The idea is good, in fact many rally cars use this type of spring at the front and rear. However, a number of car makers have gone overboard looking for a smooth ride so much so that the spring is initially far too soft, allowing excessive body roll. Such a spring may have a spring rate of say 170–310lb per in, very soft initially and finally quite stiff. A replacement spring for performance driving could have a rate of 230–290lb per in, stiffer initially but a little softer at full compression. If a single rate spring were used it would probably be about 255 or 265lb per in, which would give a harder ride and the same handling as the 230–290lb progressive spring.

Many suspension people are now advocating the replacement of rubber 239 suspension bushes with bushes made of polyurethane or other hard plastic-like material. I'm not at all in favour of this because of increased noise and vibration within the car. Naturally there are some exceptions; the only general exception which applies to all cars is that the stabiliser bar "D" bushes and also the link bar bushes can be replaced without increasing harshness. Personally I feel that it is a waste of money replacing the rubber link bar bushes with polyurethane bushes. They are quite expensive. Equally effective is to fit thicker washers and wind the link bar rubbers down until they are fully compressed. This ensures that full suspension motion is transmitted to the stabiliser bar. If the bushes are left semi-compressed, as they are when the car leaves the factory, the suspension has to move at least half an inch before the stabiliser bar starts working. Another budget measure it to use rubber "D" bushes designed for a slightly smaller diameter stabiliser bar. Hence if the bar diameter is 28mm use bushes made for a 26mm bar. This pre-compresses the bush, ensuring that the stabiliser bar works more effectively.

One area where I do not believe in saving money is when it comes to deciding if a limited slip diff should be fitted. I firmly believe that any rear wheel drive car which is regularly driven in a spirited manner over wet or slippery roads should have an LSD. Without it the car will be dangerous to drive if it has more than about 110hp, particularly if the suspension is fairly stiff and tyre widths have been increased over stock. The LSD should not be a savage race-type unit, rather it should be a "soft" clutch or cone type with about 25% lock up torque. This means that 25% of axle torque will be transferred to the wheel which has traction. This ensures some drive out of the corners; without the LSD all of the torque would go to the spinning inside wheel. To help the LSD work properly and last a long time, use the correct type of LSD oil for your unit, and change the oil at least every 30,000 miles. It is not easy accurately to check if an LSD requires adjustment or is still working correctly. However, this is a quick check which I have found works well on many units. Raise one wheel off the ground and using a tension wrench determine how much pressure has to be applied before the wheel will turn. A new LSD will read about 80lbf ft; less than 45lbf ft usually indicates that repair is required.

Limited slip diffs are not really suitable for general road use in front wheel drive vehicles due to problems with torque steer. A lot of work is being carried out with viscous drives and as these become more reliable and freely available for a wide variety of front drive cars they should prove invaluable, particularly in powerful, torquey turbo cars.

Most present day cars have excellent brakes which work quite well on the road at higher speeds. The usual arrangement is ventilated discs at the front and drums at the rear, although in recent years more vehicles are fitted with discs at the rear. Personally I don't see the need to devote a lot of attention to brakes; very few roads require more than the occasional dab on the pedal to slow from 85mph to 50mph for a corner. This doesn't demand big, efficient and well-cooled brakes like a car on the race track, which may have to slow from 130mph to 50mph at the end of the main straight every lap with very little time for cooling between each brake application.

Some people feel that they must have rear discs and competition brake materials. This can be a mistake. A big, heavy car weighing around 3200lb plus driven briskly on tight, twisty roads will benefit from being fitted with rear disc brakes. However, few public roads are so demanding that light vehicles require rear discs. After all, the front

Table 18.1   Pressure drop in Subaru intake

rpm	Point 1	Point 2	Point 3	Point 4
4000	12	17	17	20
5000	20	24	26	30
6000	27	32	34	41
7000	36	44	48	60

Point 1 – in the air box before the filter element

Point 2 – in the air box after the filter element

Point 3 – in the air duct after the air flow meter

Point 4 – in the air duct after the resonator box

Now, what do the figures mean? Standard air pressure at sea level is 14.7 psi which equals 29.92in mercury or 406.9in water. Thus 1in mercury equals about 0.5 psi and 1in water equals about 0.036 psi. Clearly, this Subaru has a problem which won't be solved by replacing the air filter element. At 7000rpm there is enough flow resistance caused by the air muffler before the air filter to cause a depression of 36in water. That's a restriction of 1.3 psi even before you get to the filter! Again, at 7000rpm the filter restriction is only 8in water (44 – 36 = 8) or 0.29 psi. The other major restriction is the little resonator box stuck in the air duct right after the air meter. It is causing a depression of 12in water (60 – 48 = 12) or 0.43 psi. In total the system has a pressure drop of 60in before you get to the throttle body (and that's another story). That is almost 2.2 psi, so instead of air pressure of 14.7 psi to force air into the cylinders this car is working with only 12.5 psi. Is that costing horsepower? Well, let's put it this way, by getting rid of that flow restriction it's like getting 2.2 psi of free supercharging without adding any heat to the air! In hp terms it means that a 200hp engine when restricted like this is going to be limited to around 170–180hp.

Some say toss out the intake muffler, the air box and filter and fit a high flow performance pod type filter with tapered neck to attach to the air flow meter. This would be a bad move unless the pod filter is boxed in to prevent hot underbonnet air from entering the intake. The underbonnet air temperature can easily rise by 50°C (122°F) above ambient temperature with a turbo engine, and usually about 40°C (104°F) for non-turbo engines. You can reckon on a power decrease of at least 1% for every 10°C (50°F) the intake air temperature rises. Thus, if the outside air temperature is 25°C (77°F) and the intake air temperature is 75°C (167°F) you are giving away 7–8hp in a 150hp engine. This illustrates why a cold air intake is so important for maximum power. However, at lower engine speeds, particularly during cooler weather, fuel economy may be poorer as a result of inferior fuel atomisation, even with fuel injected engines.

To give some idea of just how misleading air filter flow figures can be, consider what was found with a modified 1.3 litre Suzuki Swift GTi producing 117hp. These little engines really get up and go, and looking at the tiny air filter it would seem that the very first modification to obtain an easy 5–7hp gain would be to bin the standard air filter and air box. Table 18.2 shows how wrong appearances can be. When the standard air box was removed and big pod type filters which flowed about 15% better than stock were fitted, power went up by less than 2% at the top of the power band.

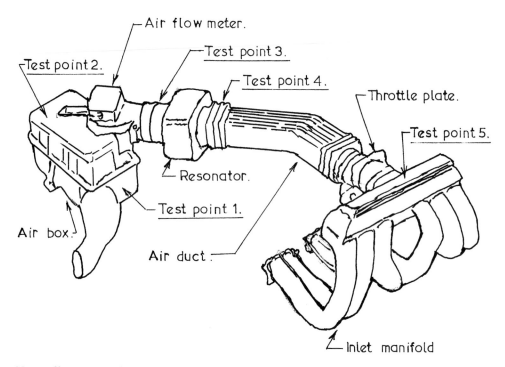

Naturally aspirated engines should be tested with a water manometer at all five test
points to determine what parts of the intake system are causing flow resistance. Turbo
engines cannot be checked with a water manometer between the turbo and the inlet
manifold but flow resistance up to point 4 can be investigated.

Test point 1 – before the air filter element but after any inlet silencers.
Test point 2 – after the air filter element but before the air flow meter.
Test point 3 – after the air flow meter but before the resonator.
Test point 4 – after the resonator but before the throttle plate.
Test point 5 – after the throttle plate.

Down in the mid-range power was up 1%. All of these figures were obtained with a
cold air feed from a blower fan onto the filter. Drawing hot under-bonnet air it is
probable these filters would have shown power figures lower than the factory set-up.

Table 18.2   Suzuki 1.3 GTi air filter comparison

Filter type	Air flow (cfm)	Flow increase (%)	hp increase
Stock factory*	195	–	–
Uni-Filter*	175	–10	–
K & N*	197	1	1hp above 7250rpm
K & N pod†	231	18.5	2hp above 6000rpm
Uni-Filter pod†	223	14.4	2hp above 6500rpm
HKS pod†	226	15.9	2hp above 4000rpm

   * filter element enclosed within standard air box

   † pod type filter with cold air feed

One interesting figure was the very poor flow of the Uni-Filter element. Its maximum flow when fitted in the standard air box was 10% less than stock, yet the power output was virtually identical to the factory element at all engine speeds. Equally perplexing was the K & N element. It flowed only 1% better than the standard item, but at 7250rpm power was up a full 1%. Also note the HKS pod which flowed about 2 1/2% less than the K & N pod, yet it produced identical maximum power, and from 4000rpm to 5000rpm it produced about 1hp more than the K & N.

Statement: Our exhaust system with equal length header tubes and mandrel bends will give up to 10hp increase.

Fact: Note the claim is not "will give a 10hp increase" but "will give up to". In reality this is an ambiguous claim to say the very least. Did any engine with that exhaust actually show a 10hp increase? Were comparisons done using a new factory exhaust or was an old exhaust which was partially blocked with soot and rust or a collapsed CAT used? Was the test engine standard or modified, as obviously a 200hp rally engine will show a larger benefit from a free-flow exhaust than a lightly modified 140hp performance/economy engine? Does the new exhaust meet government noise standards?

With turbo cars it is relatively easy to gain power with big bore exhausts; a 7% increase from 3000rpm upwards is quite usual, and at some points it may be in excess of 10%. However, such large exhausts, typically 3in dia. are expensive and prone to damage because of reduced ground clearance. An unexpected problem is drumming and resonance within the car which can take away all driving pleasure.

Grinding the manifold ports to match the gasket improves exhaust flow out of the engine. Tubular headers should also have the flanges matched to the manifold gasket, and any welding "dags" must also be ground out.

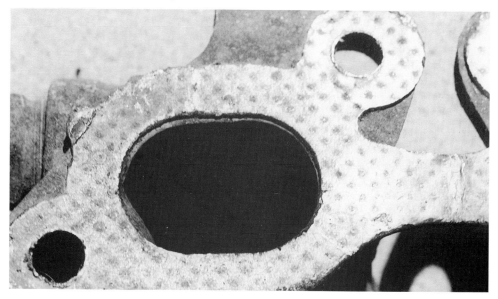

For non-turbo engines, power increases around 3–4% are more typical and you probably could get a similar increase for a lot less money without going to tube headers and a full system with mandrel bends. As shown in Chapter 6, factory cast-iron manifolds and factory tube headers work very well with mild road cams. Apart from grinding out the ports to match the manifold gasket, about the only other improvement which can be made to cast-iron manifolds is to weld in divider plates to increase the length of the "primaries" and reduce cylinder to cylinder exhaust backflow.

With 4-cylinder cast manifolds there is often a problem with exhaust backflow into cylinders No. 1 and No. 4 because of the shape of these "branches". For example, when the exhaust gas flows out of cylinder No. 1 it loses direction and rushes virtually straight ahead into the No. 4 branch rather than taking the sharp turn into the engine pipe. This creates a lot of turbulence, with exhaust gas racing into the No. 4 branch, then having to turn around 180° to flow back to the outlet. Then, just before the No. 1 exhaust valve closes, this turbulent flow can send a pressure wave back up the No. 1 branch forcing exhaust gas back into the cylinder, contaminating the fuel/air charge. Welding a divider into the manifold "steers" the exhaust gas in the right direction, reducing turbulence and exhaust reversion into the cylinder.

The No. 2 and No. 3 branches usually aren't such a problem, but they too can benefit from having a divider welded in. Typically these branches are quite short, often 7in or 8in. Welding a divider in place usually adds about 3in to the primary length and again "steers" the exhaust gas in the right direction, which reduces turbulence and reverse flow. With these dividers in place, a cast-iron manifold can be expected to work almost as well as mandrel bent equal length tube headers. I usually find that this modification on 1.8–2.0 litre engines producing 135–150hp is worth about 2hp at

Some cast-iron manifolds can be improved by welding in 1mm thick divider plates where the primary branches join.

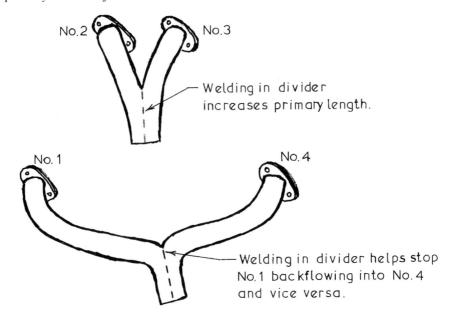

No.2   No.3

Welding in divider increases primary length.

No. 1   No. 4

Welding in divider helps stop No.1 backflowing into No.4 and vice versa.

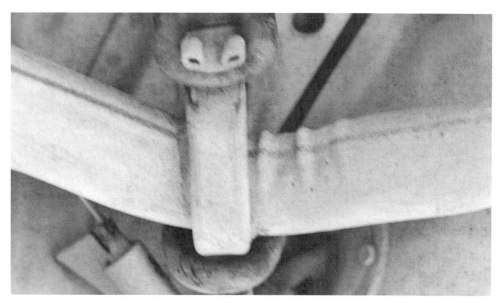

Poorly formed exhaust bends which reduce the pipe size or are creased like this cost hp right through the power range, particularly when the bend is up close to the engine.

3000rpm and 3–4hp at 7000rpm with an otherwise standard exhaust.

Further down the system the main problem I see with the factory exhaust is poorly formed bends. When bends toward the end of the system are flattened and creased it isn't such a problem, but when there is a major bend up close to the engine which is squeezed in or creased, that single bend can be knocking 2% off right through the power range. This is the primary benefit of increasing the size of the exhaust; a horribly formed bend in big bore pipe will flow just as well as a perfectly formed mandrel bend in a conservatively sized pipe.

To obtain that big bore pipe there are a number of options which work very well and are a fraction of the price of comparable big bore high-performance systems. Often manufacturers fit engines of many different capacities and performance levels into the same body shape. A system off the 2 litre version may be just perfect for your 1.6 if it has 2in pipe and yours has 1⁵⁄₈in. Rather than buy new why not check a breaker's yard as frequently the larger engine performance/luxury versions have very well-made stainless steel systems.

Statement: Unleash the real potential of your engine – Fit our performance chip.

Fact: Car manufacturers spend millions developing a package which offers reliability, performance, driveability and economy, and which meets government regulations. Their chip is correct for an average engine coming off the assembly line. A performance chip will only improve your engine if the supplier is able to dial it in, tailoring it to your non-average engine, while it is being run on a wheel dyno.

I once read an advertisement which invited enthusiasts to "get into the darker side" of their cars by fitting a performance chip. The originators of the advert probably didn't 251

There are many aspects to consider before purchasing a plug-in performance chip or having a new chip soldered onto the stock ECU circuit board.

have any idea of how honest they were being. Remember that if your engine is unmodified and is not fitted with a turbo or supercharger from the factory there is no way it can make more power with a different chip (or exchange ECU for those cars which don't have a plug-in chip). The glossy ads might indicate that the manufacturer got the fuelling or spark advance wrong and, because of extraordinary understanding of engines and performance, Blooper chips alone were able to get it right and "discover hidden power". If indeed Blooper chips did find hidden power then it is going to cost you something in addition to the price of the chip. Manufacturers are very sensitive about fuel economy, consequently if they lose 10% economy and gain 3hp they don't consider it a good trade-off. Indeed, if you lose only 10% economy for a 3hp power gain consider yourself very fortunate. There are numerous chips out there in the market which are not only costing more than 10% in lost economy but are down on power from the factory chip! I've seen over-fuelling so serious that the exhaust was emitting black smoke. Even before it becomes as visibly apparent as this the rings and bores are being rapidly worn away because the scant amount of lubricant available is being washed off the cylinder walls.

All kinds of weird things are being programmed into, or left out of so-called "performance chips". Most chips move the factory rev limit up; some by only 200rpm, but 500 or 1000rpm is more usual, while some remove any rev limiting function. As most engines have the rev limit set way above what is necessary for maximum acceleration, why do chip programmers set it even higher or not set any limit at all? For example, one popular factory hot rod produces maximum power at 6500rpm. Best performance is obtained keeping the revs below 7500rpm. The factory cut-out is at 7800rpm. Replacement chips routinely raise the limit to 8800rpm!

Another common ploy of chip reprogrammers is to specify that the vehicle must no longer be operated on standard grade fuel but high octane must be used, "because spark advance has been optimised for ultimate performance". Table 18.3 shows the result of dyno testing of an Opel Ecotec 2 litre. At 10.8:1 the standard compression ratio is quite high, demanding the use of fuel with 95 RON minimum. Where I live, standard pump unleaded is 91–93 octane RON; high octane unleaded is 95 or 96 RON octane depending on the refiner. Interestingly, instructions with the performance chip stipulated a "fuel requirement of 98 RON minimum". Group A unleaded race fuel (100 RON) was used instead, but at nearly every pull power was down compared to the factory chip and 96 octane. Next the engine was run with the race fuel and the standard chip, and power went up fairly uniformly right through the range, indicating that the knock sensor was allowing more ignition advance. As a final check a 50/50 blend of race fuel and 96 RON was mixed to produce a fuel of 98 octane as per the instructions, and the performance chip was retested. The result was a miserable failure; power was down even on the poor results obtained in Test 2.

Table 18.3   Opel Ecotec 2 litre chip comparison

rpm	Test 1 hp	Test 1 Torque	Test 2 hp	Test 2 Torque	Test 3 hp	Test 3 Torque
2000	42	110	40	105	44	116
2500	61	128	62	129	62	130
3000	82	144	81	142	84	147
3500	89	134	89	133	90	135
4000	105	138	106	139	108	142
4500	118	138	117	137	121	141
5000	137	144	139	146	140	147
5500	139	133	135	129	141	135
6000	138	121	133	116	139	122
6500	129	104	128	103	133	107
7000	119	89	117	88	122	91

Test 1 – standard chip and 96 octane unleaded fuel

Test 2 – performance chip and 100 octane Group A unleaded fuel

Test 3 – standard chip and 100 octane Group A unleaded fuel

From what I have observed I would summarise that in non-turbo vehicles performance chips from those who really know what they are doing will provide very modest power gains in the order of 1–2% at the expense of increased fuel consumption and perhaps a more expensive high octane fuel; raise the rpm at which the rev limiter operates; disable the speed limiter function.

Factory turbo and supercharged engines are a different story. Usually a replacement chip will give a substantial power improvement, basically because boost pressure is raised and the chip is programmed to provide additional fuel to match the increased air flow into the engine. Manufacturers tend to be reasonably cautious, so most engines can handle a 15–20% power increase without running into reliability problems. However, when I see claims being made for power increases in the order of   253

30% and 40% with boost pressures being elevated to 17–20 psi I am concerned; this is well into "meltdown" territory where competition engines operate.

A question demanding an answer is: "Why re-chip for a 15–20% power increase when a similar improvement can be achieved by improving engine breathing?" A chip change may be less time-consuming than fabricating a new exhaust and intake system, and it may initially cost less, but the overall package will not work as well. With the intake and exhaust freed up, the extra power will always be on tap, but when the chip is changed that additional performance will probably only be available when the ambient temperature is cooler. This occurs because the chip raises the power by raising boost pressure; in turn, intake temperature increases reducing cylinder filling, and detonation sets in sooner, so the knock sensor retards ignition advance. However, when it is cooler the chip improves hp because the air is much more dense to begin with, so cylinder filling is improved and, additionally, the intercooler works more efficiently at removing heat from the compressed air, which lowers charge temperature and also improves cylinder filling.

Raising the boost pressure can also lead to increased problems with turbo lag and wheelspin, so the car may not be so pleasant to drive, particularly on twisting or wet roads. Elevated boost pressure brings with it elevated turbo temperatures with a subsequent reduction in turbo life. The chip programmer may endeavour to combat this with increased fuelling, but rather than lowering turbo temperature extra fuel may raise turbo temperature because of exhaust afterburn. Whether the extra fuel improves

Raising boost pressure increases intake charge temperature, so re-chipping a turbo engine with stock intercooler may show power gains only when the ambient temperature drops below about 15°C (59°C).

the situation or not, fuel consumption increases. However, when the intake and exhaust are modified to give improved breathing there is usually a reduction in fuel consumption, relative to the increase in hp, and the turbo spins up to boost more quickly, which reduces turbo lag.

Statement: Our spark plugs improve starting in winter, provide smoother engine idle and increase engine power due to their exclusive electrode design.

Fact: A high voltage electric current will jump across an air gap ionising the air in its path regardless of the shape of the air gap, initiating combustion when fuel molecules of the correct size are surrounded by the correct proportion of air molecules within that air gap. The number of earth electrodes or whether they are shaped like a "U", or whether the centre electrode has a "V" in it does not alter the speed or the efficiency of this process.

What does alter the speed and efficiency of initiating the combustion process with regard to the influence of the spark plug gets down to two basics: the width of the gap, and the "cleanness" of metals forming the air gap.

The width of the gap depends on what you adjust it to when you fit the spark plugs. How long the gap remains that size, if we leave the ignition system out of the equation, is dependent on the specifications of the electrode materials and their width. Hence some modern cars with terrible access to the spark plugs are being fitted from the factory with platinum tip centre electrode plugs (and sometimes platinum tip earth electrodes too) to keep the gap within limits for 50,000 and more miles. Similarly, commercial vehicles which are expected to do long distances between services may use a so-called "truck plug" with a wider 0.120in centre electrode. This type of plug requires more voltage to get the plug fired, but the gap width is maintained for about 40–50% more miles than a conventional plug with a 0.100in centre electrode. Conversely, race plugs may use a 0.080in or 0.052in centre electrode; this sacrifices durability for reduced firing voltage.

Because platinum erodes and oxidises much more slowly than conventional electrode materials, platinum tip plugs not only "hold gap" longer but the air gap stays "cleaner". This means the electrode surface stays sharper with square, rather than rounded, edges. Also the electrode surface remains relatively free of scale or oxide. Both situations reduce firing voltage requirements, which improves cold engine fire-up and reduces the number of higher speed-lean mixture misfires. Regular filing and regapping of a spark plug with conventional electrode materials does a similar thing; clean virgin metal with square sharp edges, along with the correct air gap width produces a spark at reduced ignition voltage.

Over the years engine tuners have worried themselves with "flame masking". The fear has been that the earth electrode standing above the centre electrode to form an air gap somehow disrupts even flame propagation throughout the combustion chamber. Hence they decided to chop off part of the earth electrode, fully exposing the tip of the centre electrode to the combustion chamber. I don't think anyone got a measurable power increase, but firing voltage requirements sure went through the roof!

Split or forked earth electrodes are also supposed to unmask the centre electrode   255

Filing the earth electrode back to the middle of the centre electrode, and then filing the corners off to taper it, reduces the spark plug's firing voltage requirement. This means that more electrical energy is available to generate a spark of high intensity over a longer duration.

and provide quicker and improved combustion. When testing this style of spark plug I have not seen any power increase, and interestingly the engines required the same amount of spark advance, which seems to cancel out the quicker burn theory.

One thing I do with conventional plugs is to file the earth electrode back to the middle of the centre electrode and then I "taper" it by filing the corners off. Technically this unmasks the centre electrode, but I don't change the earth electrode shape for that reason. Filing it that shape has three beneficial effects: the firing voltage requirement is reduced as three sharp edges are exposed to encourage a spark to jump across from the centre electrode, improving cold-engine starting and reducing high speed-lean misfires; reducing the length of the earth electrode allows it to run cooler, thus there is less risk of pre-ignition damage from a "glowing" earth electrode and consequently, thirdly, a warmer plug with greater resistance to low speed fouling can be used. The down side of filing back the earth electrode is the plugs must be filed and regapped more frequently as the centre electrode erodes more rapidly, much like race plugs with thin 0.080in electrodes.

Statement: Switch to our 100% synthetic engine oil and you won't have to change your oil for 25,000 miles or 12 months.

Fact: Modern engine oil is remarkably good stuff, and 100% synthetic is doubly remarkable, but the additive package still wears out and it still becomes contaminated by combustion by-products. Consequently, when Mobil advertising advised me many years back that Mobil 1 was good for 40,000km or 12 months, rather than being attracted to the product I was put off from ever giving it a try. In time I got to hear stories from conservative race engine builders of how race engines, seriously overheated or down on oil pressure, were able to finish races without damage thanks to Mobil 1. Rather than test it out in customer engines I gave it a run in an old test "mule" used to check out ideas I come up with; and, yes, all the claims were true. Notably, by then Mobil had modified its line about being "good for 40,000km or 12 months". The technical department advised me that "the vehicle manufacturer's recommended oil change intervals should be adhered to" but that "extended oil drain intervals were permissible under certain (unspecified) conditions". Later I found out that Mobil had tested the oil in the USA in both domestic and European engines and the oil stood up well using 15,000 mile oil change intervals.

I use 15W–50 as it suits the climate where I live; 10°C (50°F) winter and 28°C (82°F) summer being the seasonal average. I don't like wide range multi-grade, however, Mobil assure me that as Mobil 1 does not contain polymer viscosity index improvers their 0W-40 and 5W-50 grades perform just as well as the narrower range stuff.

The first thing I noticed when changing to Mobil 1 was that oil consumption was halved. Customers operating their cars both on the highway and with some stop-start driving every day are not topping up the oil between oil changes. The oil is supposed to be changed every 15,000km, but one customer stretched it out to 18,000km and even then the oil was only 3/4 litre below full in spite of the engine having covered over 200,000km since new. Another engine was consuming 2 litres of top grade mineral oil between 10,000km oil changes. That same engine, now with over 280,000km on it, is consuming less than 2 litres, between 25,000km oil changes; a 60% reduction in oil

A 100% synthetic oil provides superior lubrication and vastly improved oxidation resistance over premium mineral oil.

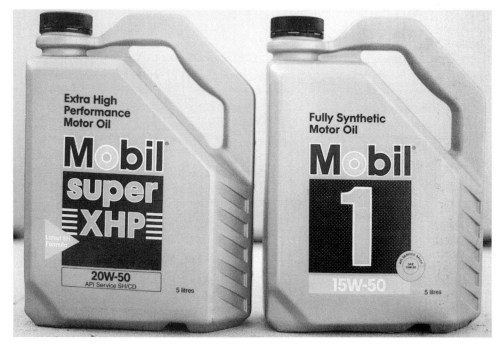

consumption. This car isn't driven short distances and doesn't do any stop-start work, hence the long oil change period, but the filter is changed every 12,500km.

The other very obvious thing was significantly reduced "oil stink". Two things cause oil stink; combustion by-products entering the sump and oil oxidation and break-down. Reduced oil stink means the oil is holding up and doing its job more effectively.

Less obvious was the very slight power advantage when using synthetic. It seems to be in the order of 0.8–1% but is only measurable using later sophisticated engine dynos. Also, fuel economy is improved. It is difficult to measure but I've found a consistent improvement of around 3–5%.

When you begin stripping high mileage engines which have been run on synthetic, the lack of engine sludge is immediately noticeable, as is the lack of varnish on the pistons. However, it is when you begin measuring parts that you realise just how little wear there is. High wear areas like the cylinder bores and piston rings regularly show at least 30% less wear than similar engines lubricated with mineral oil. In some other areas wear is almost undetectable.

Some people complain that 100% synthetic is too expensive, but by my reckoning it is actually cheaper than top grade mineral oil when calculated just on the cost of an oil change and subsequent top up before the next change. When fuel savings and savings from reduced engine wear are entered into the equation it is no contest – Mobil 1 is much cheaper than the best mineral oils. Around here, other synthetics are up to 50% more expensive than Mobil 1, but whether they offer superior lubrication is questionable.

Many oil companies now produce a blended synthetic/mineral oil which may be advertised as semi-synthetic or as a synthetic fortified mineral oil. I do not recommend such oils as I do not believe they offer value for money when compared with the initial price of Mobil 1 and the extended oil drain periods which it offers. I am also concerned as to just how much synthetic stock is blended in. Rumour has it that around 40% synthetic base is about average, but some claim it is as little as 20%.

One unresolved debate surrounding the use of synthetic oil is whether a new engine should be run-in on mineral oil and then later switched to synthetic or can synthetic be used while running in a new engine? One line of reasoning is that synthetic lubricates so efficiently – keeping metal parts so well separated by a strong oil film – that the parts never properly wear into each other. Hence the piston ring to cylinder wall seal will be inferior and parts subjected to heavy loading, such as camshaft lobes, never work-harden.

Over in the other camp the reasoning is that with the very accurate cylinder bores and piston rings which we produce today these parts don't really have to wear into each other very much to give a proper seal. Also, if synthetic is so effective at keeping the lifters and cam lobes separated when the engine is being run-in, won't it work just as efficiently at maintaining an oil film to prevent damage to these components as the engine ages?

I personally feel that cylinder preparation is the key to which direction to take. New cars leaving the Porsche factory have Shell Helix synthetic in them, and new quad cam 4 valve Chev Corvettes leave the factory with Mobil 1 100% synthetic in their sumps. Numerous professional race teams run all their engines in on 100% synthetic. I don't know what process Porsche and General Motors use to ensure

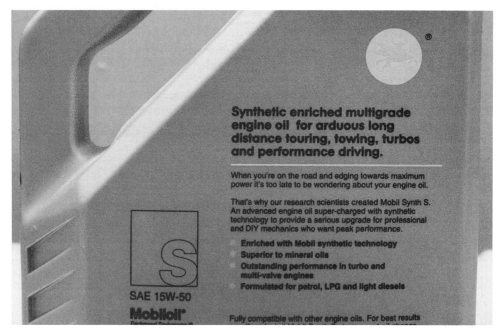

Some oils are a blend of synthetic and mineral oil, but such oils cannot be recommended without reservation because of uncertainty over exactly how much base stock is actually synthetic. Without knowledge of the percentage of synthetic base there is a question mark over value for money and extended oil drain period feasibility.

accurate cylinder walls, but I do know the painstaking procedures which professional race engine builders employ.

This varies according to the type of engine, but a fairly standard procedure is to bore the cylinder about 0.004in undersize taking fine cuts with the boring bar. Next a 2in thick steel honing plate, together with a head gasket are fitted and carefully tensioned to normal head bolt tension. Using a Sunnen CK-10 automatic hone fitted with 220 grit stones, about 0.003in of material is removed to bring the bore to 0.001in from its final diameter. Then another 0.0005in is removed with 280 grit stones, and after that 400 grit stones are used to bring the bore to its final size. The end result is a very accurate bore with a fine finish which requires very little break-in.

When cylinders are prepared in this manner, synthetic oil will not impair engine break-in and subsequent ring seal. However, very few road engines are reconditioned with such care using a state-of-the-art CK-10 hone. Many, in fact, are being hand honed without the benefit of a honing plate to replicate the bore distortion which occurs when the cylinder head is bolted down. In a situation such as this I believe there is definite merit in running-in with a mineral oil and then later changing to synthetic.

Statement: Tests prove that our unique oil additive reduces engine wear by up to 50%, reduces engine friction and improves fuel economy by up to 20%.

Fact: I first had a good close look at the outrageous claims being made by oil additive 259 companies about 30 years ago, and I was disgusted by the methods used to trap the unwary. In one demonstration, designed to prove how the additive treats the metal, the sales rep claimed that "rather than use oil in the engine, with our product you could use water as a carrier to circulate our additive throughout the engine." He then carried out a test similar to the Four-Ball Wear Test in which a rotating 1/2in steel ball is forced at high pressure against three other 1/2in balls bound in a triangular formation. In the first test ordinary engine oil was used as the lubricant and, as you can guess, in a few minutes the steel balls were hot and smoking. Next, another four balls were produced, but this time the lubricant was straight additive. Naturally the balls didn't seize and begin smoking, leaving many in the audience believing that this is just what their engines need; less friction naturally means more available hp.

The point is, what has a test like this got to do with what is happening inside a car engine? Where do you find one steel ball being forced against three other steel balls, and where in the engine do you find parts which are expected to survive without a continuous flow of lubricant? The only thing which a test like this proves is that the oil additive would work well as an anti-seize agent in an extreme pressure environment such as a hypoid type differential.

I recall another time seeing an engine up on a test stand idling at about 800rpm. The sump had been removed to prove that "with our oil treatment, if the sump plug falls out and the wife is alone in the car she will get home safely without oil." Alongside the engine was a large clock indicating that the engine had been operating for over 30 hours without oil. This test was also supposed to prove that "your engine doesn't need oil, just our additive plating engine parts."

What does a test like this prove? Basically, that an engine with no load on it will rotate at low speed for a long time without oil. You could buy any rusty old "banger" from a car dealer, drain the oil and set off down a relatively flat road at 40mph, driving until the engine locks up. Be sure to have someone following in a back-up vehicle or you could very easily have a 40–60 mile walk home.

A third dodgy test, which is supposed to prove how the oil additive reduces friction, involves several engines being set running on test stands with a large tacho being prominently displayed on each. As the "show" progresses throughout the day the special friction-reducing additive will be poured first into one engine and then into another as each new audience assembles. These unsuspecting folk will be asked to observe that the engine idle speed significantly increases when the additive is poured in. Close observation of what actually occurs shows why the idle speed increases from, say, 700rpm to 1100rpm, and also why the idle picks up as the additive is being poured rather than after several minutes circulating in the oil and "plating" engine parts.

How does the scam work? Before the show commences the engines are richened right up, and the innards are pulled out of the PCV valve to allow the free passage of air from the tappet cover to the inlet manifold. When an unvented oil filler cap is in place the engine can only draw blow-by gas from inside the engine but as soon as the oil filler cap is removed to pour in the additive, air is freely drawn into the manifold, correcting the rich mixture condition and allowing the engine to speed up. Usually the filler cap is left off after the oil treatment has been added. However, if the filler cap is replaced it will not be the original non-vented cap. Rather it will be a look-alike with a concealed vent hole, or perhaps the gasket will be grooved to permit air to be drawn through to the manifold.

Throughout this time I was getting excellent results in high performance and competition engines using freely available over-the-counter lubricants. I also knew what factory race and rally teams were pouring into their engines and, as far as I could tell, none was using any kind of oil additive. Then, less than 10 years ago I began to hear reports of a few well-respected engine builders using Slick 50 PTFE (poly-tetra-fluro-ethylene) additive with good results. (PTFE is commonly known by its trade name Teflon.)

You can very quickly be left behind being a complete sceptic, so I decided to investigate in spite of my earlier experiences with oil treatment products. In a few days a 50-page brochure arrived describing how "PTFE is the slipperiest solid substance ever invented" and how this company has been able to produce a special PTFE which "bonds" to metal surfaces rather than just circulating around in the oil. A number of independent organisations had tested the PTFE oil treatment in a variety of cars and found significant improvements in fuel economy and engine power. For

Testing indicates that Slick 50 oil treatment may provide marginal improvements in fuel consumption and cylinder wear.

example, a Ford Granada 2.3: 4.7% improvement in fuel economy and cranking compression up about 7.5 psi per cylinder; Ford Sierra 1.8: power up 3% at 2500rpm, rising to 5.35% improvement at 5500rpm; Saab 900 turbo: 10.1% improvement in fuel consumption; Opel Rekord 2.2: 11.4% improvement in fuel consumption; Volvo 245: 14.6% improvement in fuel consumption. All very impressive figures for a product which didn't have to be added with each oil change but which treats the engine's metal surfaces "for up to 160,000km", according to the brochure.

Before testing this PTFE engine treatment product, a freshly rebuilt engine was carefully run-in and operated for 14,370km with Valvoline's top mineral oil (XLD 20W–50). During that period fuel consumption averaged 7.767 litres per 100km. At that time the cranking compression pressure was measured and the vehicle was run on the wheel dyno to check power output. The cylinder head was removed and upper cylinder wear was measured.

For the following 13,032km this engine was tested as previously but with the recommended dose of 750ml of PTFE engine additive added to the engine oil, and a 80ml dose of PTFE transmission additive added to the transaxle. At about the 1500km mark it appeared to me the engine was running smoother, and then at 2530km the engine began to ping under heavy load or brisk acceleration. I didn't have time to test engine compression, but assumed that the PTFE had improved cylinder sealing as one other test organisation had noted. On the off chance that I had somehow got a tankful of bad fuel, I did not alter the spark advance until I refilled 450km later at a different service station. The pinging persisted and only went away when the timing was retarded 3°. At the conclusion of the test, fuel consumption was found to average out at 7.589 litres per 100km; a 2.29% improvement. Then the cranking compression was checked; two cylinders were identical to those previously recorded one was up 2 psi and one was down 1 psi. This raised the question of why the spark advance had had to be reduced to stop the pinging. Again, on the rolling road, the hp was checked and it produced the same result as the compression test; small rises at some rpm and corresponding small decreases at other points. While on the dyno an ignition swing was attempted, but any increase in advance only produced detonation and a decrease in power. Oil consumption was unchanged at $1^1/_2$ litre per 10,000km, so obviously octane reduction from oil leakage into the combustion chamber was not a problem.

Finally the engine was stripped and inspected for wear. As expected, the crankshaft and bearings were in excellent condition. The piston rings were all in good condition, and wear was in the range of what I would have expected from this type of engine with less than 30,000km on it. Upper cylinder wear was measured next. Up in the top ring area it was 16% less than the amount of wear recorded prior to the PTFE being added to the engine. In the second ring area it was 24% less. However, considering the engine covered 9.3% fewer kilometres with the PTFE treated engine oil and was not exposed to the accelerated wear of engine break-in, I would conclude that wear in the top ring area of the bore was not reduced (or at most 2–3% reduced) with PTFE treatment. In the second ring area of the upper cylinder I believe wear was down 11%.

After this the cylinders were honed and the engine was rebuilt, so I cannot confirm if in the longer term this pattern of reduced bore wear would be maintained. Personally I doubt it as any microscopic "plating" of PTFE would be quickly worn

through. Of course, regularly re-treating the engine with a new dose of PTFE would correct this apparent deficiency. However, since that time major oil companies have been able to produce 100% synthetic engine oils of consistent quality at reasonable prices which reduce engine wear way below what was achieved with PTFE treatment.

Statement: Use our injector cleaner every 2000 miles to remove power robbing varnish deposits from your injectors.

Fact: For many years oil companies have been adding injector cleaner, "detergent", to ordinary pump petrol to ensure injectors provide consistent long-term fuel metering. Where I live, this detergent is added only to unleaded petrol, the reasoning being that most older vehicles running on leaded don't have injectors. However, even on these older cars which have never had a detergent type petrol through their injectors, I seldom see an injector which has a restricted or erratic spray pattern.

Those who market injector clearers, and also those who market injector cleaning machines maintain that you need their product or service because, when a vehicle is switched off, engine heat quickly boils fuel in the injector tip leaving behind a varnish deposit which will not be removed by the detergent fuel companies add to their petrol. Fuel companies counter this by saying they have the chemist and lab facilities to formulate what is required to keep injectors clean, and they add that introducing another detergent into the fuel could cause injector deposits to form from the two detergents reacting against each other, or from one cancelling out the detergent effects of the other.

This injector came out of a Nissan after 180,000 miles of service. It is remarkably clean and free of deposits, even though the engine was operated on fuel which did not contain injector detergent.

Where fuel companies do not add detergent to their petrol, injector cleaner may be of some benefit. However, injector cleaner will not satisfactorily clean injectors which are already blocked and spraying abnormally.

Personally, I see no need to add an injector cleaner into the fuel if the fuel company is already doing so. However, if the petrol is a non-detergent type, injector cleaner may be of minor benefit. Certainly, when I find an injector with restricted flow I wouldn't waste my money adding bottles of injector cleaner to the fuel tank to unblock the injector. It just won't happen, the injectors will have to be cleaned in an ultra-sonic cleaner and then be flow tested and matched to bring their flow to within 5% of each other.

Appendix

Table of Useful Equivalents

1 inch = 25.4mm

1 cubic inch = 16.387cc

1 horsepower = 0.7457 kilowatts

1 pound foot torque = 1.3558 Newton metres

1 pound inch torque = 0.11298 Newton metres

1 psi = 6.89476 kilopascals

     or 68.95 millibars

     or 2.0345 inches of Mercury (Hg)

     or 27.67 inches of water

$$°F = \left(\frac{9}{5} \times °C \right) + 32$$

1 gallon (Imperial) = 160 fluid oz

         or 4.546 litres

1 gallon (US) = 128 fluid oz

        or 3.785 litres

1mm = 0.03937in

1 litre = 61.024cu in or 1000cc

1 kilowatt = 1.341hp

1 Newton metre = 0.7376 pound foot

$$°C = (°F - 32) \times \frac{5}{9}$$

1 fluid oz (Imperial) = 28.4cc

1 fluid oz (US) = 29.57cc

Index